Praise for *Continuous API Management*

Impressively, the authors have managed to make this a book about APIs in general, as opposed to being about specific technologies. Regardless of your API technology of choice, you'll definitely get valuable guidance from this book.

—*Stefan Tilkov, CEO and principal consultant at INNOQ*

APIs are the fabric of the modern enterprise. This book will be your guide to implementing and managing a pervasive API landscape, covering architecture, team structure, and evolution.

—*Gregor Hohpe, author of* The Software Architect Elevator

Continuous API Management offers an excellent guide for those responsible for establishing and scaling their API program. From practical advice to deep dives into all aspects of delivering an API program, this is an essential resource for everyone from executives to API practitioners.

—*James Higginbotham, executive API consultant and author of*
Principles of Web API Design

Copious print details the intimates of web API creation. However, the CAM book stands alone as a holistic guide through the API creation landscape. This reference is mandatory insight for technology leaders (and leaders-in-training).

—*Matthew Reinbold, author of the Net API Notes newsletter
and director of API ecosystems and digital transformation at Postman*

Mike, Mehdi, Ronnie, and Erik created a far-reaching, insightful book that captures what is needed to create, evolve, and manage complex API systems that thrive in the connected world.

—*Hibri Marzook, principal consultant at Contino*

Continuous API Management is the most comprehensive book out there when it comes to managing API products. It is full of practical guidance, and I have seen numerous organizations use its lessons to help advance their digital strategies using APIs.

—*Matt McLarty, global leader for API strategy at*
MuleSoft, a Salesforce company

SECOND EDITION

Continuous API Management

*Making the Right Decisions
in an Evolving Landscape*

*Mehdi Medjaoui, Erik Wilde,
Ronnie Mitra, and Mike Amundsen*

Beijing · Boston · Farnham · Sebastopol · Tokyo

Continuous API Management

by Mehdi Medjaoui, Erik Wilde, Ronnie Mitra, and Mike Amundsen

Published by O'Reilly Media, Inc., 1005 Gravenstein Highway North, Sebastopol, CA 95472.

O'Reilly books may be purchased for educational, business, or sales promotional use. Online editions are also available for most titles (*http://oreilly.com*). For more information, contact our corporate/institutional sales department: 800-998-9938 or *corporate@oreilly.com*.

Acquisitions Editor: Melissa Duffield
Development Editor: Gary O'Brien
Production Editor: Kate Galloway
Copyeditor: Kim Wimpsett
Proofreader: Piper Editorial Consulting, LLC

Indexer: Judith McConville
Interior Designer: David Futato
Cover Designer: Karen Montgomery
Illustrator: Kate Dullea

November 2018:   First Edition
October 2021:   Second Edition

Revision History for the Second Edition

2021-10-18:   First Release

See *http://oreilly.com/catalog/errata.csp?isbn=9781098103521* for release details.

978-1-098-10352-1

[LSI]

To those who coached me during the book writing, to my fellow partners who helped me to be useful in the industry, to Kin Lane who shared with me his passion for APIs, and to all the API practitioners who shared their API practices with me that inspired this book. To my parents.

—Mehdi Medjaoui

To all the people in my life who made this book possible. It's been quite a ride!

—Erik Wilde

To Kairav, for helping me write this dedication.

—Ronnie Mitra

To all the companies that invited us to come share what we've learned and, in the process, taught us so much that we had to try to capture it in this book.

—Mike Amundsen

Table of Contents

Foreword to the First Edition

APIs are a journey for any company, organization, institution, or government agency learning to properly manage their digital resources across an ever-expanding and evolving competitive digital landscape. This digital transformation, which has been building over the last five years, is beginning to result in a shift across the API landscape, where companies are beginning to stop asking *if they should be doing APIs* and have begun seeking more knowledge on *how to do APIs properly*. Organizations are realizing that there's more to APIs than just creating them; a lot goes into delivering APIs throughout the entire API lifecycle. The authors behind *Continuous API Management* possess a unique understanding of what it takes to move an API from ideation to realization consistently, at scale, and in a repeatable way—providing the makings for a pretty unique learning opportunity.

Most API practitioners operate with a view of the API landscape spanning a single set of APIs. Medjaoui, Wilde, Mitra, and Amundsen, the authors of this book, possess a unique view of the API landscape at a 250,000-foot level, spanning thousands of APIs, multiple industries, and some of the largest enterprise organizations out there today. I can count the top-tier API talent that exists around the globe on both my hands, and Medjaoui, Wilde, Mitra, and Amundsen are always first to be counted on my right hand. These authors bring a wealth of experience to the table when it comes to understanding what you need to move APIs from inception to design, from development to production, and back again. There just isn't another team of API experts out there who have the scope and the breadth of API knowledge that this team possesses, making this book destined to become that tattered O'Reilly tome that lives within reach on the corner of your desk—something you read again and again.

I've read numerous books on the technical aspects of creating APIs, including books about hypermedia and everything you need to know about REST and how to deliver on this vision in a variety of programming languages and platforms. This is the first API book that I've read that holistically approaches the delivery of APIs from start to finish, addressing not only the technological details but also the critical business elements of operating APIs—which also includes the critical human side of API education, realization, and activation across large enterprise organizations. The book methodically lays out the essential building blocks any enterprise API architect will need to deliver reliable, secure, and consistent APIs at scale; it will help any API team quantify their operations and think more critically about how APIs can be improved upon and evolved, while also establishing and refining a structured yet agile approach to delivering APIs in a standardized way across teams.

After putting down this book, I felt I had a refreshed look at the modern API lifecycle—but more importantly, I was left with a wealth of ideas about how I actually quantify and measure my API operations, and the API lifecycle strategy I am using to manage my operations. Even with my knowledge of the space, this book forced me to look at the landscape in some important new ways. I walked away saturated with information that reinforced some of what I already knew, but also shifted and moved around some of what I *thought* I knew, forcing me to evolve in some of my existing practices. For me, this is what the API journey is all about: continually being challenged, learning, planning, executing, measuring, and repeating until you find the desired results. *Continuous API Management* reflects this reality of delivering APIs, providing us with a reusable guide to the technology, business, and politics of doing APIs at scale within the enterprise.

Don't just read this book once. Read it; then go out and execute on your vision. Evolve your API strategy, and define a version of the API lifecycle that is all your own, taking what you've learned from Medjaoui, Wilde, Mitra, and Amundsen and putting it to work. However, every once in a while, pick this book up again and give it another read. I guarantee there will be little nuggets throughout the book that you'll rediscover and see in a new light each time you work through it—something that will build and improve your understanding of what is happening across the API landscape and help you more confidently participate (or lead) when it comes to doing business with APIs across the expanding online economy.

— *Kin Lane, The API Evangelist*

Preface

Welcome to the second edition of *Continuous API Management*. The opening paragraph for the previous edition, released in 2018, stated:

> As society and business have grown increasingly digital in nature, the demand for connected software has exploded. In turn, the application programming interface (API) has emerged as an important resource for modern organizations because it facilitates software connections. But managing these APIs effectively has proven to be a new challenge. Getting the best value from your APIs means learning how to manage their design, development, deployment, growth, quality, and security while dealing with the complicating factors of context, time, and scale.

And, in the intervening years, not much has changed when it comes to the growth and challenges of API management. The good news is that, in the years since our first edition, more tooling, more training, and more experience has help grow and mature the API management space. The not-so-good news is that the authors still see lots of organizations struggling to meet the demands of connecting people, services, and companies using APIs. This new edition is our chance to provide updates on how companies are progressing, share some new success stories, and refine some of the material we first introduced in 2018.

While we've added new examples and updated existing ones, we've still retained the same basic approach and outline for this new release. Hopefully these changes will help you extend your own journey on the road to continuous API management.

Who Should Read This Book

If you are just starting to build an API program and want to understand the work ahead of you, or if you already have APIs but want to learn how to manage them better, then this is the book for you.

In this book, we've tried to build an API management framework that can be applied to more than one context. In these pages you'll find guidance that will help you to manage a single API that you want to share with developers around the world, as well as advice for building a complex set of APIs in a microservice architecture designed only for internal developers—and everything in between.

We've also written this book to be as technologically neutral as possible. The advice and analysis we provide is applicable to any API-based architecture, including Hyper-Text Transfer Protocol (HTTP), Create/Read/Update/Delete (CRUD), REpresentational State Transfer (REST), GraphQL, and event-driven styles of interaction. This is a book for anyone who wants to improve the decisions being made about their APIs.

What's in This Book

This book contains our collective knowledge from many years spent designing, developing, and improving APIs—both our own and others'. We've distilled all that experience into this book. We've identified two core factors for effective API development: adopting a product perspective and implementing the right kind of team. We've also identified three essential factors for managing that work: governance, product maturity, and landscape design.

These five elements of API management form a foundation on which you can build a successful API management program. In this book, we introduce each of these topics and provide you with guidance on how to shape them to fit your own organizational context.

The Outline

We've organized the book so that the scope of management concerns grows as you progress through the chapters. We start by introducing the foundational concepts of decision-based governance and the API as a product. This is followed by a tour of all the work that must be managed when building an API product.

From this simple view of a single API, we then add the aspect of time as we dive into what it means to change an API and how the maturity of the API impacts those change decisions. This is followed by an exploration of the teams and people who do that change work. Finally, in the last half of the book, we tackle the complexities of scale and the challenges of managing a landscape of API products.

Here is a short summary of what you'll find in each chapter:

- Chapter 1, "The Challenge and Promise of API Management" introduces the API management domain and explains why it's so difficult to manage APIs effectively.
- Chapter 2, "API Governance" explores governance from the perspective of decision-based work—a foundational concept for API management.

- Chapter 3, "The API as a Product" establishes the API-as-a-product perspective and why it's an essential part of any API strategy.

- Chapter 4, "The Pillars of an API Product" outlines the ten essential pillars of work in the API product domain. These pillars form a set of decision-making tasks that must be managed.

- Chapter 5, "Continuous API Improvement" provides insight into what it means to change an API continuously. It introduces the need to adopt a continuous change mentality and provides an understanding of the different types of API changes (and their impacts) that you'll encounter.

- Chapter 6, "API Styles" is a new chapter for this edition. It explores the five most common API styles we see as we visit with companies around the world and digs into the strengths and drawbacks of each style to help you select the ones appropriate for each use case you encounter.

- Chapter 7, "The API Product Lifecycle" introduces the API product lifecycle, a framework that will help you manage API work across the ten pillars over the life of an API product.

- Chapter 8, "API Teams" addresses the people element of an API management system by exploring the typical roles, responsibilities, and design patterns for an API team over the life of an API product.

- Chapter 9, "API Landscapes" adds the perspective of scale to the problem of managing APIs. It introduces the eight Vs—variety, vocabulary, volume, velocity, vulnerability, visibility, versioning, and volatility—that must be addressed when multiple APIs are changing at the same time.

- Chapter 10, "API Landscape Journey" outlines a continuous landscape design approach for managing API changes continuously and at scale.

- Chapter 11, "Managing the API Lifecycle in an Evolving Landscape" maps the landscape perspective back to the API-as-a-product perspective and identifies how API work changes when the landscape evolves around it.

- Chapter 12, "Continuing the Journey" ties together the story of API management that has emerged and provides advice on preparing for the future and starting your journey today.

What's Not in This Book

The scope of API management is big, and there is a massive amount of variation in contexts, platforms, and protocols. Given the constraints of time and space when writing a book, it was impossible for us to address all the specific implementation practices of API work. This book isn't a guide for designing a REST API or for picking a security gateway product. If you are looking for a prescriptive guide to writing API code or designing an HTTP API, this isn't the right book for you.

While we do have examples that talk about specific practices, this isn't an API implementation–focused book (the good news is there are plenty of books, blogs, and videos available already to help you fill that need). Instead, this book tackles a problem that is rarely addressed: how to effectively manage the work of building APIs within a complex, continuously changing organizational system.

Conventions Used in This Book

The following typographical conventions are used in this book:

Italic
> Indicates new terms, URLs, email addresses, filenames, and file extensions.

`Constant width`
> Indicates program elements such as variable or function names, data types, statements, and keywords.

`Constant width italic`
> Shows text that should be replaced with user-supplied values or by values determined by context.

 This element signifies a tip or suggestion.

 This element signifies a general note.

 This element indicates a warning or caution.

O'Reilly Online Learning

 For more than 40 years, *O'Reilly Media* has provided technology and business training, knowledge, and insight to help companies succeed.

Our unique network of experts and innovators share their knowledge and expertise through books, articles, and our online learning platform. O'Reilly's online learning platform gives you on-demand access to live training courses, in-depth learning paths, interactive coding environments, and a vast collection of text and video from O'Reilly and 200+ other publishers. For more information, visit *http://oreilly.com*.

How to Contact Us

Please address comments and questions concerning this book to the publisher:

O'Reilly Media, Inc.
1005 Gravenstein Highway North
Sebastopol, CA 95472
800-998-9938 (in the United States or Canada)
707-829-0515 (international or local)
707-829-0104 (fax)

We have a web page for this book, where we list errata, examples, and any additional information. You can access this page at *https://oreil.ly/cam-2e*.

Email *bookquestions@oreilly.com* to comment or ask technical questions about this book.

For news and information about our books and courses, visit *http://oreilly.com*.

Find us on Facebook: *http://facebook.com/oreilly*

Follow us on Twitter: *http://twitter.com/oreillymedia*

Watch us on YouTube: *http://youtube.com/oreillymedia*

Acknowledgments

Once again, we have many people to thank for all the help and support we received as we pulled together new material for this second edition. As usual, our first thanks goes to all the people we consulted with and had the privilege to interview, and all those who attended our workshops and online webinars. The feedback was great, and we learned something new with every encounter. Additional thanks goes to the folks at NGINX who encouraged us to revise this book and who helped sponsor the work. Special thanks goes to all those who read early drafts and helped us shape the final book you see before you. We'd also like to thank James Higginbotham, Hibri Marzook, Marjukka Niinioja, and Matthew Reinbold for all the time they took to read and review our work and point out ways we could make it better. And, of course, none of this would be possible without the support of the folks at O'Reilly Media. Our thanks go to Melissa Duffield, Gary O'Brien, Kate Galloway, Kim Wimpsett, and many others who devoted their time and talent to helping us pull everything together.

CHAPTER 1
The Challenge and Promise
of API Management

Management is, above all, a practice where art, science, and craft meet.
—Henry Mintzberg

According to an IDC report from 2019, 75% of the companies surveyed expected to be "digitally transformed" in the next decade and expected that 90% of all new apps would feature microservice architecture powered by APIs.[1] It was also noted that, for API-focused organizations, up to 30% of revenue was generated via digital channels. At the same time, these companies identified key barriers to API adoption as "complexity," "security," and "governance."

Finally, this was one of the key summary findings: "Defining the right app architecture requires a deep understanding of the challenges related to governing, managing and orchestrating these foundational technology components."[2] This survey, like the one from Coleman Parkes (*https://oreil.ly/pAWGs*) we cited in the first edition of this book, contains a mix of encouragement and caution.

An interesting trend we have seen in the last few years is a widening gap between the "API haves" and "API have-nots." For example, when asked the question "Does your company have an API management platform?" 72% of media and services companies answered "yes," while only 46% of companies in the manufacturing sector replied in the affirmative.[3] All indications are that APIs will continue to drive business growth

---

1 Jennifer Thomson and George Mironescu, "APIs: The Determining Agents Between Success or Failure of Digital Business," IDC, *https://oreil.ly/9yshw*.

2 Thomson and Mironescu, "APIs: The Determining Agents Between Success or Failure of Digital Business."

3 Ibid.

going forward, and it is imperative that companies from all segments of the economy step up to the challenge of digital transformation.

The good news is there are many companies out there successfully managing their API programs. The not-so-good news is that their experience and expertise is not easily shared or commonly available. There are several reasons for this. Most of the time, organizations that are doing well in their API management programs are simply too busy to share their experiences with others. In a few cases, we've talked to companies that are very careful about how much of their API management expertise they share with the outside world; they are convinced API skills are a competitive advantage and are slow to make their findings public. Finally, even when companies share their experience at public conferences and through articles and blog posts, the information they share is usually company-specific and difficult to translate to a wide range of organizations' API programs.

This book is an attempt to tackle that last problem—translating company-specific examples into shared experience all organizations can use. To that end, we have visited with dozens of companies, interviewed many API technologists, and tried to find the common threads between the examples companies have shared with us and with the public. There are a small handful of themes that run through this book that we'll share here in this introductory chapter.

A key challenge to identify right up front is sorting out just what people mean when they talk about APIs. First, the term *API* can be applied to just the *interface* (e.g., an HTTP request URL and JSON response). It can also refer to the code and deployment elements needed to place an accessible service into production (e.g., the customerOnBoarding API). Finally, we sometimes use *API* to refer to a single *instance* of a running API (e.g., the customerOnBoarding API running in the AWS cloud versus the customerOnBoarding API running on the Azure cloud).

Another important challenge in managing APIs is the difference between the work of designing, building, and releasing a *single API* and supporting and managing *many APIs*—what we call an *API landscape*. We will spend a good deal of time in this book on both ends of this spectrum. Concepts like *API as a product* (AaaP) and the skills needed to create and maintain APIs (what we call *API pillars*) are examples of dealing with the challenges of a single API. We will also talk about the role of API maturity models and the work of dealing with change over time as important aspects of managing an API.

The other end of that spectrum is the work of managing the API landscape. Your landscape is the collection of APIs from all business domains, running on all platforms, managed by all the API teams in your company. There are several aspects to this landscape challenges, including how scale and scope change the way APIs are designed and implemented as well as how large ecosystems can introduce added volatility and vulnerability just because of their size.

Finally, we touch on the process of decision making when managing your API ecosystem. In our experience, this is the key to creating a successful *governance* plan for your API programs. It turns out that the way you make decisions needs to change along with your landscape; holding on to old governance models can limit your API program's success and even introduce more risk into your existing APIs.

Before we dive into the details on how you can learn to deal with both challenges—your individual APIs and your API landscape—let's take a look at two important questions: what is API management, and why is it so hard?

What Is API Management?

As mentioned, API management involves more than just governing the design, implementation, and release of APIs. It also includes the management of an API ecosystem, the distribution of decisions within your organization, and even the process of migrating existing APIs into your growing API landscape. In this section, we'll spend time on each of these concepts—but first it is important to talk about the ultimate reason for APIs, the *business of APIs*.

The Business of APIs

Beyond the details of creating APIs and managing them, it is important to keep in mind that all this work is meant to support business goals and objectives. APIs are more than the technical details of JSON or XML, synchronous or asynchronous, etc. They are a way to connect business units together to expose important functionality and knowledge in a way that helps the company be effective. APIs are often a way to unlock value that is already there in the organization, for example, through creating new applications, enabling new revenue streams, and initiating new business.

This kind of thinking focuses more on the needs of API consumers instead of those producing and publishing the APIs. This consumer-centric approach is commonly referred to as "Jobs to Be Done," or JTBD. It was introduced by Harvard Business School's Clayton Christensen, whose books *The Innovator's Dilemma* and *The Innovator's Solution* (Harvard Business Review Press) explore the power of this approach in depth. For the purposes of launching and managing a successful API program, it serves as a clear reminder that APIs exist to solve business problems. In our experience, companies that are good at applying APIs to business problems treat their APIs as *products* that are meant to "get a job done" in the same sense that Christensen's JTBD framework solves consumer problems.

Access to data
   One way APIs can contribute to the business is by making it easy to access important customer or market data that can be correlated to emerging trends or unique behaviors in new customer segments. By making this data safely

and easily available (properly anonymized and filtered), APIs may enable your business to discover new opportunities, realize new products/services, or even start new initiatives at a reduced cost and faster time to market.

Access to products

Another way an API program can help the business is by creating a flexible set of "tools" (the APIs) to build new solutions without incurring a high cost. For example, if you have an `OnlineSales` API that allows key partners to manage and track their sales activity and a `MarketingPromotions` API that allows the marketing team to design and track product promotional campaigns, you have an opportunity to create a new partner solution: the `SalesAndPromotions` tracking application.

Access to innovation

In our experience, many companies have internal processes, practices, and production pipelines that—while effective—are less than efficient. Some have been around for quite a while (in some cases, decades), and we've even found cases where no one can remember when (or why) the organization put a certain process in place. Changing existing processes is not easy. It can also be costly. By creating an infrastructure of APIs within your company, you can unleash the creativity within your organization and, in some cases, bypass gatekeeping mechanisms and enable improvements and efficiencies within your company.

We cover these important aspects of AaaP in Chapter 3. But, first, let's explore a short explanation of what we mean by the term *API*.

What Is an API?

Sometimes when people use the term *API*, they are talking about not only the interface but also the functionality—the code behind the interface. For example, someone might say, "We need to release the updated Customer API soon so that other teams can start using the new search functionality we implemented." Other times, people may use the term to refer only to the details of the interface itself. For example, someone on your team might say, "What I'd like to do is design a new JSON API for the existing SOAP services that support our customer onboarding workflow." Both are correct, of course—and it seems pretty clear what is meant in both cases—but it can be confusing at times.

To try to clear up the distinction and make it easier for us to talk about both the interface and the functionality, we are going to introduce some additional terms: interface, implementation, and instance.

Interface, implementation, and instance

The acronym API stands for *application programming interface*. We use *interfaces* to gain access to something running "behind" the API. For example, you may have an API that exposes tasks for managing user accounts. This interface might allow developers to:

- Onboard a new account.
- Edit an existing account profile.
- Change the status of (suspend or activate) an account.

This interface is usually expressed using shared protocols such as HTTP, Message Queuing Telemetry Transport (MQTT), Thrift, Transfer Control Protocol/Internet Protocol (TCP/IP), etc., and relies on standardized formats like JSON, XML, YAML, or HTML.

But that's just the interface. Something else actually needs to perform the requested tasks. That something else is what we'll be referring to as the *implementation*. The implementation is the part that provides the actual functionality. Often this implementation is written in a programming language such as Java, C#, Ruby, Python, or some other language. Continuing with the example of the user account, a `UserManagement` implementation could contain the ability to create, add, edit, and remove users. This functionality could then be exposed using the interface mentioned previously.

Decoupling the Interface from the Implementation

Note that the functionality of the implementation described is a simple set of actions using the Create, Read, Update, Delete (CRUD) pattern, but the interface we described has three actions (`OnboardAccount`, `EditAccount`, and `ChangeAccountStatus`). This seeming "mismatch" between the implementation and the interface is common and can be powerful; it decouples the exact implementation of each service from the interface used to *access* that service, making it easier to change over time without disruption.

The third term in our list is *instance*. An API instance is a combination of the interface and the implementation. This is a handy way to talk about the actual running API that has been released into production. We manage instances using metrics to make sure they are healthy. We register and document instances in order to make it easy for developers to find and use the API to solve real-world problems. And we secure the instance to make sure that only authorized users are able to execute the actions and read/write the data needed to make those actions possible.

Figure 1-1 clarifies the relationship between the three elements. Often in this book, when we write API, we're talking about the instance of the API: a fully operational combination of interface and implementation. In cases where we want to highlight *just* the interface or *only* the implementation, we'll call that out in the text.

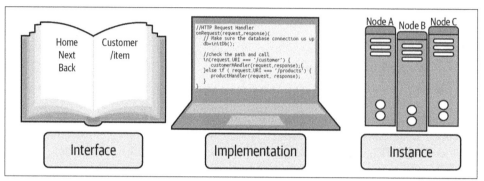

Figure 1-1. Three API elements

API Styles

Another important element of APIs is what can be called *style*. Like styles in other fields (painting styles, decor, fashion, and physical architecture), API styles are coherent, identifiable approaches to creating and using APIs. It is important to know what style of API your client applications want to consume and provide a consistent implementation of that style when creating your API implementations.

The most common API style today is the REST or RESTful API style. But this is just one possibility. In fact, we see an ever-growing trend of using non-REST, non-HTTP APIs within organizations large and small. The rise of event-driven architecture (EDA) is one example of this new reality for API management.

 While there are many styles, each with unique names, in our experience, there are five general styles you need to be aware of when managing your API program. We cover the importance of API styles and review each of them in Chapter 6.

It is rare that any company can get along relying on only one API style throughout the company. And it is unlikely that any single style you implement will last forever. Taking style into account when designing, implementing, and managing your API ecosystem is a critical element in establishing the success and stability of your API program.

This multistyle API reality leads to another important aspect of successful API management programs: the ability to govern many APIs in a coherent and consistent way.

More Than Just the API

The API itself—the technical details of interface and implementation—is just part of the story. The traditional elements of design-build-deploy are, of course, critical to the life of your APIs. But actually *managing* APIs also means testing them, documenting them, and publishing them to a portal so that the right audience (internal developers, partners, third-party anonymous app developers, etc.) can find and learn how to use them properly. You also need to secure your APIs, monitor them at runtime, and maintain them (including handling changes) over their lifetime. All these additional elements of an API are what we call *API pillars*: elements that all APIs need and all API program managers need to deal with. We'll dig into pillars in Chapter 4, where we walk through the list of ten key practices vital to creating and maintaining healthy APIs.

The good news about these practice areas is that they transcend any single API. For example, the skill of documenting APIs well is transferable from one API team to the next. The same goes for learning proper testing skills, security patterns, and so forth. That also means that even when you have separate teams for each API domain (sales team, product team, back-office team, etc.), you also have "cross-cutting" interests that bind people within teams to other people in other teams.[4]

Another important aspect of managing APIs is enabling and engineering the teams that build them. We talk more about how this works in different organizations in Chapter 8.

API Maturity Stages

Understanding the API pillars is not the entire picture. Each API in your program goes through its own "lifecycle"—a series of predictable and useful stages. Knowing where you are in the API journey can help you determine how much time and resources to invest in the API at the moment. Understanding how APIs *mature* allows you to recognize the same stages for a wide range of APIs and helps you prepare for and respond to the varying requirements of time and energy at each stage.

On the surface, it makes sense to consider that all of the API pillars need to be dealt with when designing, building, and releasing your APIs. But reality is different. Often, for early-stage APIs it is most important to focus on the design and build aspects and reduce efforts on documentation, for example. At other stages (e.g., once a prototype is in the hands of beta testers), spending more time on monitoring the use of the API and securing it against misuse is more important. Understanding

---

4 At music streaming service Spotify, they call these cross-cutting groups *guilds*. See "Scaling Up Your Teams" on page 209 for more on this topic.

maturity stages will help you determine how to allocate limited resources for maximum effect. We'll walk you through this process in Chapter 7.

More Than a Single API

As many readers may already know, things change when you start managing a lot of APIs. We have customers with thousands of APIs that they need to build, monitor, and manage over time. In this situation, you focus less on the details of how a single API is implemented and more on the details of how these APIs coexist in an ever-growing, dynamic ecosystem. As mentioned earlier, we call this ecosystem the API landscape, and we devote several chapters to this concept in the second half of the book.

Much of the challenge here is how to assure some level of consistency without causing bottlenecks and slowdowns due to centralized management and review of all the API details. This is usually accomplished by extending responsibility for those details to the individual API teams and focusing central management/governance efforts on normalizing the way APIs interact with one another, ensuring that there is a core set of shared services or infrastructure (security, monitoring, etc.) in place and available for all API teams, and generally providing guidance and coaching to more autonomous teams. That is, it's often necessary to move away from the usual centralized command-and-control model.

One of the challenges when working toward distributing decision making and autonomy deeper in the organization is that it can be easy for those higher up in the organization to lose visibility into important activities happening at the team level. Whereas in the past a team might have had to ask permission to take an action, companies that extend additional autonomy to the individual teams will encourage them to act without waiting for upper-level review and permission.

Most of the challenges of managing a landscape of APIs have to do with *scale* and *scope*. It turns out that as your API program grows, it doesn't just get bigger; it also changes in *shape*. And that's what we'll discuss next.

Why Is API Management Difficult?

As we mentioned at the beginning of this chapter, while most companies have already launched an API program, some sectors of the economy are more advanced in their APIs than others. What's going on here? Why is it that some companies are better at this than others? What are the common challenges, and how can you help your company overcome them?

As we visit with companies all over the world, talking about API lifecycle management, a few basic themes emerge:

Scope

Just what is it that central software architecture teams should be focusing upon when governing APIs over time?

Scale

Often, what works when companies are just starting out on their API journey doesn't scale as the program grows from a few small teams to a global initiative.

Standards

As programs mature, management and governance efforts need to move from detailed advice on API design and implementation to more general standardization of the API landscape, freeing teams to make more of their own decisions at a detailed level.

Essentially, it is the continued balance of these three elements—scope, scale, and standards—that powers a healthy, growing API management program. For this reason, it is worth digging into these a bit more.

Scope

One of the big challenges of operating a healthy API management program is achieving the proper level of central control and, to make it even more challenging, the proper level of changes as the program matures.

Early in the program, it makes sense to focus on the details of designing the API directly. In cases where APIs are in their infancy, these design details might come directly from the team creating the API—they look at existing programs "in the wild," adopt tooling and libraries that make sense for the style of API they plan to create, and go ahead and implement that API.

It is at this "first stage" in the life of APIs within your company that detailed recommendations and clear roles can lead to early success. Chapters 3 and 4 list much of the material we find helpful for companies just starting out on their API journeys.

In this "early-stage" API program, everything is new; all problems are encountered (and solved) for the first time. These initial experiences often end up being chronicled as the company's "API best practices" or company guidelines, etc. And they make sense for a small team working on a few APIs for the very first time. However, those initial guidelines may turn out to be incomplete.

As the number of teams working on APIs at the company grows, so does the variety of styles, experiences, and points of view. It gets more difficult to maintain consistency across all the teams—and not just because some teams are not adhering to the published company guidelines. It may be that a new team is working with a different set of off-the-shelf products that constrain their ability to follow the initial guidelines. Maybe they don't work in an event-streaming environment and are supporting XML-based call-and-response-style APIs. They need guidance, of course, but it needs to fit *their* domain and fit *their* customers' needs.

At this "middle stage" of your API management program, the leadership and guidelines need to shift from specific guidance on how to design and implement APIs to a more general guidance on the lifecycle of your APIs and the ways in which they need to interact with one another. Chapters 6 and 7 contain the kinds of things we see successful organizations doing for middle-stage API programs.

There are certainly some guidelines that all teams need to share, but that guidance needs to fit their problem domains as well as their API customers' needs. As your community widens, your diversity increases, and it is essential that you don't make the mistake of trying to eliminate that diversity. This is where your lever of control needs to move from giving *orders* (e.g., "All APIs *must* use the following URL patterns…") to giving *guidance* (e.g., "APIs running over HTTP *should* use one of the following URL templates…").

In this "later-stage" API management, the perspective of governance telescopes out even further to focus on how APIs interact over time and how your APIs interact with the APIs of other companies in your market space and industry sector. Chapters 9, 10, and 11 all reflect the kind of "big-picture" thinking needed to maintain a healthy and stable API ecosystem well into the future.

As you can see, as your program's scope expands, your collection of guidelines needs to expand appropriately. This is especially important for global enterprises where local culture, language, and history play an important role in the way teams think, create, and solve problems.

And that leads us to the next key element: scale.

Scale

Another big challenge for creating and maintaining a healthy API management program is dealing with changes in scale over time. As we discussed in the previous section, growing the number of teams and the number of APIs created by those teams can be a challenge. The processes needed to monitor and manage the APIs at runtime will also change as the system matures. The tooling needed to keep track of a handful of APIs all built by the same team in a single physical location is very different from the tooling needed to keep track of hundreds or thousands of API entry points scattered across multiple time zones and countries.

In this book we talk about this aspect of API management as the "landscape." As your program scales up, you need to be able to keep an eye on lots of processes by lots of teams in lots of locations. You'll rely more on monitoring runtime behavior to get a sense of how healthy your system is at any one moment. In the second part of this book (starting with Chapter 9) we'll explore how the notion of managing the API landscape can help you figure out which elements deserve your focus and what tools and processes can help you keep a handle on your growing API platform.

API landscapes pose a new set of challenges. The processes you use to design, implement, and maintain a single API are not always the same when you need to scale your ecosystem. This is basically a game of numbers: the more APIs you have in your system, the more likely it is that they will interact with one another, and that increases the likelihood that some of those interactions will result in unexpected behavior (or "errors"). This is the way large systems work—there are more interactions and more unexpected results. Trying to remove these unexpected results gets you only part of the way. You can't eliminate all the bugs.

And that leads to the third challenge most growing API programs encounter: how can you reduce unexpected changes by applying the appropriate level of standards within your API program?

Standards

One of the key shifts that happen when you begin managing at the landscape level instead of the API level is in the power of standards in providing consistent guidance for teams designing, implementing, and deploying APIs in your organization.

As groups grow larger—including the group of teams responsible for your organization's APIs—there is a coordination cost that is incurred (see "Decisions" on page 18). The growing scale requires a change in scope. And a key way to deal with this challenge is to rely more on general standards instead of specific design constraints.

For example, one of the reasons the World Wide Web has been able to continue to function well since its inception in 1990 is that its designers decided early on to rely on general standards that apply to all types of software platforms and languages instead of creating tightly focused implementation guidance based on any single language or framework. This allows creative teams to invent new languages, architecture patterns, and even runtime frameworks without breaking any existing implementations.

A common thread that runs through the long-lived standards that have helped the web continue to be successful is the focus on standardizing the *interaction* between components and systems. Instead of standardizing the way components are implemented internally (e.g., use this library, this data model, etc.), web standards aim to make it easy for parties to understand one another over the wire. Similarly, as your API program grows to a more mature level, the guidance you provide to your API community needs to focus more on general interaction standards instead of specific implementation details.

This can be a tough transition to make, but it is essential to moving up the ladder to a healthy API landscape where it is possible for teams to build APIs that can easily interact with both the existing and the future APIs in your system.

Managing the API Landscape

As mentioned at the start of this chapter, there are two key challenges in the API management space: managing the life of a single API and managing the landscape of all the APIs. In our visits to many companies and our research into API management in general, we find many versions of the "managing a single API" story. There are lots of "lifecycles" and "maturity models" out there that provide solid advice on identifying and mitigating the challenges of designing, building, and deploying an API. But we have not found much in the way of guidance when it comes to an ecosystem (we call it a *landscape*) of APIs.

Landscapes have their own challenges and their own behaviors and tendencies. What you need to take into account when you design a single API is not the same as what you must consider when you have to support tens, hundreds, or even thousands of APIs. There are new challenges *at scale* that happen in an ecosystem—things that don't happen for a single instance or implementation of an API. We dive deep into the API landscape later in the book, but we want to point out three ways in which API landscapes present unique challenges for API management here at the start of the book:

- Scaling technology
- Scaling teams
- Scaling governance

Let's take a moment to review each of these aspects of API management with regard to landscapes.

Technology

When you are first starting your API program, there are a series of technical decisions to make that will affect all your APIs. The fact that "all" your APIs is just a small set at this point is not important. What is important is that you have a consistent set of tools and technologies that you can rely upon as you build out your initial API program. As you'll see when we get into the details of the API lifecycle (Chapter 7) and API maturity, API programs are not cheap, and you need to carefully monitor your investments of time and energy into activities that will have a high impact on your API's success without risking lots of capital too early in the process. This usually means selecting and supporting a small set of tools and providing a clear, often detailed set of guidance documents to help your API teams design and build APIs that both solve your business problems and work well together. In other words, you can gain early wins by limiting your technical scope.

This works well at the start, for all the reasons we've mentioned. However, as your program scales up in volume (see "Volume" on page 242) and its scope widens (e.g., more teams building more APIs to serve more business domains in more locations, etc.), the challenges also change. As you grow your API program, relying on a limited set of tools and technologies can become one of the key things that slow you down. While at the beginning, when you had a small set of teams, limiting choices made things move faster, placing limits on a large set of teams is a costly and risky enterprise. This is especially true if you start to add teams in geographically distant locations and/or when you embrace new business units or acquire new companies to add to your API landscape. At this point, variety (see "Variety" on page 236) becomes a much more important success driver for your ecosystem.

So, an important part of managing technology for API landscapes is identifying when the landscape has grown large enough to start increasing the variety of technologies instead of restricting them. Some of this has to do with the realities of existing implementations. If your API landscape needs to support your organization's existing SOAP-over-TCP/IP services, you can't require all these services to use the same URL guidance you created for your greenfield CRUD-over-HTTP APIs. The same goes for creating services for new event-driven Angular implementations or the legacy remote procedure call (RPC) implementations.

A wider scope means more technological variety in your landscape.

Teams

Technology is not the only aspect of API management that surfaces a new set of challenges as the program grows. The makeup of the teams themselves needs to adjust as the landscape changes, too. Again, at the start of your API program, you can operate with just a few committed individuals doing—for the most part—everything. This is when you hear names like "full-stack developer" or "MEAN developer" or some other variation on the idea of a single developer that has skills for all aspects of your API program. (MEAN stands for MongoDB, Express.js, Angular.js, Node.js.) You also may hear a lot of talk about "startup teams" or "self-contained teams." It all boils down to having all the skills you need in one team.

This makes sense when your APIs are few and they all are designed and implemented using the same set of tools (see "Technology" on page 12). But as the scale and scope of your API program grows, the number of skills required to build and maintain your APIs grows, too. You can no longer expect each API team to consist of a set number of people with skills in design, database, backend, frontend, testing, and deployment. You might have a team whose job is to design and build a data-centric dashboard interface used by a wide range of other teams. Their skills may, for example, need to cover all the data formats used and tools needed to collect that data. Or you might have a team whose primary job is to build mobile apps that use a single technology like GraphQL or some other query-centric library. As technological variety grows, your teams may need to become more specialized. We'll have a chance to explore this in detail later, in Chapter 8.

Another way in which teams will need to change as your API landscape grows is the way in which they participate in day-to-day decision-making processes. When you have a small number of teams and their experience is not very deep, it can make sense to centralize the decision making to a single, guiding group. In large organizations, this is often the Enterprise Architecture group or something with a similar name. This works at smaller scales and scopes but becomes a big problem as your ecosystem becomes less homogeneous and more wide-ranging. As tech gets more involved, a single team is unlikely to be able to keep up with the details of each tool and framework. And as you add more and more teams, decision making itself needs to be distributed; a central committee rarely understands the realities of the day-to-day operations in a global enterprise.

The solution is to break down the decision-making process into what we call *decision elements* (see "The Elements of a Decision" on page 28) and distribute those elements to the proper levels within your company. A growing ecosystem means teams need to become more specialized on a technical level and more responsible at the decision-making level.

Governance

The last area that we want to touch on in regard to the challenge of API landscapes is the general approach to *governance* of your API program. Again, as in other cases mentioned here, it is our observation that the role and levers of governance will change as your ecosystem grows. New challenges appear, and old methods are not as effective as they were in the past. In fact, especially at the enterprise level, sticking to old governance models can slow or even stall the success of your APIs.

Just as in any area of leadership, when the scope and scale are limited, an approach based on providing direct guidance can be the most effective. This is often true not just for small teams, but also for *new* teams. When there is not a lot of operating experience, the quickest way to success is to provide that experience in the form of detailed guidance and/or process documents. For example, we find that early API program governance often takes the form of multipage process documents that explain specific tasks: how to design the URLs for an API, or which names are valid for URLs, or where the version number must appear in an HTTP header. Providing clear guidelines with few options makes it hard for developers to stray from the approved way of implementing your APIs.

But again, as your program grows, as you add more teams and support more business domains, the sheer size and scope of the community begin to make it difficult to maintain a single guidance document that applies to all teams. And while it is possible to "farm out" the job of writing and maintaining detailed process documents for the entire enterprise, it is usually not a good idea anyway—as we mentioned in "Technology" on page 12, technology variety becomes a strength in a large ecosystem, and attempting to rein it in at the enterprise governance level can slow your program's progress.

That's why as your API landscape expands, your governance documents need to change in tone from offering direct process instructions to providing general principles. For example, instead of writing up details on what constitutes a valid URL for your company, it is better to point developers to the Internet Engineering Task Force's guidelines on URI design and ownership (RFC 7320) and provide general guidance on how to apply this public standard within your organization. Another great example of this kind of *principled guidance* can be found in most UI/UX guidelines, such as the "10 Usability Heuristics for User Interface Design" (*https://oreil.ly/qU66X*) from the Nielsen Norman Group. These kinds of documents provide lots of options and rationales for using one UI pattern over another. They offer developers and designers guidance on why and when to use something instead of simply setting requirements for them to follow.

Finally, for large organizations, and especially companies that operate in multiple locations and time zones, governance needs to move from distributing principles to collecting advice. This essentially reverses the typical central governance model. Instead of telling teams what to do, the primary role of the central governance committee becomes to collect experience information from the field, find correlations, and echo back guidance that reflects "best practice" within the wider organization.

So, as your API landscape grows, your API governance model needs to move from providing direct advice to presenting general principles to collecting and sharing practices from experienced teams within your company. As we'll see in Chapter 2, there are a handful of principles and practices you can leverage to create the kind of governance model that works for your company.

Summary

In this opening chapter, we touched on a number of important aspects of API management that appear within this book. We acknowledged that while APIs continue to be a driving force, barely 50% of companies surveyed are confident of their ability to properly manage these APIs. We also clarified the many uses of the term API and how these different uses may make it harder to provide a consistent governance model for your program.

Most importantly, we introduced the notion that managing "an API" (as in a single API) is very different from managing your "API landscape." In the first case, you can rely on AaaP, API lifecycle, and API maturity models. Change management for APIs is also very much focused on this "an API" way of thinking. But this is just part of the story.

Next, we discussed managing your API landscape—the entire API ecosystem within your organization. Managing a growing landscape of APIs takes a different set of skills and metrics; these are skills that deal with variety, volume, volatility, vulnerability, and several other aspects. In fact, these landscape aspects all affect the API lifecycle, and we'll review them in detail later in this book.

Finally, we pointed out that even the way you make your decisions about your API program will need to change over time. As your system grows, you need to distribute decision making just as you distribute IT elements like data storage, computational power, security, and other parts of your company's infrastructure.

With this introduction as a background, let's start by focusing on the notion of *governance* and how you can use decision making and the distribution of decisions as a primary element in your overall API management approach.

CHAPTER 2

API Governance

Hey, a rule is a rule, and let's face it, without rules there's chaos.
—Cosmo Kramer

Governance isn't the kind of thing people get excited about. It's also a topic that carries a bit of emotional baggage. After all, few people want to be governed, and most people have had bad experiences with poorly designed governance policies and nonsensical rules. Bad governance (like bad design) makes life harder. But in our experience, it's difficult to talk about API management without addressing it.

In fact, we'll go as far as saying that it's *impossible* to manage your APIs without governing them.

Sometimes, API governance happens in a company, but the term *governance* is never used. That's perfectly fine. Names matter, and in some organizations, governance implies a desire to be highly centralized and authoritative. That can run counter to a culture that embraces decentralization and worker empowerment, so it makes sense that governance is a bad word in those kinds of places. No matter what it's called, some form of decision governance is always taking place.

The question "Should you govern your APIs?" isn't very interesting, because in our opinion, the answer is always yes. Instead, ask yourself: "Which decisions need to be governed?" and "Where should that governance happen?" Deciding on the answers to these types of questions is the work of designing a governance system. Different styles of governance can produce vastly different working cultures, productivity rates, product quality, and strategic value. You'll need to design a system that works for you. Our goal in this chapter is to give you the building blocks to do that.

We'll start by exploring the three foundational elements of good API governance: decisions, management, and complexity. Armed with this understanding, we'll take a closer look at how decisions can actually be distributed in your company and how that impacts the work you do. That means taking a closer look at centralization, decentralization, and the elements of what makes a decision. Finally, we'll take a look at what it means to build a governance system and take a tour of three governance styles.

Governance is a core part of API management, and the concepts we introduce in this chapter will be built upon throughout the rest of this book. So, it's worthwhile to spend some time understanding what API governance really means and how it can help you build a better API management system.

Understanding API Governance

Technology work is the work of making decisions—lots of decisions, in fact. Some of those decisions are vitally important, while others are trivial. All this decision making is the reason that we can say a technology team's work is *knowledge work*. The key skill for a knowledge worker is to make many high-quality decisions, over and over again in a timely fashion. When that happens, products get delivered, changes become easier to make, and teams hit their goals.

No matter which technologies you introduce, how you design your architecture, or which companies you choose to partner with, it's the decision-making abilities of everyone involved that dictate the fate of your business. That's why governance matters. You need to shape all of those decisions in a way that helps you achieve your organizational goals.

That's harder to do than it sounds. To give yourself a better chance of success, you'll need a better understanding of the foundational concepts of governance and how they relate to one another. Let's start by taking a quick look at API decisions.

Decisions

If you can make better decisions, you'll produce better results. APIs are primarily a technology product, but to build better APIs you'll need to make decisions that go well beyond writing good code. Consider the following list of choices API teams often make:

- Should our API's URI be /payments or /PaymentCollection?
- Which cloud provider should we host our API in?
- We have two customer information APIs—which one do we retire?
- Who's going to be on the development team?
- What should I name this Java variable?

From this short list of decisions, we can make a few observations. First, API management choices span a wide spectrum of concerns and people—making those choices will require a lot of coordination between people and teams. Second, the individual choices people make have different levels of impact—the choice of a cloud provider is likely to affect your API management strategy much more than the name of a Java variable. Third, small choices can have a big impact at scale—if 10,000 Java variables are named poorly, the maintainability of your API implementations will suffer greatly.

All of these choices, spanning multiple domains, being made in coordination and at scale, need to come together to produce the best result. That's a big and messy job. Later in this chapter we'll pick this problem apart and give you some guidance for shaping your decision system. But first, let's take a closer look at what it means to *govern* these decisions and why governance is so important.

Decision Management

If you've ever worked on a small project by yourself, you know that the success or failure of that work relies solely on you. If you make good decisions consistently, you can make something good happen. A single, highly skilled programmer can produce some amazing things. But this way of working doesn't scale very well. When the thing you produce starts getting used, the demand for more changes and more features grows. That means you need to make many more decisions in a shorter space of time—which means you'll need more decision makers. Scaling decision making like this requires care. You can't afford for the quality of your decisions to drop just because there are more people making them.

That's where governance comes in. Governance is the process of managing decision making and decision implementation. Notice that we aren't saying that governance is about control or authority. Governance isn't about power. It's about improving the decision-making quality of your people. In the API domain, high-quality governance means producing APIs that help your organization succeed. You may need some level of control and authority to achieve that, but it's not the goal.

Keep in mind that governance always has a cost. Constraints need to be communicated, enforced, and maintained. Rewards that shape decision-making behavior need to be kept valuable and attractive to your audience. Standards, policies, and processes need to be documented, taught, and kept up-to-date. On top of that, constant information gathering is needed to observe the impact of all of this on the system. You may even need to hire more people just to support your governance efforts.

Beyond those general costs of maintaining the machinery of governance, there are also the hidden costs of applying governance to your system. These are the impact costs that come up when you actually start governing the system. For example, if you mandate the technology stack that all developers must use, what is the organizational cost in terms of technological innovation? Also, what will be the cost to employee happiness? Will it become more difficult to attract good talent?

It turns out that these kinds of costs are difficult to predict. That's because in reality you're governing a complex system of people, processes, and technology. To govern an API system, you'll first need to learn what it takes to manage a complex system in general.

Governing Complex Systems

The good news is that you don't need to control every single decision in your organization to get great results. The bad news is that you'll need to figure out which decisions you *will* need to control in order to get those good results. That's not an easy problem to solve, because the answer is that "it depends."

If all you wanted to do was bake a sponge cake, we could give you a pretty definitive recipe for making one. We'd tell you how much flour and how many eggs you'd need and what temperature to set your oven at. We could even tell you exactly how to check if the cake is done. That's because there is very little variability in modern baking. The ingredients are reasonably consistent no matter where you purchase them from. Ovens are designed to cook at specific, standardized temperatures. Most importantly, the goal is the same—a specific kind of cake.

But you aren't making a cake, and this isn't a recipe book. You'll need to deal with an incredible amount of variability. For example, the people in your company will have varying levels of decision-making talent. The regulatory constraints you operate in will be unique to your industry and location. You'll also be serving your own dynamically changing consumer market with its own consumer culture. On top of all that, your organizational goals and strategy will be entirely unique to you.

All this variability makes it tough to prescribe a single correct "recipe" for API governance. To make things even harder, there's also the small problem of knock-on effects. Every time you introduce a rule, create a new standard, or apply any form of governance, you'll have to deal with unintended consequences. That's because all the various parts of your organization are intertwined and connected. For example, to improve the consistency and quality of your API code, you could introduce a standard technology stack. That new stack might result in bigger code packages as programmers start adding more libraries and frameworks. And that could result in a change to the deployment process because the bigger deployment packages can't be supported with the existing system.

With the right information, maybe you could predict and prevent that outcome. But it's impossible to do that for every possible eventuality, especially within a reasonable amount of time. Instead, you'll need to accept the fact that you are working with a complex adaptive system. As it turns out, this is a feature, not a bug. You'll just need to figure out how to use it to your advantage.

Complex adaptive systems

When we say that your organization is a complex adaptive system, we mean:

- It has lots of parts that are interdependent (e.g., people, technologies, process, culture).
- Those parts can change their behavior dynamically and adapt to system changes (e.g., teams changing deployment practices when containerization is introduced).

The universe is full of these kinds of systems, and the study of complexity has become an established scientific discipline. Even you yourself are a complex adaptive system. You might think of yourself as a single unit—a self—but "self" is just an abstraction. In reality, you're a collection of organic cells, albeit a collection of cells that is capable of amazing feats: thinking, moving, sensing, and reacting to external events as an emergent whole "being." At the cellular level, your individual cells are specialized; old, dying cells are replaced, and groups of cells work together to produce big impacts in your body. The complexity of the biological system that you are composed of makes your body highly resilient and adaptable. You're probably not immortal, but you're equally likely to be able to withstand massive amounts of environmental change and even bodily damage, thanks to your complex biological system.

Usually, when we talk about "systems" in technology, we focus on software systems and network-based architecture. Those kinds of systems can definitely grow to be complex. For example, the web is a perfect example of system-level complexity and emergence. Individual servers in a network run independently, but through their dependencies and interconnections produce an emergent whole that we call "the web." But most of that software isn't really *adaptive*.

APIs are no exception. The APIs we write today aren't very adaptive. If they are any good, they do exactly what they are programmed to do. Once an API is released, it's unlikely to change the way it works, unless someone fixes it. The fundamental truth about API governance is that governing APIs alone won't get you very far. Instead, you need to govern the people in your organization and the decisions they make about their APIs. The only way to get better APIs is to help your people make better API decisions.

People are very good at adapting (especially when compared to software). Your API organization is a complex adaptive system. All of the individual people in your organization make many *local* decisions, sometimes collectively and sometimes individually. When all those decisions happen at scale and over time, a system emerges. Just like your body, that system is capable of adapting to a lot of change.

But managing people's decisions requires a special kind of approach. It's difficult to predict the impact of changes in a complex system—making a change to one part of your organization can lead to unintended consequences in another part. That's because the people in your organization are constantly adapting to the changing environment. For example, introducing a rule that deploying software in "containers" is forbidden would have a wide-reaching impact, affecting software design, hiring, deployment processes, and culture.

All of this means that a big, up-front plan and execution approach to API governance is unlikely to work. Instead, you'll need to "nudge" the system by making smaller changes and assessing their impact. It requires an approach of continuous adjustment and improvement, in the same way you might tend to a garden, pruning branches, planting seeds, and watering while continuously observing and adjusting your approach. In Chapter 5, we'll explore the concept of continuous improvement in more detail.

Governing Decisions

In the previous section, we introduced the concept of governing decisions inside a complex system. Ideally, that's helped you to understand a fundamental rule for API governance: if you want your governance system to be effective, you'll need to get better at influencing the decisions that people make. We think one of the best ways to do that is to focus on where decisions are happening and who is making them. It turns out that there isn't a single best way to map out those decisions. For example, consider how API design governance could be handled in two different fictional companies:

Company A: Pendant Software
> At Pendant Software, all API teams are provided with access to the *Pendant Guidelines for API Design* ebook. These guidelines are published quarterly by Pendant's API Center of Excellence and Enablement—a small team of API experts working inside the company. The guidelines contain highly prescriptive and very specific rules for designing APIs. All teams are expected to adhere to the guidelines, and APIs are automatically tested for conformance before they can be published.

> As a result of these policies, Pendant has been able to publish a set of industry-leading, highly consistent APIs that developers rate very favorably. These APIs have helped Pendant differentiate itself from competitors in the marketplace.

Company B: Vandelay Insurance
> At Vandelay, API teams are given the company's business goals and expected results for their API products. These goals and results are defined by the executive teams and are updated regularly. Each API team has the freedom to address

an overall business goal in the manner they choose, and multiple teams can pursue the same goal. API teams can design and implement APIs however they like, but every product must adhere to Vandelay's enterprise measurement and monitoring standards. The standards are defined by Vandelay's System Commune, a group made up of individuals from each of the API teams who join voluntarily and define the set of standards that everyone needs to follow.

As a result of these policies, Vandelay has been able to build a highly innovative, adaptive API architecture. This API system has enabled Vandelay to outmaneuver its competition with innovative business practices that can be delivered very quickly in its technology platform.

In our fictional case studies, both Pendant and Vandelay were wildly successful in their management of decision making. But the way they governed their work was incredibly different. Pendant found success with a highly centralized, authoritative approach, while Vandelay preferred a results-oriented method. Neither approach is "correct," and both styles of governance have merit.

To govern decisions effectively, you'll need to address three key questions:

- Which decisions should be managed?
- Where should those decisions be made (and by whom)?
- How will the system be impacted by your decision management strategy?

 There are lots of decisions to make in an API-enabled system, both at the API level and at the collective, "landscape" level. We'll catalog the breadth of the decisions you need to make and manage in Chapters 4 and 9, respectively.

For now, we'll focus on the second question of where in the system the most important decisions should be made. To help you address decision distribution, we are going to dig deeper into the subject of governing a decision. We'll tackle the trade-off between centralized and decentralized decision making, and we'll take a closer look at what it means to distribute a decision.

Centralization and Decentralization

Earlier in this chapter, we introduced the concept of a complex adaptive system, and we used the human body as an example. These kinds of systems abound in nature, and you are surrounded by them. For example, the ecosystem of a small pond can be thought of as a complex adaptive system. It continues to survive thanks to the activities and interdependence of the animals and vegetation that live in it. The ecosystem adapts to changing conditions thanks to the localized decision making of each of these living things.

But the pond doesn't have a manager, and there is no evidence that the frogs, snakes, and fish hold quarterly management meetings. Instead, each agent in the system makes individual decisions and exhibits individual behaviors. Taken together these individual decisions and actions form a collective, emergent whole that can survive even as individual parts of the system change or appear and disappear over time. Like most of the natural world, the pond system succeeds because system-level decisions are *decentralized* and *distributed*.

As we established earlier, your organization is also a complex adaptive system. It's a product of all the collective individual decisions made by your employees. Just like in a human body or a pond ecosystem, if you were to allow individual workers to have complete freedom and autonomy, the organization as a whole would become more resilient and adaptive. You'd have a bossless, decentralized organization that could find its way thanks to the individual decisions of its employees (see Figure 2-1).

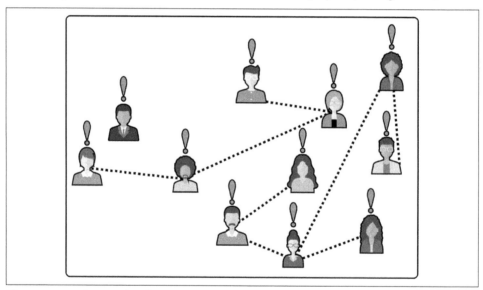

Figure 2-1. A decentralized organization

You could do this, but you might run into some problems, primarily because it's difficult to succeed with a free-market organization in the same way that complex systems succeed in nature. The biosystem of a pond is directed by the hand of natural selection. Every agent in the system has become optimized for the survival of its species. There's no system-level goal beyond survival. On top of that, in nature it's normal for systems to fail. For example, if an invasive species is introduced, the entire pond system might die. In the natural world, that can be OK because something else might take its place—the system as a whole remains resilient.

However, businesses leaders don't respond well to this level of uncertainty and lack of control. Chances are you'll need to steer your system toward specific goals that go beyond survival. Also, it's likely that you aren't willing to risk letting your company die for the sake of a better company taking its place. You'll almost certainly want to reduce the risk that any individual agent can destroy the whole company because of a bad decision. That means you'll need to reduce decision-making freedom for individuals and introduce some accountability. One way of doing that is to introduce decision *centralization* (Figure 2-2).

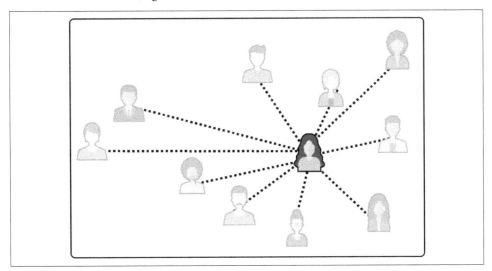

Figure 2-2. A centralized organization

By this, we mean that decision making is constrained to a particular person or team in your organization. That centralized team makes a decision that the rest of the company will need to adhere to. Decentralization is the opposite case: individual teams can make decisions that only they need to adhere to.

The truth is that there is no perfectly centralized or perfectly decentralized organization. Instead, different types of decisions are distributed within the organization in different ways—some are more centralized, while others are more decentralized. You'll need to decide how to distribute the decisions that impact your system the most. So, which ones should be more centralized, and which ones should be more decentralized?

Remember, a primary goal of governing decisions is to help your organization succeed and survive. What that means is entirely dependent on your business context, but generally speaking it means that decisions need to be timely enough to enable business agility and of sufficient quality to improve the business (or at the very least avoid damaging it). There are three factors that impact the ability to make decisions:

Availability and accuracy of information

It's really difficult to make a good decision if you base it on information that is incorrect or missing. That could mean being misled about the goal or context of the decision, but it could also mean not knowing what the decision's impact will be on the system. Most of the time, we assume the responsibility for gathering decision-making information rests at the feet of the decision makers. But for the purposes of distributing decisions, we also need to think about how centralizing or decentralizing a decision affects the information that's available.

Decision-making talent

Generally speaking, decision quality improves if the decision maker is good at making high-quality decisions. Or, in simpler language—highly talented people with lots of experience will make better decisions than less-talented people with no experience. When it comes to distributing decision making, the challenge is to also distribute your talent in a way that helps you the most.

Coordination costs

Complex decisions can't be made in a timely manner unless the decision making is shared. But whenever you share decision-making work, you'll incur a coordination cost. If that coordination cost grows too high, you won't be able to make decisions quickly enough. Centralization and decentralization of decisions can have a big impact on coordination costs.

Thinking about decisions in terms of these factors will help you decide when a decision should be centralized or decentralized. To help you understand how to do that, we'll take a look at it from two perspectives: scope of optimization and scale of operation. Let's start by digging into scope and its relationship with decision-making information.

Scope of optimization

The big difference between a centralized decision and a decentralized decision has to do with their scope. When you make a centralized decision, you are making it for the entire organization. So, your scope for the decision includes the whole system, and your goal is to make a decision that improves that system. Another way of saying this is that the decision you are making is meant to *optimize the system scope*. For example, a centralized team might decide on a development methodology for the entire company to follow. The same team might also make decisions about which APIs in the system should be retired. Both of these decisions would be made with the goal of doing what's best for the entire system.

Conversely, the primary characteristic of a decentralized decision is that it is *optimized for a local scope*. When you are optimizing for the local scope, you are making a decision that will improve your local context—the set of information that pertains only to your local situation. While your decision might have an impact on the wider system, your goal is to improve your local results. For example, an API team can make a local decision to use a waterfall development process because they're sharing the work with an external company that insists on it.

The great thing about decentralized decision making is that it can help you make big gains in efficiency, innovation, and agility for your business overall. That's because decentralized decision makers are able to limit their scope of information to a local context that they understand. This means they can form a decision based on accurate information about their own problem space, which helps them produce better decisions. For any modern business that is trying to succeed with a strategy of agility and innovation, the decentralized decision pattern should be the default approach.

However, making decisions that focus only on optimizing the local scope can cause problems, particularly if those decisions have the potential to impact the system negatively and in irreversible ways. When former Amazon CEO Jeff Bezos (*https:// oreil.ly/v5Ois*) talks about the impact of decisions, he splits them into two types: "type 1" decisions that can be easily reversed if they are wrong and "type 2" decisions that are near impossible to recover from. For example, a lot of big companies choose to centralize decisions about API security configuration to prevent a local optimization from creating a system vulnerability.

Beyond dangers to the system, there are times when system-level consistency is more valuable than local optimization. For example, an individual API team might choose an API style that makes the most sense for their problem domain. But if every API team chooses a different API style, the job of learning to use each API becomes more difficult due to a lack of consistency, especially when many APIs need to be used to accomplish a single task. In this case, optimizing the API style decision for the system scope might be better.

You'll need to think about the scope of optimization carefully when you plan where a decision should happen. If a decision has the potential to impact your system in an irreversible way, start by centralizing it so that it can be optimized for system scope. If decision quality could benefit from the local context of information, start by decentralizing it. If decentralizing a decision could result in unacceptable inconsistency at the system level, consider centralizing it.

Scale of operation

If you had unlimited resources for making good decisions, you'd only need to think about scope for decision making. But you don't. So, in addition to scope, you'll need to think about the scale of decisions being made. That's because if there is a bigger decision demand, there will be more pressure on your decision-making talent supply and an upward pressure on your coordination costs. If you want your API work to scale as your organization grows, you'll need to plan your decision distribution pattern carefully.

Decentralizing a decision creates a big talent demand when you are operating at scale. When you decentralize a decision, you are distributing it to more than one team. If you want all of those decisions to be high quality, you'll need to fill each of those teams with talented decision makers. If you can't afford to do that, you'll end up generating lots of bad decisions. So, it's worthwhile to hire the best decision makers you can for every decision-making position in your company.

Unfortunately, hiring good people isn't an industry secret. There are a limited number of talented and experienced people available and a lot of companies competing to hire them. Some companies are willing to spend whatever it takes to make sure that they get the best talent in the world. If you are lucky enough to be in that situation, you can decentralize more of your decisions because you have the talent to make them. Otherwise, you'll need to be more pragmatic with your distribution decisions.

If your supply of top-level, "grade A" decision-making talent is limited, you may choose to pool that talent together and centralize the most important decisions to that group of people. That way, you have a greater chance of producing better decisions, faster. But an increasing scale of decision demand wreaks havoc on this model too, because as the demand for decision making grows, the centralized team will need to grow along with it. As the team grows, so too will the cost of coordinated decision making. No matter how talented the people are, the cost of coordinating a decision grows as you add more people. Eventually you'll reach a number that makes it impossible to reach decisions affordably.

All of this means that decision distribution will involve a lot of trade-offs. If the decision is highly impactful, like the "type 1" decisions that Jeff Bezos describes, you'll need to centralize it and pay the price of lower decision-making throughput. Conversely, if speed and local optimization are most important, you can decentralize the decision and either pay for better people or accept the net reduction in quality of decisions.

That said, there is a way to manage this trade-off in a more nuanced and flexible way. It involves distributing the *parts* of the decision instead of the entire decision itself, and it's what we are going to focus on in the next section.

The Elements of a Decision

It's difficult to distribute a decision in the way we've described so far because it's a bit of an all-or-nothing affair. Do you let your teams decide which development method they want to use, or do you choose one and make every team use it? Do you let the teams decide when their API should retire, or do you take the choice away from them completely? In reality, governance requires more nuance. In this section, we'll explore a way of distributing decisions with more flexibility by breaking them up into pieces.

Instead of distributing the entire decision, you can distribute parts of the decision. That way you can get the benefits of system-level optimization along with highly contextual local optimization at the same time. Some parts of a decision can be centralized, while other parts are decentralized. To help you accomplish distribution with this kind of precision, we've broken down API decisions into the six *decision elements* you'll need to distribute (see Figure 2-3).

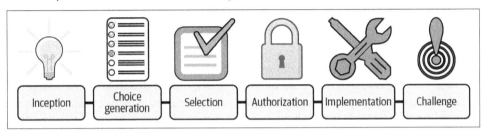

Figure 2-3. Decision elements

This isn't meant to be an authoritative, universal model for decision making. Instead, it's a model that we've developed to distinguish the parts of a decision that have the biggest impact on a system when they are either centralized or decentralized. These parts are based on the various five-, six-, and seven-step models of decision making that abound in the business management domain. Although the steps we'll describe could be applied to a decision made by a single person, they're most useful when we are talking about decisions made in coordination between a group of people.

Let's start by taking a look at how distributing the inception of a decision impacts your system.

Inception

Every decision happens because someone thinks that decision needed to be made. It means that someone has identified that a problem or opportunity exists with more than one possible solution. Sometimes this is obvious, but in many cases spotting a decision-making opportunity requires talent and expertise. You'll need to think about which decisions will naturally ignite on their own and which ones will need special handling to make sure that they happen.

Kicking off decisions about API work happens naturally in the course of day-to-day problem solving. For example, choosing which database to use for storing persistent data would be a difficult decision for a typical implementer to ignore. The decision happens because the work can't continue without it. But there will also be situations where you'll need to force inception to happen. This is usually for one of two reasons:

Habitualized decision making

Over time, if a team makes the same decision over and over, the decision may disappear. That is, the possibilities are no longer considered, and instead an assumption is made that work will continue in the same way it always has. For example, if every API implementation is written in the Java programming language, it may not occur to anyone to consider a different choice of language.

Decision blindness

Sometimes, teams will miss opportunities to make impactful decisions. This can happen because of habit but also because of limited information, experience, or talent. For example, a team may focus on the choice of which database to use for storage but fail to identify that the API could be designed in a way that doesn't require persistent storage.

Not every decision needs to happen, and it's perfectly fine for decisions to be missed or for a cultural habit to make them implicit. It's only a problem if not making a decision negatively impacts the results you are getting from your APIs. Arbitrarily demanding that more decisions happen could have a nightmarish impact on productivity. Instead, the role of API governance is to generate more of the decisions that will lead to optimal results and less of the decisions that will provide little value.

Choice generation

It's hard to choose if you don't know your options, and that's what this element is all about. Choice generation is the work of identifying the choices to choose from.

If you're making a decision in a domain you have a lot of experience in, generating choices can be pretty easy. But if there are lots of unknowns, you'll need to spend more time identifying the possibilities. For example, an experienced C programmer already has a good idea of their options when they are deciding on a loop structure, but a beginner will probably need to do some investigation to learn that they can use a `for` loop or a `while` loop and the differences between the two.

Even if you know a domain fairly well, you'll probably spend more time on choice generation if the cost and impact of the decision are very high. For example, you may have intimate knowledge of the different cloud hosting environments, but will still perform your due diligence of research when it comes time to sign a contract with one of them. Are there new vendors available that you didn't know about? Are the prices and terms still the same as you remember?

From a governance perspective, choice generation is important because it's where the *boundaries* of decision making are set. This is especially useful when the people coming up with the list of choices are not the same as the people making the selection. For example, you could standardize a list of possible API description formats but let individual teams decide which format they like best. If you take this approach, you'll need to be careful about the quality of the "menu" you are providing. If the choices are overly restrictive or of poor quality, you'll run into problems.

Selection

Selection is the act of choosing from the list of possible options. Selection is the heart of decision making, and it's the step most people focus on, but the importance of the selection element depends a lot on the scope of choices that have been made available. If that scope is very wide, then the selection process is integral to the quality of the decision. But if that scope has been constrained to safe choices with little differentiating them, the selection step can be quick and less impactful.

Let's walk through an example of this in action. Suppose you're responsible for configuring Transport Layer Security (TLS) for your HTTP API. Part of that work includes a decision on which cipher suites (sets of cryptography algorithms) the server should support. It's an important decision because some cipher suites have become vulnerable with age, so picking the wrong ones can make your API less secure. Also, if you choose cipher suites that your users' client software doesn't understand, nobody will be able to use your API.

In one scenario, you might be given a list of all the known cipher suites and asked to select the ones that the server should support. In this case, selection would need special care. You'd probably do a lot of research and only feel comfortable making a selection once you'd gathered as much information as possible. In fact, if you didn't have a good amount of experience securing servers, you'd probably look for someone who did and ask them to make a selection for you.

But what if instead of being given the set of all possible cipher suites, you were given a curated list of them? The list of options might also include relevant information about how well supported each cipher suite is and what the known vulnerabilities are. Armed with this information, you could probably make a faster choice. Equally, your choice is likely to be safer because your decision scope is limited to choices that have been deemed safe enough to use. In this case, you'd make a decision based on what you know about the clients using the API and the sensitivity and business importance of the API.

Finally, you might be given only one choice: a single cipher suite that you must use. A single-choice decision makes selection a trivial affair—the decision has been made for you. In this case, the quality of the decision is entirely dependent on the people who generated that choice. Ideally it's a good fit for the specific requirements you have.

So, the importance of selection depends a lot on the scope of the choices offered. There's a bit of a trade-off at work here. If you push more of the decision-making investment into choice generation, you'll spend less time on selection, and vice versa. That has implications for how you distribute decision elements and who should be responsible for them. Whichever decision element becomes more important will require a suitably talented decision maker to make it.

It also means you can combine system scope and local scope by distributing choice *generation* and choice *selection*. For example, you can centralize the generation of development method choices based on the system context while still allowing individual teams to choose their preferred method using their local context. This happens to be a particularly useful pattern for governing large API landscapes at scale and preserving both safety and speed of change.

Authorization

Just because a choice has been selected doesn't mean the decision is done. The selection needs to be authorized before it can be realized. Authorization is the work of deciding on the validity of the selected choice. Was the right selection made? Is it implementable? Is it safe? Does it make sense in the context of other decisions that have been made?

Authorization can be implicit or explicit. When authorization is explicit, it means that someone or some team must expressly authorize the decision before it can go forward. It becomes an approval step in the decision-making process. We're sure you've been involved in many decisions that required some kind of approval. For example, in many companies, workers can select their holiday time from a list of work dates, but it's up to their manager to make the final approval decision on the schedule.

Implicit authorization means that authorization happens automatically when some set of criteria has been met. Examples of this are the role of the person making the selection, the cost of the selection that was made, or adherence to a specific policy. In particular, authorization can become implicit when the person making the selection is also the person authorizing the selection. In effect, they become their own approver.

Explicit authorization is useful because it can further improve the safety of the decision. But if there are lots of decisions being made and all of them are being *centrally* authorized, then there is likely to be a reduction in decision speed. Lots of people will end up waiting for their approvals. Implicit authorization greatly increases the speed of decision making by empowering selection, but comes with greater risk.

How authorization should be distributed will be an important decision for you to make in your governance design. You'll need to consider the quality of decision makers, the business impact of bad decisions, and the amount of risk built into the choices offered. For highly sensitive decisions, you'll probably want more explicit authorization. For time-sensitive, large-scale decisions, you'll need to figure out how to introduce an implicit authorization system.

Implementation

The decision-making process doesn't end when the choice is authorized. A decision isn't realized until someone does the work of executing or implementing the choice that has been made. Implementation is an important part of API management work. If the implementation of decisions is too slow or of poor quality, then all of your decision making is for naught.

Oftentimes a decision isn't implemented by the people who made the selection. In these cases it's important to understand what that means for the availability of accurate information gathering. For example, you might choose to introduce the hypermedia style of APIs into your landscape, but if the implementation of hypermedia APIs turns out to be too difficult for the designers and developers, you'll need to reevaluate your decision. A good governance design will have to take these practicalities into account. It's no good managing decisions in a way that makes them only *theoretically* better. When you are determining the quality of decision making, you'll need to include the implementability of the decision you are managing.

Challenge

Decisions aren't immutable, and each decision you make for your API management system should be open to being challenged. Oftentimes we don't consider how the decisions we make may need to be revisited, altered, or even reversed in the future. Defining a challenge element allows us to plan for continuous change at the decision-making level.

For example, if you've defined a "menu" of choices for API teams to choose from, it's wise to also define a process to go "off-menu." That way you can sustain a decent level of innovation and prevent bad decisions from being made. But if everyone can challenge the decision to constrain these choices, then there aren't really any constraints. So, you'll need to identify who can challenge the decision and in what circumstances.

It's also important to allow decisions to be challenged over time. As business strategies and context change, so too should the decisions of your system. To plan for that kind of adaptability, you'll need to build the challenge function into your system. That means you'll need to think about who in your organization will have the ability to "pull the cord" and challenge an existing decision.

Decision Mapping

We now know that decisions are composed of a number of elements. Understanding that decisions have atomic elements allows us to distribute the pieces of a decision rather than the entire decision process. This turns out to be a powerful feature of organizational design and will allow you to exert greater influence over the balance of efficiency and thoroughness.

For example, a decision about the style a new API should have is an important one. In the clumsy, binary centralization versus decentralization discussion, the API management designer might consider whether the members of the API team should own the API style decision (decentralized) or a central body should maintain control of it (centralized). The advantage of distributing the decision-making power to the API teams is that each team can make the decision within a local context. The advantages of centralizing the decision within a single strategic team are that the variation in API styles is reduced, and control over the quality of the style choice is maintained and controlled.

This is a difficult trade-off to make. But, if instead you distribute the *elements* of the decision, it's possible to design an API management system that lives somewhere in between these two binary options. For example, you might decide that for an API style decision, the elements of *research* and *choice generation* should be owned by a centralized, strategic API management team, while the elements of *choice selection*, *authorization*, and *implementation* are owned by the API teams themselves. In this way, you choose to sacrifice some of the innovation that comes from distributing choice generation in order to gain the benefits of a known set of API styles within the company. At the same time, distribution of the API style selection and authorization elements allows the API teams to continue to operate at speed (i.e., they do not need to ask permission in order to choose a suitable style).

To get the most out of decision mapping, you'll need to distribute decisions based on your context and goals. Let's take a look at two fairly common decision scenarios to see how decision mapping can be a useful tool.

Decision mapping example: Choosing a programming language

You've identified that the decision of which programming language to choose for API implementation is highly impactful, and you'd like to govern it. Your organization has adopted a *microservices* style of architecture, and freedom to choose the programming language for implementation has been raised as a requirement. But after running a few experiments, you've noticed that variation in programming languages makes it harder for developers to move between teams and harder for security and operations teams to support applications.

As a result, you've decided to try the decision distribution in Table 2-1 for deciding on a programming language.

Table 2-1. Programming language decision map

Inception	Choice generation	Choice selection	Authorization	Implementation	Challenge
Centralized	Centralized	Decentralized	Decentralized	Decentralized	Decentralized

This way you constrain the programming languages to a set of choices that are optimized for the system as a whole but allow the individual teams to optimize for their local contexts within those constraints. You've also allowed API teams to challenge the decision so that you can accommodate new language choices and changing situations.

Decision mapping example: Tool selection

Your chief technical officer (CTO) is trying to improve the level of agility and innovation of your software platform. As part of this initiative, they have decided to allow API teams to choose their own software stacks for implementations, including the use of open source software. However, your procurement and legal teams have raised concerns based on legal risks and risks to supplier relationships. To get started with this cultural transition, you've decided to implement the decision map in Table 2-2 for the software stack decision on a trial basis.

Table 2-2. Tool selection decision map

Inception	Choice generation	Choice selection	Authorization	Implementation	Challenge
Decentralized	Decentralized	Decentralized	Centralized	Decentralized	Centralized

Local optimization is one of the keys to your CTO's strategy, so you choose to completely decentralize inception, choice generation, and selection. However, to reduce the system-level risk of a choice, you've mapped the authorization element to the centralized procurement and legal teams. This should work for now, but you are also aware that over time and at scale this has the potential to be a big bottleneck in your system, so you make a note to keep measuring the process and tune it accordingly.

Decision Design in Practice

In our own API management work, we've rarely documented decisions using the decision-mapping structure we've defined in this section. That's because a decision map isn't a great way to communicate how work should be done or how a team can achieve their goal. Think of the decision map as a useful mental model that you can keep in your API management "toolbox."

In practice, the decision map isn't a great way of describing how people should work or how teams should communicate with one another to get work done. That's because the decision map is a high-level abstraction: it focuses purely on the elements of a decision. Instead, you'll need to communicate your design in a language that fits your context.

For example, in the enterprise management space, you might realize the decision design by creating a target operating model (TOM). The TOM describes organizational structures, process models, and the tools that teams will need to succeed. If you're working in the world of technology and architecture, you could use *Team Topologies* and draw a coordination model that can be translated into a software architecture. Ultimately, you'll need to express your target state in the language of the work, decisions, and concepts that your people will understand.

Team Topologies

Team Topologies (https://oreil.ly/wmJZY) is a book that outlines a design approach by the same name created by Matthew Skelton and Manuel Pais. It provides a useful model and language for designing software by first focusing on teams and the way they work together.

Understanding that the decision-making process can be broken up into distributable parts is important because it encourages more precision in your governance approach. It will help you get better results when it comes time to design the important parts of your governance system. You'll be able to consider which parts of your organization should own the individual elements of key decisions. With that understanding, you'll be able to start applying solutions to focus on introducing constraints and changing behaviors for those teams and people.

Designing Your Governance System

We've spent a lot of time going into the details of decision distribution because we think it's a foundational concept for a governance system. But it's not the only thing you'll need to pay attention to if you want to introduce effective API governance. A good API governance system should have the following features:

- Decision distribution based on impact, scope, and scale
- Enforcement of system constraints and validation of implementation (from centralized decisions)
- Incentivization to shape decision making (for decentralized decisions)
- Adaptiveness through impact measurement and continuous improvement

It's difficult to get the advantages of decision centralization if the rest of the organization doesn't conform to the decision. That's why enforcement and validation needs to be a feature of an API governance system. We've purposefully steered away from the authoritative parts of governance so far, but ultimately you'll need to build at least some constraints into your system. Even the most decentralized organizations have rules that need to be followed. Of course, validation and enforcement will require some level of obedience. If the centralized decision-making team has no authority, the decisions will carry no weight.

If you don't have authority, you can use incentivization instead of enforcement. This is especially useful when you've decided to decentralize decisions but still want to shape the selections that are being made. For example, an architecture team could alter a deployment process so that deployment of immutable containers is made much cheaper and easier than any other type of deployment. The goal here would be to incentivize API teams who have authority over their own implementation decisions to choose containerization more often.

In truth, neither the "carrot" of incentivization nor the "stick" of enforcement is enough to steer your system on its own—you'll need to use both. Generally speaking, if a decision's authorization element has been decentralized, you'll have to use incentivization if you want to shape it. If selection and authorization have been centralized and implementation is decentralized, you'll need to make sure you've instituted some level of enforcement or validation. Table 2-3 highlights when you should enforce or incentivize a decision based on your decision-mapping design.

Table 2-3. When to enforce and when to incentivize

Enforce or incentivize?	Choice generation	Choice selection	Authorization
Enforce	Centralized	Centralized or decentralized	Centralized or decentralized
Incentivize	Decentralized	Decentralized	Decentralized

No matter how you distribute your decisions or change decision-making behavior, it's crucial that you measure the impact you are having on the system itself. Ideally, your organization should have some existing process indicators and measurements that you can use to assess the impact of your changes. If there isn't anything like that, instituting organizational measurements should be one of your first priorities. Later, in Chapter 7, we'll talk about product measurement patterns for APIs. Although we'll be focusing on API product measurement specifically, you can still use that section as an introductory guide for designing governance measurements for your system.

To help tie all this together, let's take a look at three API governance patterns. These patterns capture different approaches to API governance, but all of them use the core principles of decision distribution, enforcement, incentivization, and measurement. Keep in mind, we aren't offering you a menu—you aren't supposed to choose one of these to be *your* governance system. We are offering you these patterns as a way of illustrating how an API governance system can be implemented at a conceptual level.

For each governance pattern described, we'll identify a few key decisions and how they are mapped, how desired behaviors are enforced and incentivized, how talent is distributed, and the costs, benefits, and measures for the approach.

Governance Pattern #1: Design Authority

A design authority acts as a gatekeeper, ensuring that the outputs of API teams conform to a minimum level of quality. Design authorities are centralized teams that provide assurance for the quality of decision making in the organization. They can be implemented as formal review boards that meet on a regular basis or as an on-demand review service. Mature design authorities may even provide self-service tooling to make the work of conformance testing cheap and easy.

PayPal's Central Design Team

At PayPal, a central design authority team validates all new API designs using a four-step process.[1] They begin by examining proposals for new APIs to make sure they are a good fit for the business and don't already exist. Next, they test API designs to make sure that they conform to PayPal's published standards. After the API is developed, the design team runs a set of tests to make sure that the implementation matches the design contract. Finally, the published API is checked to make sure that it meets PayPal's security requirements.

Enforcement and incentivization

Design authorities are most effective when they have the power to prevent low-quality, high-risk decisions from being made. That usually means they have the authority to stop a change from being deployed if their quality requirements are not met. In some companies, design authorities must function without authority. Instead, these teams issue *audit notes* that highlight risks. In these cases, decision-making quality relies on a team's desire to address the notes that the design authority has made. Whether this works or not depends a lot on the culture of the organization and the people involved. To be effective, a design authority should be more than a gate-keeping team, even when they have the authority to be one. The team should endeavor to both validate that good decisions have been made as well as inform teams on how to meet their quality requirements. That means they'll need to provide consumable information and guidance to help teams avoid an endless cycle of conformance validation.

Talent distribution

In this pattern, a small number of expert decision makers are centralized in the design authority team. But, they must be supported by API teams that have competent decision makers who can make decisions that conform to the design authority's requirements. Otherwise, the system becomes bogged down by

---

1 Thomas Bush, "PayPal's Four-Step Process for Building Governance-Friendly APIs," Nordic APIs (blog), June 9, 2020, *https://oreil.ly/H6Ahj*.

low-quality designs that need continuous help. In this pattern, it's common for the talent level of API teams to increase over time as they go through the design and review process.

Costs and benefits

The primary benefit of this pattern is that *all* APIs are run through the same team for quality control. This gives the organization maximum assurance that the right decisions have been made and risks have been addressed. This kind of thoroughness is crucial for decisions that could adversely impact a business. For example, in large companies, API designs are almost always validated to make sure they implement security and access controls correctly. But, the design authority's strength is also its greatest weakness. Running all API changes through a single centralized team is a bottleneck waiting to happen. In the early stages of an API-enabled company, a design authority can help immensely, but over time it can become an enormous problem, causing API projects to stall as they wait to get time with the team.

Governance Pattern #2: Embedded Centralized Experts

In this pattern, instead of validating the outputs of an API team, experts are embedded into the team to help with decision making. A typical implementation of this pattern is an internal consulting model, in which a central pool of API experts are distributed to API teams. These experts either enable key decisions or are given the authority to make decisions on behalf of the team. But, the key characteristic of this pattern is that the experts become part of the API team, investing their time to help produce better outputs.

The Embedded Expert pattern relies on a central team of API experts who can be distributed to work in API teams. Counterintuitively, this means that the research and choice selection parts of decisions are centralized (even though they are executed within federated teams). This works when the central team of experts have a shared understanding of the "right" decisions for the company. Think of it like a distributed version of the design authority. But, the actual authorization and implementation of those choices are usually still owned by the teams themselves, leaving those elements decentralized. We'll discuss this type of centralized team structure later in "The Center for Enablement" on page 254.

HSBC's API Champions

HSBC is a globally diverse and distributed organization, with many different teams building APIs for their clients to use. To help their teams build better APIs, they've created a network of *API champions* (*https://oreil.ly/Gezig*) who understand and apply HSBC API standards for local project teams. This helps them distribute API expertise across the organization at scale.

Enforcement and incentivization

Embedding experts in a project team is the ultimate form of enforcement. That's because the embedded experts either own or directly inform the decision-making process. If your experts make decisions aligned with your central objectives, so will the teams they are embedded within.

Talent distribution

A big challenge of running a consulting team is finding and maintaining a group of experts. For this pattern to work, you'll need a pool of API subject-matter experts that can be distributed to project and product teams. That talent can be centrally funded but is distributed decentrally to API teams and will need to scale to meet the demand for API work in the system.

Costs and benefits

Being at the "coalface" of API work has several distinct advantages. First, it ensures that better decisions are made early due to the involvement of a central team's experts in the work. Second, experts are able to bring back experiences and knowledge from the work to ensure that central guidance is continually improved to meet the needs of product and project teams. However, there are severe operational challenges to this pattern. It requires an adequately large team of experts to help every team. Depending on the scale of your organization, this can be a challenge. Finally, it takes a concerted effort to maintain a shared system-level optimization view among experts who are facing the day-to-day challenges of delivering API products. Over time, this can result in a fully decentralized decision model with little consistency or management.

Governance Pattern #3: Influenced Self-Governance

We've noticed a trend in modern organizations toward less central control and more team autonomy, within reason. As the business and technology world continues to strive for more innovation and faster speed of change, there is less appetite for central teams that control decision making with absolute authority. That's given rise to a third kind of governance pattern that relies heavily on influence rather than control.

In this pattern, API teams have autonomy in a decision space. They have decision-making agency and own all elements of the decision-making process. Their decisions are "governed" by influencing the decisions that they make. A common way of phrasing this is to make it difficult to do the wrong things and easier to do the right things.

Spotify's Golden Path

Spotify has embraced a platform approach called the *Golden Path* (*https://oreil.ly/chT9y*) that provides a catalog of tools and services to Spotify engineering teams. These are the recommended tools within the Spotify system. It's easier for Spotify teams to use these tools because they know that they are "blessed" by the platform team and are supported. However, if needed, a team can go *off-menu* and use a tool of their choice.

Enforcement and incentivization

This pattern relies completely on incentivization to influence decision making. This pattern embodies the Netflix principle of Freedom and Responsibility (*https://oreil.ly/DdTxl*). Teams are provided with a "Golden Path" of recommended decisions, driven by a central team. Teams have the freedom to make a different decision; however, they are also responsible for the success of their products. Ideally, this balance drives teams to make decisions that conform to the central team's offering.

Talent distribution

For this type of pattern to work, teams must be capable of making good decisions independently. That means that talent must be distributed so that every team has at least one expert who can guide API decision making properly. In organizations where this scale of talent distribution is not possible, this pattern is often combined with a design authority ("Governance Pattern #1: Design Authority" on page 38) as a safeguard.

Costs and benefits

The key benefit of this pattern is speed. Teams can move very fast when they are given autonomy over their decisions. But, that speed comes with the risk that decisions will be inconsistent and or inadequate. In addition, local teams may over-optimize for their local context to the detriment of the system. In practice, self-governance is often combined with a centrally driven governance pattern to balance these factors.

Implementing Governance Patterns

As we mentioned earlier in this chapter, if your API organization is a complex adaptive system, it needs a lot of "nudges" to get good results. We've also introduced a set of patterns that can help you distribute experts and tools to guide decisions in the right direction. In this section, we'll detail some strategies for implementing and introducing these decision-guiding patterns in a practical manner.

We'll outline the high-level parts of a governance solution that you'll need to tackle, including how to get started, how to get information, and how to produce tools and assets. Later in this book, we'll dive into specific aspects of management and governance in more detail. For example, in Chapter 9 we'll cover considerations when forming a central team and the concept of a "platform."

Evolving Your Solution

A central tenet of this book is that API management must be *continuous* to be successful. That means that you'll need to continuously adapt and evolve your governance implementation as your organization grows and changes. The truth is that you won't create a perfect governance system on day one.

But, we still need to strive to start with a governance solution that works as well as possible immediately. We also need to ensure that we don't introduce a solution that will be costly to change. With that in mind, we provide the following practices when implementing a new governance solution:

Embed early

When embarking on a new governance solution, try to start by implementing the pattern covered in "Governance Pattern #2: Embedded Centralized Experts" on page 39 with a small set of indicative products or projects. This isn't always possible to do, especially when there is a large backlog of APIs that need to be validated quickly. But, if you can afford to do it, starting with embedding gives you a chance to test and learn your standards before you ratify and communicate them to the organization. It's usually easier to change a design decision in a project than it is to change a published standard that the company has adopted en masse. Another benefit of starting this way is that your team of experts can build a network of relationships with product teams and experiences from the front lines. If you plan to move to a centralized design authority (as covered in "Governance Pattern #1: Design Authority" on page 38), this can help to counteract the "ivory tower," out-of-touch syndrome that often develops in highly centralized teams.

Implement observability early

You'll never succeed at improving your system if you can't observe what is happening. In our experience, it's worth investing in observability and visibility early in the life of your governance solution. The more information you can get, the better. From a practical perspective, it makes sense to start by focusing on data collection. You can improve your insight and observability features as your solution matures.

Automate after

When it comes to API governance, automation provides a massive benefit. Tools and automation reduce operational costs, provide more data to collect, and make it easier for everyone to conform to your quality standards. But, you don't get automation for free. It takes effort and investment to implement an automation solution. Changes to the solution can also come at high cost. This change cost can result in organizations not wanting to change their governance advice because they are limited by the tools they've chosen. In our experience, automation and tooling are ideal for the more established decision areas of your API system. For example, we recommend that you use a human review process for API designs first before you establish a *linting* tool to automate design validation. This ensures that you have the flexibility to establish the right checks before you land on a tool-based solution.

Create centralized teams cautiously

As the number of APIs (and API teams) grows in your company, there will inevitably be pressure to create central teams to help manage the decision-making work. In fact, central teams are an essential part of scaling all of the governance patterns we defined earlier. However, be cautious when starting a new centralized team. Unlike standards and tools, teams are often difficult to downsize or disband. In some cases, a central team may start to make its own existence its goal. Once the genie is out of the bottle, it can be difficult to put back in. Creating these teams cautiously may mean starting with a pool of *borrowed resources* from other teams or keeping the team small and lean until demand necessitates growth. Another approach we've heard of is to make the dissolution of the central team a key goal. Ultimately, the central team serves a strong and necessary purpose: optimizing APIs for system concerns. The challenge is to strike the balance between meeting that need and creating an unnecessary overhead.

Observability and Visibility

As we've mentioned, getting data early is an important factor in implementing a good governance solution. At a minimum, you should focus on gathering information across these data points when you get started:

- All APIs that have been released and are currently running in production systems
- Ownership and funding of APIs in the organization
- Runtime traffic per API

- Adoption (or conformance) levels of your standards and tools for each API

The difficulty of gathering this information will depend greatly on the size of your organization and its investment in APIs. In fact, in large enterprises, this kind of data collection can be a project in its own right. We'll get into this in more detail in "Understanding the Landscape" on page 234.

But, achieving adequate observability will require more than a data collection project. You'll need to influence API decisions so that API teams provide you with the data you need. You can also use infrastructure and tooling to automate the gathering of data at runtime. Our recommendation is to focus on these aspects of your system early.

Operating Models

If you're implementing a design authority (covered in "Governance Pattern #1: Design Authority" on page 38) for some of your decision space, you'll need to set up formal meetings, checkpoints, or forums for reviews. But, even if you don't implement this pattern, you'll still need to think about how you'll gather and share information across your organization. This requires you to think about how your teams will operate on a day-to-day basis and how they will coordinate with one another.

This is actually an essential part of your governance design and implementation. Your operating or coordination model will have the biggest impact on the autonomy and speed of your API teams as well as the quality of the decisions that they make. The way that you share information and make decisions will depend a lot on your organizational culture. We'll talk a bit more about team designs and coordination models later in the book in Chapter 8. For now, keep in mind that this is a key ingredient for the solution you develop.

Develop a Strategy for Standards Management

We've yet to meet an API team that doesn't work with some kind of standard for their API development. In rare cases, those standards aren't written down and shared through a spoken history of how "things are done." But, most of the time API standards are documented in written form.

Standards are useful because they document a constrained set of choices for a decision space. So, it's worth spending some time thinking about how you'll capture, manage, and share the standards for your system. But, keep in mind that every standard you write comes with its own management and operational costs. Sadly, we've seen many examples of companies that start with a small set of useful standards, only to have them balloon into an unmanageable, difficult-to-consume (and often out-of-date) mess of documentation.

Ideally, standards should be managed like a product or a platform. At a minimum, you should define how they should be created, how they will be edited, how they will be distributed, and how they will be maintained. For example, you could open up standards authoring to anyone in the organization but have a design authority determine which standards get published. You could also follow an IETF-like process (*https://oreil.ly/UA97h*) that provides a transparent, community-based review process for standards acceptance.

Standards management and processes aren't unique to the API domain. But, due to the variability of solutions in the API space, standards are an inevitability. Make sure that you do the work to evolve a standards process that makes sense for your teams and goals.

Summary

In this chapter we gave you our definition of governance: *managing decision making and decision implementation*. From that definition, we took a closer look at what it means to make a decision and what it means to govern a decision. You learned that API decisions can be small ("What should my next line of code be?") or big ("Which supplier should we partner with?") and can range massively in scope. Most importantly, you learned that the system you are trying to govern is a *complex adaptive system*, which means it's difficult to predict the results of any decision management strategy you apply.

Next, we took a closer look at decision distribution and compared centralization and decentralization. To help you understand the differences, we compared them in terms of the *scope of optimization* and *scale of operation*. Then we discussed how you can break decisions down into their essential elements of inception, choice generation, selection, authorization, implementation, and challenge. By putting all of these concepts together, along with some enforcement and incentivization, you can build an effective API governance system.

Governance is at the heart of API management, so it's not a big surprise that it's a core concept for this book. Our goal in this chapter was to introduce the major concepts and levers of governance. In the rest of the book, we'll dive deeper into the domain of API governance by tackling the specific challenges of which decisions matter the most, how to manage the people involved, and what to do as APIs mature and the scale of the APIs grows. In the next chapter, we'll start that journey by investigating how product thinking can help you identify the API work decisions that matter the most.

CHAPTER 3

The API as a Product

Anything humans create—be it product, communication, or system—is a result of making inspiration real.

    —Maggie Macnab

The phrase "API as a product" (AaaP) is something we often hear when talking to companies that have built and maintained successful API programs. It's a play on the *<Something> as a Service* monikers that are often used in technical circles (software as a service, platform as a service, etc.) and is usually meant to indicate an important point of view when designing, implementing, and releasing APIs: that the API is a *product* fully deserving of proper design thinking, prototyping, customer research, and testing, as well as long-term monitoring and maintenance. "We treat our APIs just like any other product we offer" is the common meaning of the phrase.

In this chapter, we'll explore the AaaP approach and how you can use it to better design, deploy, and manage your APIs. As you may have gathered from Chapter 2, the AaaP approach involves understanding which decisions are critical for the success of your APIs and where within your organization those decisions should be made. It can help you think about what work needs to be centralized and what you can successfully decentralize, where enforcement and incentives are best applied, and how you can measure the impact of these decisions in order to quickly adapt your products (your APIs) when needed.

There are lots of decisions to make when creating new products for your customers. This is true whether you are creating a portable music player, a laptop computer, or a message queuing API. In each of these cases, you need to: (1) know your audience, (2) understand and solve their most pressing problems, and (3) pay attention to customers when they give you feedback on how you can improve your product. These three necessities can be encapsulated in three key lessons, which we will focus on in this chapter:

- Design thinking as a way to make sure you know your audience and understand their problems

- Customer onboarding as a way to quickly show customers how they can succeed with your product

- Developer experience as a way to manage the post-release lifecycle of your product and to gain insights for future modifications

Along the way, we'll learn from companies like Apple about the power of design thinking and customer onboarding. We will also see how Jeff Bezos helped the Amazon Web Services (AWS) division create an implementation mandate that establishes a clear, predictable developer experience. Most companies we talk to understand the notion of AaaP, but not all of them are able to turn this understanding into tangible action. However, the organizations that have a good track record for designing and releasing successful API products have all figured out how to leverage the three key lessons we've just mentioned—the first of which has to do with how your teams *think* about the API products they are creating.

The Programmable Economy Is API-Led

APIs are the interface for enabling the programmable economy, but to do so, they must be designed in such a way that they are discoverable, scalable, and fulfill the capabilities they claim to provide to solve developers' problems. For that, companies will need to manage their developer communities' expectations and aspirations with the right approach. This is where developer relations come into play. It establishes the link between what each of your APIs can provide and the skilled people who will integrate them into other applications: the developers. In the following sections, we'll explore how APIs are changing the game in the programmable economy, by providing greater reach, scalability, and ubiquity, and we'll also look at the role of developer relations in the context of API management, advocacy, and evangelism.

To talk about the importance of APIs, we need to understand why they are so important to a business strategy. In 2011, one of the most renowned investors in Silicon Valley and the founder of Netscape, Marc Andreessen, quipped "Software is eating the world." Before then, information technology (IT) capabilities were integrated within organizations to support the business. However, with the emergence of network and infrastructure technologies that enabled the "as-a-service model" where software could be executed from someone else's infrastructure (SaaS, PaaS, Iaas), IT *became* the business, where third parties could offer self-service, automated, programmable, and traceable functionalities while allowing the business to maintain full control and maintenance. And the key that enabled these third-party organizations to deliver *as-a-service* capabilities to others? That's open APIs.

These programmable interfaces enable companies and their applications to open their businesses to third parties and to grow beyond their own walls and development capabilities. There are more developers, resources, ideas, market knowledge, enthusiasm, innovation, and capital outside the organization than inside. So when it makes sense, why not open assets and capabilities to a larger number of economic and societal actors that can be involved in value creation?

Competition used to be product versus product, but this has shifted to platform versus platform and will then evolve to ecosystems versus ecosystems. APIs are the programmable interfaces that lead from one form to the other.

Price, Promotion, Product, Place → Everywhere

Classic marketing managers know the 4Ps from marketing guru Michael Porter: Price, Promotion, Product, Place are the four variables that you manage and control in a product marketing strategy. But in the digital world where APIs are eating software, to quote Andrew Bosworth, head of growth at Facebook, "It is not the best product which wins, it is the one everybody uses."[1] This is the same for your API products, which means that sometimes the experience of the product that is delivered can have more importance for the customer compared to some extra features on the product you may want to add. As such, the developer experience you give to your API users will make the competitive difference.

In a digital world where IT capabilities are delivered as a service via APIs, the goal is not to be at the right place but to be everywhere. It is not about the place you can control; it is about all the places possible, in any applications. For instance, the banking and finance industry is being disrupted by APIs that are enabling embedded finance. Paul Rohan, author and Open Banking API expert, explains that the future of banking is not "in the bank" but everywhere where banking is needed: embedded in third-party customer experiences, on real estate platforms, in wedding planning applications, in car dealer website widgets, in ecommerce websites—everywhere.[2] Thanks to APIs, banks could be in every customer experience they don't own but still able to deliver banking value propositions. In a 2020 blog post, platform thought leader and industry consultant Simon Torrance estimated that within five years, embedded finance will represent a $7.2 billion opportunity: twice the total market value of current banking and finance.[3] When you are everywhere, your new reach

---

1 Brian Balfour, "Growth Wins," Reforge (blog post), last modified July 25, 2018, *https://oreil.ly/UJDIU*.

2 Paul Rohan, "Driving Business Growth and Brand Strategy in the Api-Powered *Age of Assistance*," APIdays London, 2019, *https://oreil.ly/IcxbV*.

3 Simon Torrance, "Embedded Finance: A Game-Changing Opportunity For Incumbents," August 10, 2020, *https://oreil.ly/L6I3n*.

enables you to deliver value in unprecedented and untackled places, enlarging the size of your market.

Consider how this has evolved over the last 20 years. In 2000, you had to have a website to distribute your value digitally. In 2010, you had to have a mobile application. In 2020, you need an API. Indeed, the new way to conquer the digital experience is to be integrated into other people's websites and applications. It is no longer about controlling only one or two channels but about being integrated into as many channels as possible, where your users are. As Chris Anderson describes in his book, *The Long Tail* (Hachette), while the first distribution channels (web and mobile) represented a significant part of the total traffic, the long tail of all the other smallest niches and channels actually represented increasing traffic over time, which in some cases became even bigger than traditional channels. Some applications, like Salesforce or eBay, get the major part of their traffic via third-party platforms, more than via their own website or mobile applications. More than 50% of their traffic is directly from APIs. The only problem for companies is that it was too hard and too costly to address them all at once, but now with APIs, it is possible to address multiple channels with the same application programming interfaces.

Now APIs are the product of our programmable world, and we will see in the following chapter how to treat them like products, from inquisitive onboarding and initial steps to delightful developer experiences and successful integrations.

Design Thinking

One of the things that Apple is known for in product design circles is its ability to engage in *design thinking*. For example, when describing the work that went into Apple's Mac OS X, one of the key software architects, Cordell Ratzlaff, said, "We focused on what we thought people would need and want, and how they would interact with their computer."[4] And this focus played out in real and tangible ways. "There were three evaluations required at the inception of a product idea: a marketing requirement document, an engineering requirement document, and a user-experience document," explained one-time Apple vice president (and one of the people credited with founding the field of human–computer interaction design) Donald Norman.[5]

---

4 Scott Meade, "Steve Jobs: Mac OS, Designed by a Bunch of Amateurs," Synap Software, LLC (blog), June 16, 2007, *https://oreil.ly/jRURa*.

5 Daniel Turner, "The Secret of Apple Design," *MIT Technology Review*, May 1, 2007, *https://oreil.ly/ehrgv*.

This attention to meeting people's needs definitely resulted in creating viable business for Apple. A continuing string of products over multiple decades contributed to Apple's reputation for defining new trends in technology and helped it capture greater market share more than once.

Tim Brown, CEO of the California-based design and consulting firm IDEO, defines the term *design thinking* as:[6]

> A design discipline that uses the designer's sensibility and methods to match people's needs with what is technologically feasible and what a viable business strategy can convert into customer value and market opportunity.

There is a lot to unpack in that definition. For our purposes, we'll focus on the ideas of "match people's needs" and a "viable business strategy."

Match People's Needs

One of the key reasons to build an API at all is to solve a problem. Discovering problems to solve and deciding which problems have priority is just part of the challenge of the AaaP approach—this is the *what* of APIs. An even more fundamental element is knowing the *who*. Who are the people you are serving with this API? Correctly identifying the audience and their problem can go a long way toward ensuring you build the *right* product: one that works well and is used often by your target audience.

Harvard Business School's Clayton Christensen calls this work of understanding the needs of your audience the theory of *Jobs to Be Done*. He says, "People don't simply buy products or services, they 'hire' them to make progress in specific circumstances."[7] People (your customers) want to make progress (solve problems), and they will use (or hire) whatever products or services they find will help them do that.

Should You Apply AaaP to Both Internal and External APIs?

Yes. Maybe not with the same level of investment of time and resources—we will cover that in the next section—but this is one of the lessons Jeff Bezos taught us in "The Bezos Mandate" on page 52 that led Amazon to open the initially internal AWS platform for use as a revenue-generating external API. Because Amazon adopted AaaP from the start, not only was it *possible* (e.g., safe) to start to offer the same internal API to external users, but it was also *profitable*.

---

6 Tim Brown, "Design Thinking," *Harvard Business Review*, June 2008, *https://oreil.ly/VRA7Y*.

7 "Jobs to Be Done," Christiansen Institute, last modified October 13, 2017, *https://oreil.ly/l1s63*.

In most companies, the IT department is in the business of helping others (customers) solve problems. Most of the time, these customers are fellow employees within the same company (private internal developers). Sometimes the customers are important business partners or even anonymous public developers of third-party applications (external developers). Each of these developer audiences (private, partner, and public) has its own set of problems to solve and its own way of thinking about (and resolving) those problems. Design thinking encourages teams to get to know their audience before starting the process of creating APIs as a solution. We'll explore this topic in "Knowing Your Audience" on page 60.

Viable Business Strategy

Another important part of design thinking is determining a *viable business strategy* for your API product. It doesn't make sense to invest a lot of time and money in an API product that has little to no return value. Even when you do a good job of designing the right product for the right audience, you need to make sure you spend an appropriate amount of time and money and that you have a clear idea of what the payback will be when the API is up and running.

For most companies, there is only a finite amount of time, money, and energy that can be devoted to creating APIs to solve problems. That means that deciding *which* problems get solved is of critical importance. Sometimes we encounter companies where the APIs that were built don't solve important business problems. Instead, they solve known problems in the IT department: things like exposing database tables or automating internal department processes. These are usually important problems to solve, but they might not be solutions that have a big impact on the day-to-day business operations or "move the needle" when it comes to meeting the company's annual sales or product goals.

Figuring out which problems matter for the business can be tricky. It might be difficult for leadership to communicate company goals in ways that the IT department can easily understand. And even when the IT team has a grasp of what problems could make a difference to the company, the department may not have good measures and metrics to confirm their assumptions and track their progress. For these reasons, it is important to have a standardized way to communicate key business objectives and relevant performance indicators. We'll talk more about this aspect of assessing your API's success in "Measurements and Milestones" on page 162.

The Bezos Mandate

No matter how old or new your company is, launching a successful API program— one that will transform your company—is not a simple task. One of the most well-respected companies that worked through this process (and continues to transform itself more than a decade later) is Amazon, with its AWS platform. First created in the early 2000s, the platform is widely regarded as a brilliant master stroke executed cleanly by a savvy team of IT and business executives. Although the AWS platform has become a huge success, it was born out of an internal need: a deep frustration with the amount of time needed for Amazon's IT programs to act upon and deliver the business team's requests. The AWS team was too slow to act, and what they eventually created was less than adequate at both the technical (scaling) and business (product quality) level.

As current AWS CEO Andy Jassy tells it, the AWS team (along with Amazon CEO Jeff Bezos and others) spent time identifying just what it was they were good at and what it would take to design and build out a core set of shared services on an interoperable platform.[8] Their plan took more than three years to develop, but in the end formed the basis for Amazon's ability to offer its now famous infrastructure-as-a-service (IaaS) platform. This now $45 billion business ($13.5 billion profit in February 2021) happened only because of careful attention to detail and relentless iterations to improve upon the original idea. Much the same way as Apple has transformed the way consumers thought of handheld devices, AWS has transformed the way that businesses think of servers and other infrastructure.

One of the important ways in which AWS was able to change the point of view *internally* was through what is now known as the *Bezos mandate*. Steve Yegge, former senior manager of software development at Amazon, describes the mandate in his "Google Platforms Rant".[9] One of the key points in the blog post is that Bezos issued a mandate that all teams must expose their functionality through APIs and that the only way to consume other teams' functionality must be through APIs. In other words, APIs are the only way to get things done. He also required that all APIs be designed and built *as if they would be exposed outside the company boundaries*. This idea that "APIs must be externalizable" was another key constraint that affected the way the APIs were designed, built, and managed.

So, design thinking is about matching the needs of your audience and committing to supporting viable business strategies when deciding which APIs are worthy of your limited resources and attention. What does that look like in real terms? How can you apply these product lessons to your API management efforts in order to express the API-as-a-product approach?

---

8 Ron Miller, "How AWS Came to Be," *TechCrunch*, July 2, 2016, *https://oreil.ly/OtRyN*.

9 "Stevey's Google Platforms Rant," GitHub Gist, October 11, 2011, *https://oreil.ly/jxohc*.

Applying Design Thinking to APIs

You can elevate your APIs from utilities to products by applying the principles of design thinking to your design and creation process. Several companies we've talked to in the last few years are doing just that. They have made the decision that their APIs, even the APIs that are just used within the organization, deserve the same level of care, study, and design sense as any product or service that company already provides. For many companies, this means teaching their API developers and others in the IT department the principles of design thinking directly. For others, it means creating a "bridge" between the product design teams and the API teams within the same organization. In a few organizations we've worked with, we've seen both activities at the same time: teaching design thinking to the developers and strengthening the bridge between the product teams and the developer teams.

The actual content of a design-thinking curriculum is out of scope for this book. However, most design-thinking courses provide a mix of topics like the ones we've already mentioned in this chapter, such as:

- Design thinking skills
- Understanding the customer
- Service/workflow design
- Prototyping and testing
- Business considerations
- Measurement and assessment

If your company already has staff dedicated to product design, they can be a great resource for teaching your developer teams how to start thinking and acting like product designers. Even if your company doesn't have dedicated design staff, you can usually find product design classes on offer at a local college or university. Many of these institutions will offer to customize a course for delivery on-site. Finally, even if you're a small company or just a single individual interested in the topic, you'll be able to find online courses in design thinking.

One company we talked to (a large consumer bank) decided to create its own internal design thinking course, with the product design staff delivering the sessions to API teams at various company locations. These trainers then became important resources that the API teams could call upon when they needed advice on how to improve their API designs. The goal was not to turn all their developers and software architects into skilled designers. What they were aiming to do was simply improve the API teams' understanding of the design process and teach them how to apply these skills to their own work.

It is important to remember that the results of design thinking are more than just improved usability or aesthetic appeal of your APIs. It can result in better understanding of the target audience (customers), a focus on creating APIs that meet viable business goals, and a more reliable process for measuring the success of the APIs into the ecosystem.

As important as design is in the overall AaaP approach, it is just the start. It is also important to pay attention to the initial customer experience once the API is released and available for use. And that's what we'll cover in the next section.

Customer Onboarding

Anyone who's purchased anything from Apple in recent years knows that unboxing its products can be a memorable experience. And that is not by coincidence. For years, Apple has had a dedicated team whose only job is to focus on delivering the best "unboxing experience."

According to Adam Lashinsky, author of *Inside Apple* (Business Plus), "For months, a packaging designer was holed up in this room performing the most mundane of tasks—opening boxes."[10] He continues:

> Apple always wants to use the box that elicits the perfect emotional response on opening...One after another, the designer created and tested an endless series of arrows, colors, and tapes for a tiny tab designed to show the consumer where to pull back the invisible, full-bleed sticker adhered to the top of the clear iPod box. Getting it just right was this particular designer's obsession.

And this attention to detail went well beyond just opening the box and taking out the device. Apple made sure the battery was fully charged, that customers could be "up and running" within seconds, and that the overall experience was pleasant and seamless. Apple's product teams wanted customers to *love* their product from the very start: as Stefan Thomke and Barbara Feinberg wrote in a Harvard Business School case, "Helping people 'love' their equipment and the experience of using it animated—and continues to motivate—how Apple products were and are designed today."[11]

---

10 Jamie Condliffe, "Apple's Packaging Is So Good Because It Employs a Dedicated Box Opener," *Gizmodo*, January 25, 2012, *https://oreil.ly/JrY6S*.

11 Stefan H. Thomke and Barbara Feinberg, "Design Thinking and Innovation at Apple," revised May 2012, *https://oreil.ly/wY4IA*.

This same attention to the initial experience of product customers applies to APIs. Making it possible for developers to *love* them may seem a far-fetched notion, but it has long-reaching implications. If your API is difficult to understand in the beginning, developers will struggle with it, and if it takes "too long" to get started, they will just walk away in frustration. In the API world, the time it takes to "get things working" is often referred to as "Time to first Hello, World." In the online application space this is sometimes called "Time to Wow!" (TTW).

Time to Wow!

In his article "Growth Hacking: Creating a Wow Moment," David Skok, part of the equity investment firm Matrix Partners, describes the importance of a customer's "Wow!" moment as a key hurdle to cross in any customer relationship: "Wow! is the moment…where your buyer suddenly sees the benefit they get from using your product, and says to themselves 'Wow! This is great!'"[13] And while Skok is talking directly to people designing and selling apps and online services to consumers, the same principles apply to people designing and deploying APIs.

A key element to the TTW approach is understanding not just the problem to solve (see "Design Thinking" on page 50) but also the time and work required to get to "Wow!" The effort it takes to reach a point where the API consumer understands how to use the API and learns that it will solve their important problems is the hurdle each and every API must cross in order to win over the consumer. Skok's approach is to map out the steps needed to experience the "Wow!" moment and work to reduce friction and effort along the way.

---

12 Ingrid Lunden, "Stripe Closes $600M Round at a $95B Valuation," *TechCrunch*, March 14, 2021, *https://oreil.ly/60fbh*.

13 David Skok, "Growth Hacking: Creating a Wow Moment," For Entreprenuers (blog), 2013, *https://oreil.ly/YyVlI*.

For example, consider the process of using an API that returns a list of hot leads for your company's key product, WidgetA. A typical process flow might look like this:

1. Send a login request to get an access_token.
2. Retrieve the access_token and store it.
3. Compose and send a request for the product_list using the access_token.
4. From the returned list, find the item where name="WidgetA" and get that record's sales_lead_url.
5. Use that sales_lead_url to send a request for all the sales leads where status="hot" (using the access_token).
6. You now have a list of hot sales leads for the WidgetA product.

That's a lot of steps, but we've seen workflows with many more than this. And each step along the way is an opportunity for the API consumer to make a mistake (e.g., send a malformed request) and for the API provider to return an error (e.g., a timeout for a data request). There are three possible request/response failures here (login, product_list, and sales_leads). The TTW will be limited to how long it takes a new developer to figure out the API and get it working. The longer it takes, the less likely they are to ever get their "Wow!" moment or to keep using the API.

There are a number of ways to improve the TTW for this example. First, we could adjust the design by offering a direct call to get the list of hot leads (e.g., GET /hot-leads-by-product-name?name=WidgetA). We might also spend time writing "scenario" documentation that shows new users exactly how to solve this particular problem. We could even offer a sandbox environment for testing examples like this one that allows users to skip the authentication work while they learn the API.

API Pillars

Design, documentation, and testing are what we call *API pillars*. Those and others are covered in detail in Chapter 4.

Anything you can do to reduce the time it takes to get to "Wow!" will improve the API consumer's opinion of your API and increase the chances that the API will be used by more developers both inside and outside your organization.

Onboarding for Your APIs

Just as Apple spends time on its "unboxing" experience, companies that are good at adopting the AaaP approach spend time making sure the "onboarding" experience for their APIs is as smooth and rewarding as possible. And just as Apple makes sure the battery is already charged up when you open your new mobile phone, APIs can be "fully charged" at first use, making it easy for developers to get started and make an impact within minutes of trying a new API.

Early in our work on APIs and API management, we used to tell our customers they needed to get a new user from the initial view of their API's landing page to a live working example in about 30 minutes. Anything more than that risked losing a potential user and wasting all the time and money put into designing and deploying the API. However, after one of us completed a presentation on API onboarding, a representative of Twilio, the SMS API company, came up to us and told us they aim for an initial onboarding experience of 15 minutes or less.

Twilio's field (SMS APIs) is notoriously fiddly and confusing. Imagine trying to design a single API that works with dozens of different SMS gateways and companies *and* is easy to use and understand. Not an easy task. One of the keys to achieving their 15-minute onboarding goal is the copious use of measurements and metrics in their tutorials to identify bottlenecks—points where API users "drop out"—and determine just how long it takes for them to complete the tasks.

Twilio's Neo Moment

In 2011, Twilio's API evangelist Rob Spectre wrote a blog post relating his experiences teaching others how to use Twilio's SMS API. He tells the story of helping a developer to use the API for the first time:[14]

> In fifteen minutes we worked through a Twilio quickstart guide for outgoing calls and after navigating a few speedbumps, his Nokia feature handset lit up as his code executed. He looked up at me, looked back at his screen, answered his phone and heard his code say, "Hello world."
>
> "Whoa dude," he said, stunned. "I just did that."
>
> And that is pure magic.

Spectre calls this the "Neo moment" (referring to the character Neo from the *Matrix* movies) and says it can be a "powerful inspiration" for developers.

Twilio has worked diligently to engineer its API and onboarding experience to maximize these inspirational moments.

So, a great onboarding experience is more than just the result of a good design process. It includes well-crafted "getting started" and other initial tutorials, and diligent tracking of API consumers' *use* of these tutorials. Gathering data helps provide you

---

14 Rob Spectre, "Introducing Rob Spectre, An Evangelist With A Story To Tell," Twilio (blog), September 15, 2011, *https://oreil.ly/daUWP*.

with the information you need to improve the experience. Just as you design the API, you need to design the onboarding experience, too. And improving the onboarding experience means acting on the feedback (both personal and automated) you get from API users.

But the AaaP approach doesn't stop with onboarding. Hopefully, you've gained a community of avid API consumers that will stick with you well past the initial introduction. That means you need to focus on the overall *developer experience* for your APIs. This can include signing up, filling out forms, agreeing to the terms of service, setting up their environment, getting their application credentials, downloading helper libraries, being redirected to the right "getting started" section, reading the docs: all of these steps need to be as simple and straightforward as possible. If you are in a company that requires lots of time for validation, for legal or compliance purposes, you can make the onboarding better by providing a sandbox that replicates the real API environment while users are waiting for their validation to complete. Another technique is to ask what stack the developer is using so you can send them directly to the right SDK in their preferred language. More generally, you should try to implement every tip and trick you come across to make onboarding as delightful as possible.

Developer Experience

Customer interactions with a product typically last well beyond the initial unboxing. Even though it is important to make sure the product "works right out of the box," it is also important to keep in mind that the customer will (ideally) continue to use the product for quite a while. And, over time, customers' expectations change. They want to try new things. They get bored with some things they loved at the beginning. They start to explore options and even come up with unique ways to use the product and its features to solve new problems not initially covered by the product release. This continuing relationship between consumer and product is typically called the *user experience* (UX).

Apple pays attention to this ongoing relationship, too. Tai Tran, CEO and founder of social app Blue (*https://oreil.ly/3bKkZ*) and former Apple employee, put it this way: "Whenever there's a question about whether we should do something or not we always come back to the question of, 'How would this impact the customer experience?'"[15] Like any good product company, Apple tells its employees that the customer is king and to pay close attention to the way they interact with Apple products. And they're not worried about making lots of changes if that means making meaningful improvements along the way. For instance, between 1992 and 1997, Apple created

---

15 Shana Lebowitz, "Apple Employees Take on Any Projects That Will Improve User Experience," *Business Insider*, July 5, 2018, *https://read.bi/2JbmgDb*.

more than 70 models of its Performa desktop computer (some of which were never even released to the public), each an attempt to take advantage of what it had learned from customer experience feedback on previous releases.

But probably the best example of managing the UX of its products is Apple's approach to customer service: the Genius Bar. As Van Baker of Gartner Research says, "The Genius Bar is a real differentiator for the stores and the fact that it is free really sets the stores apart from the other offerings in the industry."[16] By offering customers a place to go with all their questions and problems, Apple illustrates the importance of the continuing relationship between customer and product.

All these UX elements—acknowledging an ongoing relationship, dedication to making small improvements, and offering easy access to support—are key to creating successful API products and experiences.

Knowing Your Audience

A big part of creating a successful AaaP is to make sure you target the right audience. That means knowing *who* is using your API and *what* problems they are trying to solve. We covered this in "Design Thinking" on page 50, and it is also an important part of the ongoing developer relationship. By focusing on the *who* and *what* of your API, you not only gain insight into what is important, but you can also think more creatively about the *how* of your API: what it is your API has to do in order to help your audience solve their problems.

We talked earlier in this chapter about the concept to match people's needs when working through the design process. This same work needs to continue after your API is released. Gathering feedback, confirming your user stories, and paying close attention to how the APIs are used (or not used) is all part of the ongoing developer experience. Three important elements are:

- API discovery
- Error reporting
- API usage tracking

These three (and others) will be covered in depth in Chapter 4, so we'll just highlight some aspects of them that are important to the overall developer experience (DX) of your AaaP strategy.

---

16 Conner Forrest, "Decoding the Genius Bar: A Former Employee Shares Insider Secrets for Getting Help at the Apple Store," *TechRepublic*, April 3, 2014, *https://tek.io/2ykZrJl*.

API discovery

The way internal or external developers discover your APIs and the value they provide is key in starting your relationship with them. How do developers find your APIs? Since there is no search engine for APIs yet, the discovery mechanism for APIs is often described, as Bruno Pedro, cofounder of HithHQ, used to say, as "word of mouth and a little luck."

Of course, for external APIs, your communication will help a lot with search engine optimization (SEO), along with exhibiting at developer conferences, online content marketing, online advertising, and corporate events. However, discovery is still quite rudimentary and cannot really be planned in a way where the best always wins. You will need to develop your own influence network, and this is where word of mouth will be really powerful. When a CTO or a developer asks on forums, mailing lists, or social networks, "What is the best API to do something?" your API needs to be in the response provided by others. Next, when developers find you, they still need to understand the value your API provides. You will need to set up a developer portal that clearly describes the value of your API. For instance, Twilio used to market their SMS API using the slogan "We make your application talk." On its first website, Stripe declared, "Payment processing. Done right." Funnily enough, the original website was *devpayments.com*.

For internal APIs in large organizations, one of the challenges of the API program is, even when an appropriate API is available, developers end up creating their own APIs—sometimes many times over throughout the organization. While sometimes seen as a kind of rebellion inside the company ("They won't use the APIs we give them!"), this explosion of duplicate functionality is more often simply evidence that developers cannot find the API they need when they need it. The API discovery is often a combination of word of mouth, asking colleagues who have this legacy knowledge, and a catalog or a developer portal. The industry calls these knowledgeable employees the API *librarians* as they know where the API is in the system, who the owner is, and where the docs are.

API Discovery

We cover the role of this key pillar in supporting your API in "Discovery" on page 110 and how the role of discovery changes in large API landscapes in "Discovery" on page 313.

Having a central catalog for your APIs can help solve this problem. Establishing an API search hub or a portal where documentation, examples, and other important information can be accessed is another good way to improve the discoverability of your existing APIs.

At the time of the release of this book, there is no single, commonly used public search engine for APIs. One reason for this is that it is hard to index services on the web since most of them don't expose crawlable links and they rarely include links to other dependent services. Another problem is that most of the APIs in use today are behind private firewalls and gateways, which makes them "invisible" to any publicly operated API search crawlers.

There are some open source projects and formats working to make API crawlers possible, including {API}Search (*https://apis.io*), the API (*http://apisjson.org*) description format, and the Application-Level Profile Semantics (ALPS) (*http://alps.io*) service description format. These and others offer the possibility of a future API search engine available to all. In the meantime, individual organizations can use these standards internally to start the process of creating a searchable API landscape.

At least one company we talked to made publishing to a central discovery catalog a required step in the build pipeline. That meant the developers building an API could not actually release it into production until they'd added it to the company's API catalog and ensured all important APIs within the organization would be findable in one location—a big step toward improving the discovery quotient of their API program.

Error reporting

Errors happen all the time. They're part of the "landscape" of APIs. While you can use good design to try to reduce user errors and testing to try to eliminate development bugs in your own code, you will never get rid of all the errors. Instead of trying to do the impossible (eliminate all errors), a better tactic is to monitor your APIs closely so you can record and report the errors that do occur. This act of recording and reporting will give you important insight into the way your target audience is using your APIs—and that can lead to improving the developer experience.

API Monitoring

Error reporting and API usage tracking (discussed next) fall under the API pillar of *monitoring*. We'll explore that API-level skill in "Monitoring" on page 108. We'll also look at how monitoring changes as you grow your API program in "Monitoring" on page 311.

One of the challenges encountered when creating and releasing a physical product (whether it be clothing, furniture, office supplies, or something else) is that it can be difficult to see errors when they occur during use. Unless you are standing right next to the person while they use your product, you're likely to miss details and lose out on valuable feedback. For this reason, most product companies engage in extensive prototyping and in-person monitored testing. The good news is, in the age of electronics and virtual products, you can build in error reporting and collect important feedback even after the product has been released and is in the hands of users.

You can implement error reporting at a number of key touchpoints along the way for your APIs. For example:

End-user error reporting

You can add an error-reporting feature to your application. This prompts the user for permission to send detailed information if and when an error occurs. In this way you can capture unexpected conditions on the user's end of the transaction.

Gateway error reporting

You can add error reporting at the API router or gateway. This allows you to collect the state of the request when it first arrives "on your doorstep" and can help you discover malformed API requests or other network-related problems.

Service error reporting

You can add error reporting within the service being called by your API. This helps you discover errors in coding the service and some component-level problems, such as issues with dependencies or internal issues due to changes within your organization's ecosystem.

Error reporting is a great way to get important feedback on how your API is being used and where problems occur. But it is only half of the tracking story. It is also important to track *successful* API usage.

API usage tracking

API usage tracking covers more than errors. It means tracking all requests and, eventually, analyzing the tracking information to find patterns. As we mentioned in "Viable Business Strategy" on page 52, a big reason for creating and deploying APIs is to support your business. As the well-known API evangelist Kin Lane puts it, "Understanding [how] APIs will (or won't) assist [the] organization to better reach their audience is what the API(s) are all about."[17]

The data needed to determine whether your API is helping your organization to better reach your target audience is usually expressed as OKRs (objectives and key

---

17 Kin Lane, "Your API Should Reflect A Business Objective Not A Backend System," API Evangelist (blog), April 17, 2017, *https://oreil.ly/XCOTT.*

results) and KPIs (key performance indicators). We'll dig deeper into these in "OKRs and KPIs" on page 162, but for now it is important to recognize that in order to meet your goals, you need to know just how your APIs are doing along these lines. That means tracking not just the errors that occur, as described in the previous section, but also the successes.

For example, you'll want to collect data on which applications are making which API calls and whether those applications are effectively meeting the needs of their users, and if they match your business goals. Tracking has the added benefit of helping you to see patterns over a wide range of users—patterns that individual users may not be able to notice. For example, you might discover that applications continue to make the same series of API calls over and over again, such as:

```
GET http://api.mycompany.org/customers/?last-order=90days
GET http://api.mycompany.org/promotions/?flyer=90daypromo
POST http://api.mycompany.org/mailing/
customerid=1&content="It has been more than 90 days since...."
POST http://api.mycompany.org/mailing/
customerid=2&content="It has been more than 90 days since...."
...
POST http://api.mycompany.org/mailing/
customerid=99&content="It has been more than 90 days since...."
```

This pattern might indicate the need for a new, more efficient way for your target audience to send out mailings to key customer groups—a single call from the application that will combine the target customer group with the selected promotional content. For example:

```
POST http://api.mycompany.org/bulk-mailing/
customer-filter=last-order-90days&content-flyer=90daypromo
```

This call creates less client/server traffic, reduces the number of possible network failures, and is easier to use for API consumers. And it was "suggested" not by a customer, but by paying attention to the API usage tracking information.

Drink Your Own Champagne

In 2017, when coauthor Medjaoui was working as a consultant, a European national railway company decided to organize some hackathons for its developer communities: one for external developers and another for internal developers.

The external event was coordinated by the communications and product management leadership. They arranged to have the IT department produce some static data available for external use and helped the IT teams design a set of simple, task-focused APIs for accessing things like station locations and departure schedules. These were implemented quickly and viewed by the IT department as "less powerful" than its own "full-featured" internal APIs. The event went quite well.

Six months later, the IT department arranged its own hackathon using the "official" internal APIs. After a while, the hackathon organizers realized the internal developer teams had switched from using the "full-featured" internal APIs to the easier, more task-focused external APIs. And the teams were more effective and productive, too.

There are a few lessons to be learned from this experience. First, the task-focused APIs were preferred by all developers. Second, creating these "simpler" APIs did not take much time or resources. Third, it is always best for IT departments to pay attention to which APIs are popular and used more often. A last lesson can be summed up by the common phrase "Drinking your own champagne" (some say "Eating your own dog food," too). With APIs, as with any other product, it is often best for internal teams to be using the same product external teams are using.

This leads us to one more important area of developer experience (DX): making it safe and easy for developers to "do the right thing" with your API.

Making It Safe and Easy

Along with facilitating straightforward API discovery and accurate tracking of both errors and general API usage, it is important to provide easy access to ongoing support and training to your API consumers. In fact, it is the experience that occurs *after* you've successfully onboarded the developers consuming your APIs that will ensure a long-term positive relationship. We saw an example of this kind of attention to the ongoing relationship earlier in this section, with Apple's use of the Genius Bar as a source of support for existing customers. Your APIs need their own Genius Bar, too.

Another important aspect of support for developers is making your product *safe for use*. In other words, it should be somewhat difficult to misuse the product in ways that result in some sort of harm. For example, it should be hard to delete important data, remove the only admin account, and so forth. Paying attention to how your API consumers (that is, developers) *use* the product can help you identify areas where some added safety efforts can pay off.

It takes a mix of both these elements—ease and safety—to create a powerful and ongoing connection with the developers consuming your APIs.

Making APIs safe to use

There are a number of elements of an API that can represent *risk* from the developer's point of view. Sometimes certain API calls can do dangerous things, like deleting all customer records or changing all service prices to zero. Sometimes even *connecting* to an API server can represent some risk. For example, setting up a connection string to a data API might make it too easy to expose usernames and passwords in URLs or unencrypted message bodies. We've seen lots of these types of safety issues in our reviews of APIs.

Often risks can be *designed out* of the API. That is, you can make changes in the design that make encountering a particular risk less likely. For example, you can design an API that deletes critical data to also support an "undo" API call. That way, if someone mistakenly deletes important data, they can also invoke the undo call to reverse it. Or you can require elevated access rights to execute certain operations, such as requiring an extra data field (such as a passcode) to be sent with calls that update critical information.

However, sometimes it can be difficult to mitigate the risk through API design elements. There may be some cases where executing an API call is simply inherently risky. Any API call that deletes data is risky, no matter how many design changes you make to it. Some API calls might always take a long time to execute, possibly consuming lots of server-side resources. Other APIs might execute quickly and result in quite a lot of data in return. For example, a filter query might potentially return hundreds of thousands of records.

In cases where API calls represent unavoidable risk, you can reduce negative impacts by adding warnings to the API documentation itself. In this way, you can make it easier for API consumers to recognize potential dangers ahead of time and possibly avoid making critical mistakes. There are lots of ways you can format documentation to help point out possible dangers. Highlighted text telling the user of the problem ("Warning: This API call may return over a million records, depending on your filter settings") is one way to do it. Another way to warn API users is to adopt a kind of labeling method using symbols. This way, there is no need to add lots of text to your documentation: readers can just recognize the warning label instead.

Physical products use information and warning symbols quite often (see Figure 3-1).

Figure 3-1. Examples of household product labels

You can adopt a similar approach for your APIs, too (see Figure 3-2).

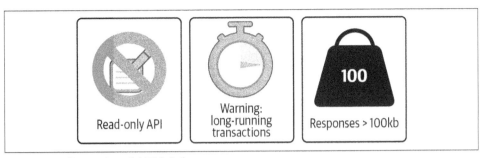

Figure 3-2. Examples of API labels

Easy-to-read warning symbols combined with design changes to make it more unlikely for API users to make regrettable mistakes are good practices for increasing the safety of your API product.

Making APIs easy to use

It is also important to make your API relatively easy to use for your API consumers. If it takes too many steps to accomplish a task, if the names and numbers of arguments API developers need to pass are confusing or complicated, or if the names of the API calls themselves don't make much sense to consumers, your API can run into problems. Not only will developers be unhappy using your API, but they might make more errors, too.

You can *design in* ease of use by adopting naming patterns that fit your developers' Jobs-to-Be-Done vocabulary. This goes back to understanding your audience ("Match People's Needs" on page 51) and solving their problems ("Viable Business Strategy" on page 52). But even when you do that, if your API is large (e.g., lots of URLs or actions) or just plain complicated (lots of options to deal with), you can't always rely on design to solve your problem. Instead, you may need to make it easier for API consumers to ask the right questions and find appropriate answers. Your API needs a kind of "Genius Bar" for developers.

Probably the easiest way to provide your developers an API Genius Bar is through the documentation. By adding more than simple reference documentation (e.g., API name, methods, arguments, and return values), you can elevate your API docs to "genius" level. For example, you can add a Frequently Asked Questions (FAQ) section where you provide answers (or pointers) to the most common consumer questions. You can expand your FAQ support by adding a "How Do I...?" section that gives short step-by-step examples on how to accomplish common tasks. You can even provide fully functional examples that developers can use as starter material for their own projects.

Documentation

We'll talk more about this API skill of documentation in "Documentation" on page 91 and discuss how your needs in this area may change as your API landscape grows in "Documentation" on page 292.

The next level up from enhanced documentation is an active online support form or chat channel. Support forums provide an ongoing conversation space where developers can ask questions to a larger group and share solutions. In the case of large API communities, these forums can even become a source of important bug fixes and feature requests. Forums can also become a valuable repository of knowledge accumulated over time, especially when you have a robust search mechanism.

Chat channels offer an even more immediate means of providing Genius Bar support for your API consumers. Chats often happen in real time and can add an additional level of personalization to your developer experience. This is also another great place to leverage and grow community knowledge about your API product.

Finally, for large API communities and/or large organizations, it can make sense to provide in-person support for your product in the form of API evangelists, trainers, or troubleshooters. Your company can arrange meetups or hack events where API users come together to work on projects or test new features. This works whether your primary API community is internal (e.g., company employees) or external (e.g., partners or public API users). The more personal you can make your connection to your developers, the more likely you are to be able to learn from them and improve the ease of use of your API.

Taking the time to make your APIs safer to use and easy to work with can go a long way toward establishing a positive relationship with your API consumers and, in turn, improving your overall developer experience.

Why Are Developers So Important in the API Economy?

How does your product evolve into a platform and, subsequently, an ecosystem? By making people work and invest in your product, instead of you working for them or investing your money and development efforts on their product. This is where APIs are a key element of value accumulation. By lowering the cost of leveraging the value that your solution provides, you incentivize people and companies to spend the time and funds to integrate your API. Instead of integrating with everybody, everybody will integrate with you, and that is a unique way to accumulate value over time. When Apple reached one million applications, those were one million applications that Apple did not have to build, which span thousands of market niches that Apple could not address due to the sheer quantity and because Apple can't hire all the necessary product managers to analyze all the market needs. By accumulating the work and the investment of others, you transform your products into platforms and ecosystems.

Readers living in Silicon Valley may remember the Twilio advertisement with ad panels on the 101 Highway and in the main streets of San Francisco, in full Twilio-red background stating, "Ask Your Developer." Twilio has been one of the first API companies to push really hard on developer evangelism because they knew before others that the doers of the programmable economy will soon be the angular stone of the corporate adoption of APIs. They understood that whether a decision maker or prescriber, the developer is a key influencer in an application economy.

By having the skills to develop applications, developers are a central stakeholder for an API strategy. Every integration and every application will pass through the hands of developers. In a marketplace strategy, they will be the first to use your API and the first to build applications on your platform. Developers will show the path to follow to other developers and help you benefit from marketplace traction. Internally in bigger corporations, they will be your internal API champions and will recommend the use of an API over another because they know it better and because it is safer to use, better designed, and/or better documented compared to another. In that context, we are shifting from business to consumer (B2C) and business to business (B2B) to business to developer (B2D) models.

In other words, in the 21st century, APIs are the new goods: the new products created and stored in servers, distributed on information highways through the network, transported by developers into applications, and promoted in digital supermarkets (aka application stores), where end users will come to download (for an app) or consume APIs.

For AaaPs to enable programmable business models and accumulate value at integration scale, a team must be dedicated to support that integration growth, always listening to the needs of developers and delivering them the best experience possible, both on the technical side and the human side of IT. That is the overall role of developer relations for APIs. As a result, some in the industry argue that in the programmable economy where every company will provide core competencies to others via APIs and consume core competencies of others via APIs, the role of developer relations will be more and more important, to the point that all companies will need to have a developer relations department, like they have a marketing department.

Developer Relations for APIs as a Product

As coauthor Medjaoui wrote in the third edition of *Developer Marketing and Relations: The Essential Guide*, there is a clear and important relationship between API strategies and developer engagement, internally or externally. It consists of understanding the relationship between community, code, and content; understanding the difference between AaaPs and product APIs; and also adopting the right metrics to measure developer engagement by developers. Finally, it is important to also spend some time discussing internal or external API monetization strategies. We will address all of these in this section.

Community, code, content

The role of developer relations when talking about APIs should be built around three blocks that the SendGrid developer relations team used to call the three Cs: community, code, and content.

Developer relations is firstly about the community. As long as humans still integrate APIs, at least until machines can do it for us, the concept of a community will remain an important part of developer relations. Being where developers are, engaging with them, listening to their feedback and ideas, inspiring them, and putting a face on the API are all part of the community's mission in developer relations.

The community aspect is important as a soft-power to enable more word of mouth. As Tim Falls from SendGrid used to say, "A personal connection is worth more than a click," and sometimes he found that developers were recommending the use of SendGrid even if they had never used it, because they knew the SendGrid team was caring.

Community is also about attending developer events or API conferences to keep in contact with the community, and participating in speaking engagements that are not directly involved with what your API does. Sometimes topics might be about a cool hack someone made thanks to your API, an open source package released for the community, or sometimes even more societal topics.

The second block is code. Integrating APIs is about code, and a developer's job is to produce code that delivers value. If they can leverage code that is already provided, they can focus on implementing the business logic faster. Then, the role of the developer relations team is to provide this as code samples, SDKs, prototype applications, or API definitions (specifications) that developers will be able to use directly. Code, to the members of the developer relations team, also means writing code themselves to maintain the developer platform and the API, with a nice developer experience that we will talk more about in a subsequent section.

The third block is content. Developers love transparent and honest communications and useful content. Content is one of the best ways to attract developers and maintain them as a loyal audience of your blog and ecosystem.

Content exists in many different forms. It can be just a technical update about recent changes, it can be a blog or email about a cool customer use case, it can be more of an engineering post about a specific way to build some features, or it can be a best practice explained in detail. It can also be broader, like the recent Stripe booklet and blog post series about how to make a company and its applications carbon neutral.

Content is the important part of your relationship with developers that makes your company and its APIs discoverable through SEO or social media sharing.

In summary, community, code, and content are the three pillars of developer relations that you should strive to fulfill.

AaaPs versus product APIs

There is a clear distinction to make when talking about developer relations and APIs. You need to consider whether your API is the product or if your API feeds and supports a product. You can then categorize it as either an AaaP or a product API, respectively. For instance, Stripe, Twilio, Mailjet, and Avalara are all AaaPs. They offer standalone capabilities for a specific purpose such as payments, SMS, email, and tax validation.

On the other hand, Salesforce APIs, Facebook APIs, eBay APIs, YouTube APIs, and Twitter APIs are product APIs, or said differently, APIs for a product. They exist to support and customize an existing platform. They often represent more than 50% of the total traffic to the platform and product, a considerable chunk. As much as they are critical for the business, they are often free to use because their use increases the value of the underlying business.

The role of developer relations is different for AaaPs and product APIs.

For AaaPs, the end goal of developer relations is to evangelize, advocate, and build relations that will directly augment the top-line business with the consumption of the API. As APIs are the product to be integrated and sold, the goal will be to maximize the number of valuable integrations according to the business model. In the case where developers are not the decision makers but just the prescribers, the goal of developer relations will be to have developers trained and acculturated about the benefits of the APIs. They can propose it inside their organization at an enterprise level, leading to enterprise integrations and the high revenues that follow.

On the other hand, developer relations for product APIs are mostly to inspire developers to build applications that will directly augment the value of the platform but not necessarily its direct revenues. When Facebook opened its platform APIs, it was free of charge for developers to build applications or games, and the rich portfolio of applications that resulted demonstrated that the Facebook platform was here to stay, always aggregating more application from developers.

In the end, users will stay not only because of the social network but for the full ecosystem of applications that is around it and powers it. This is similar for the Salesforce AppExchange, which has more than 5,000 business applications in 2021. In that context, Salesforce is not just customer relationship management (CRM) software anymore, but a full ecosystem of business applications powered by and around a CRM that fits many use cases across many industries. For product APIs, the role of developer relations is to nurture that ecosystem; this then scales the value and sales of the product among end users.

The story of Twitter API versus Slack API

Aligning KPIs with APIs is important and can completely change the future of the platform you are building. As Jason Costa from GGV Capital said in his article, "A Tale of 2 API Platforms," both Twitter and Slack had great developer traction because of their important user base and their openness to build valuable applications.[18] Twitter finally decided that its business model was not based on being a monetized application ecosystem but was to be a media platform making revenue through advertising. With this clearer identity, all the previous APIs published suddenly represented the complete opposite mindset of the platform, and this was the reason why Twitter highly restricted its API to third parties, hurting its developer ecosystem. Years later, it worked hard to rebuild relationships with developers, with a manifesto from Jack Dorsey himself, and hiring great developer advocates like Romain Huet, but trust in using the APIs by developers never completely recovered.

On the other hand, the Slack model was based on making an application ecosystem to enrich the value of the main Slack product. More business applications increased the value of the Slack communication platform, so the business KPIs were aligned with the APIs. To this day, the Slack API has never suffered from tensions within the developer community, which partly explains why developers love building bots on Slack. These two stories are the perfect reflection of how aligning your KPIs with APIs, and then your APIs with your KPIs, makes the difference for how you manage your developer relations strategy and APIs in the long term.

The DevRel ROI cheat sheet: Tracking success in developer relations

Evaluating the quality and potential of your developer community is a key element of your developer relations strategy. Many companies have tried to develop an internal tool to better understand their developer community. Many API management vendors have built what they call internally *developer relation management* software, like a CRM solution but for developers. This offers a way to better communicate, track, and differentiate developers with the most potential ROI, based on your API strategy goals, which could include reach, application ecosystem, or revenues. Also, identifying and engaging developers who are on your platform is a way to reactivate them and reinspire them to build with your API.

---

18 Jason Costa, "A Tale of 2 API Platforms," *Medium*, October 25, 2016, *https://oreil.ly/ZzAlj*.

For that, you will need what Mike Swift, founder and CEO of Major League Hacking, calls "the nuts and bolts" of developer relations. It is a mix between developer relations practices and metrics to invest and track effectively. It is split into two parts: the API usage tracking and the developer tracking.

"If you can't measure it, you can't improve it," Admiral Lord Nelson used to say. On the other side, as the Goodhart law states, "When a measure becomes a target, it ceases to be a good measure." How do you find the right balance between metrics and the goals of your developer relations strategy? You just have to match your APIs with your KPIs.

There are all sorts of KPIs for APIs, and we have provided some here to help you get started. To get the most from each, you should couple them with the Pirate Funnel inspired by Dave McClure, founder of famous startup accelerator 500 Startups, better known as the AARRR model: awareness, acquisition, activation, retention, revenue, and referrals.[19]

API awareness. API awareness is the metric that tells us how people are becoming aware of your API—how they discover your product:

Number of visits to the developer portal's home page and API docs
> There are many ways, both paid and organic, to attract developers to your home page. To attract developers to use your API, first they need to discover your value proposition and the capabilities you offer. Attracting the maximum number of developers is your main awareness metric.

Number of blog articles views and reads
> Content is key in a developer relations strategy, so everything you publish must be tracked. Be sure to always put a link to the page of your developer portal that can track referrals from your articles, and monitor your engagement analytics.

Number of developers registered to written communication channels
> Ask readers to register to your newsletter to get notified about new articles and API updates. This number is a key element to track how many community members want to keep receiving news from you and to compare it with the current developers registered to the API.

Number of public speaking engagements
> Awareness comes from offline discussions and in real life (IRL) events. Conferences, meetups, and all public or private events where you can raise awareness of your API are important to activate a key element that is not measurable but that works well: word of mouth. This also serves as the foundation for kickstarting

---

19 "AARRR Pirate Metrics Framework," ProductPlan, *https://oreil.ly/GiDgb*.

the viral referral phase, something that we will talk about later. For that, you can track the number of talks, the average audience size, and so on, to calculate audience reach. Also, if you have a booth at an event, you can add in the number of people you had interactions with.

Open source stars and contributions for API tooling
Providing useful tools or releasing valuable software under an open source license can deliver a lot of awareness for your company and API. This recently provided developer success to Strapi, which released a tool to build an API-driven CMS with GraphQL, and Hugging Face API, which released its natural language processing technology as open source. Through open source, these companies attracted developers, scaled their businesses, and raised a lot of money from investors—$10 million and $15 million, respectively—based on the success of developer relations in managing the developer community around the open source project of the company.

API acquisition. API acquisition is the metric that tells us how developers are engaging in our API onboarding process:

Number of registered developers
An important acquisition metric is the number of registered developers. But it is useful only at the start! Don't depend on it as an important metric in the long term because it loses potency when the maturity of your developer relations program evolves. This metric enables you to know if there is a match between the developer community and the perceived value of the API you provide and its associated capabilities.

Number of applications and applications/developer
Most of the time, one developer account is linked to one application, but when you gain popularity or, for instance, when your API has an intrinsic value that can be reused in other applications easily (i.e., it's a transactional or Business-Process-as-a-Service API), you will see two or more applications per developer account. That is important to track because these developers are probably your best word-of-mouth ambassadors since they understand the value of your product enough to reuse it multiple times. Tracking the total number of applications and the median of developers who have at least two applications can be a good metric in the acquisition phase.

Number of total API calls
In the beginning, the total number of API calls can be a good metric, enabling your API developer relations team to focus on increasing the use of the API and being innovative in their marketing strategy. The developer relations team will focus on inspiring developers into different usages, according to different common use cases. It should be tracked because it ceases to be a good metric

really fast, unless your strategy and/or business model is attached to a number of API calls, for instance, affiliation, pay-as-you go, or indirect models like advertisement of third-party pages.

Number of third-party integrations onto other platforms

Another way to scale the reach and acquisition of your developer relations is to work with existing companies that already have developer communities and build a plug-in, add-on, or integration on their marketplace to scale. For instance, Typeform, a platform to make survey forms with an API, was based on integrating a use case into third-party marketplaces to leverage their existing developer communities. Now that it has grown, Typeform can attract applications on its platform and reverse the API integration scheme of "I spend time and money to integrate with you" into "You spend time and money to integrate with me."

API activation. The API activation metrics help us understand the level of engagement our APIs are generating, especially early in the onboarding lifecycle:

Time to first Hello World (TTFHW)

An important conversion metric is how to transition an interested developer into an active developer. For that, you need to track the TTFHW, which is the time between when a developer registers on your platform to when they successfully invoke your API. As Twilio developer relations suggest, no more than 15 minutes is the perfect DX timing to enable developers to be successful with your API. Of course, not all internal validations and processes are possible in every organization to reach that sort of time, but reducing it to its minimum will have a direct impact on your developer activation ratio.

Number of active applications/developers

You already track the number of applications and developers as we saw earlier, but identifying the difference between developers, who are just using your API for small projects and your power developers who are integrating it into business projects can help you identify where to invest more resources, or when you need to be more reactive to a support ticket, for instance. The limit between the two needs to be defined by the API product manager, but it is important to track in order to understand the difference. This difference will also help you to define your pricing plans and help you put fair limits on your free plan, where developers have sufficiently grown their applications to become "activated" as a customer.

API retention. The API retention metrics tell us how we are doing in maintaining an acrtive relationship with the develoipers we have already onboarded:

Number of "valuable" applications

As for the difference between acquired and activated, the difference between activated and valuable needs to be defined by the API product manager, according to the API strategy. A valuable application can be an application that provides lots of visibility into your application ecosystem, an application that attracts lots of users, or one that generates significant and growing revenues.

Number of active end-user tokens

A more specific metric in the retention phase is to track the retention of end-user tokens as the users of your API consumer applications. Applications that tend to grow their user base have less tendency to change their stack and switch API providers to focus on customers. This is why companies like Stripe can still charge high fees for their APIs, because payment capability is probably the last thing you want to change when you are growing. This metric can be really useful if you target an application ecosystem for your strategy like the Facebook and Slack APIs do.

API revenue. The API revenue metric lets us track the actual revenue generated by the developer activity on our APIs:

Direct revenues generated by the API

This kind of metric is pretty straightforward if your business model is directly attached to payment. Tracking revenues can also help influence an organization's internal decision makers and C-level staff on the need to continue investment in developer relations to monetize the API.

Indirect revenues generated by the API

This metric is harder to define because it requires a subjective approach, but the exercise to link indirect API metrics with business KPIs will encourage internal support for developer relations. Developer relations pays off in the mid and long term, so some managers may want to demonstrate faster rewards internally to executives. Giving them a vision about the value created by developer relations, by translating API metrics into business KPIs, even indirectly, can help the developer relations team to continue to get support. For instance, if your API enables your application ecosystem to grow and this ecosystem increases the valuation of the company by 100% to investors and to the market, the value of developer relations needs to be linked to the market cap of the company.

API referrals. With referrals, the idea is to leverage your existing happy API users as ambassadors who foster interest in using your APIs among their networks. Here is a set of metrics to analyze that:

Conversation activity

Conversation activity is important to monitor because your developer relations team can engage developers and product managers who are actually discussing or debating "What is the best API for that?" or where to find capabilities and business processes that have been encapsulated by an API. These discussions can happen where developers are, such as on Discourse, Twitter, Medium, Hacker News, Reddit (*https://oreil.ly/DwVx3*), and public Slack forums.

Mentions from others

You can source speakers and developers who are referencing your API and its value in their talks or articles and transform them into ambassadors. For that, you must track these mentions, either in conferences or developer blogs, and begin to engage them. This is what companies like Auth0 did with its ambassador program, or Docker with its Docker Captain program, which identified its best community advocates.

API presence and use in cool hacks and at hackathons

You can only track this manually, by monitoring social networks or mentions and search engine alerts, but knowing that your API is being used by others, where it happens, and who is doing it are all an important part of your developer relations strategy. Your goal is to be sure they reach out to you next time, before they actually start making their cool tool.

Funding API Consumers with Capital

An original strategy currently in place is to create an investment fund for API consumers and developers. This strategy has been used by major API-driven companies in the ecosystem like Mailchimp, Twilio, SendGrid, Slack, and Stripe. At some point, they all created investment funds especially for developer companies using their APIs. With that fund, they can directly take ownership of a stake in their API consumer companies and align their interest with their application ecosystem. This has many benefits, but mainly it offers the potential for developers to profit from building on your platform. Even if the number of investments per year is low, it enables you to keep developers loyal to your platform instead of your competitors by showing a path to monetization and/or funding.

In another venture-friendly strategy, Salesforce encouraged developers to build on their Salesforce AppExchange over iOS because the average revenue for an app on AppExchange at the time was $450,000, instead of $3,000 for an app on iOS at the time (2015). Even a bank in France, Credit Agricole, proposed that developers be paid based on the traction of their app, with a monthly revenue based on active users of their applications using their public APIs.

API-as-a-Product Monetization and Pricing

Lots of companies want to monetize APIs, to generate revenue, and to demonstrate value for customers and the ecosystem. It is often hard to maximize value retention and at the same time spread and expand traction through the ecosystem. We help you define all the different variables in an AaaP monetization and pricing strategy.

Infrastructure pricing versus SaaS pricing for APIs

An API represents access to your capabilities as a service. But you will have to position yourself around how you want customers to rely on you, and your mindset around how you want to deliver these APIs. Two main patterns are present in the industry: the infrastructure mindset and the SaaS mindset.

An infrastructure mindset often sets the same pricing for the same service, without a gatekeeper, as we see with Amazon Web Services and other cloud vendors. The pricing is always public, matched with usage, and not correlated with the value the user creates. Whether you can generate $1 or $1 million with an Amazon Bucket, the pricing is the same. At the scale they operate, the AWS product team cannot differentiate all the customers, so the pricing is open, transparent, and matched with usage levels.

With a SaaS mindset, you may try to design different tiers of API customers matched to the potential value expected to be generated, always trying to capture the maximum value whenever possible. For instance, when a user jumps from a few thousand API calls per day to tens of thousands, it may seem that they are now in production (and have a viable business of their own with their own paying customer base), so they can pay a lot more than when just starting out and testing their product in the market. Or when they require a service level agreement (SLA), that can indicate that this is "money" time for them, and you can make them pay a lot more for the same access to your capabilities (with penalties if you don't maintain service performance and therefore impact their business value chain). Some companies even use API management to decide the threshold for selecting API consumer pricing tiers. They look at the median number of API calls for production users and then set the enterprise pricing plan around that level. This matches the price with the transition from testing to production and seeks to capture the maximum value the APIs can create for consumers.

You will have to decide on the trade-off between rentability and user acquisition. If your customers have a flywheel effect that increases the value of the ecosystem, you may choose to simplify the revenue model to maximize adoption instead of direct and short-term revenues. For instance, the Facebook business model is based on usage with ads, so the Facebook API needs to maximize third-party applications that encourage users to spend more time on Facebook. The API is free (up to 100 million requests per day). We have gathered a list of API pricing dimensions to consider when applying pricing for APIs.

Freshness: old versus new

If the API gives access to resources that get old and obsolete with time (like company information data), you can set tiered pricing dependent on the freshness of the data. Some financial APIs give you access for free for one-day-old data, but fresh data access needs to be paid.

Precision: blurry versus accurate

If the API gives access to resources that have different levels of value at different levels of precision, you can apply tiered pricing dependent on the level of precision. A weather prediction API can set a low price point for a one-day prediction but set access to three-to-five-day predictions at a larger price point. A credit score API could give a precise credit score for a higher fee but a generalized (blurry) representation of that score (for example, by applying a traffic light red, amber, green scoring) for a smaller fee.

Consumability: transactional versus process

Do you provide granular APIs that the customers integrate one by one and pay individually for a small fee, or do you gather complex business processes and encapsulate them into one API that you sell at a high price? For instance, the Checkr API does a background check in one API call that helps companies like Netflix answer one question: can we hire that person? The Checkr API gathers many API calls from different public services and legal sources and produces a result that is of higher value to API consumers than them making and assembling all the different API calls themselves.

Scope: reduced versus all

The API can give access to all your internal resources or to a smaller suite of functionalities. The tiered API pricing can then be based on how you define the scope of the API access. This could be per year, per geographic region, per datatype…you decide, as long as you know your customers well and understand what they really value in your proposition.

Quantity: few versus many

Another way to tier API plans is to decide the quantity of data or the number of requests allowed. The more API calls you want to make, the more you pay. Some businesses rely heavily on data when they deal with important customers, so if you know the quantity of data they need, you can set the pricing tier at volume levels.

Performance: fast versus slow

SLAs are an important part of the delivery value of an API. Guaranteeing fast and reliable access versus not guaranteeing it can be a strong differentiator for API pricing plans.

Maintenance: managed versus delegated

APIs need to be maintained across versions. Lots of companies version APIs to make them evolve over time. API consumers need to maintain their applications and update them with the new version. By making companies pay to maintain older versions, you can set different level of maintenance fees for the APIs.

Support: full versus limited

Supporting API customers can also be a differential factor for tiering API plans. Some customers are willing to pay fees for the stability of 24/7, multiregional, and guaranteed responses within an hour or less for API technical issues. This can be monetized at a higher price. For lower pricing points, or free plans, support can be offered via redirecting customers to the public forums or by providing support only via email.

License: all rights reserved versus open

Your API may give access to resources that may not be available for all uses. You can limit the potential uses of the API for low-paying customers and open greater access for higher-paying API customers.

Branding: white label versus "powered by"

Some API providers prefer adoption and awareness among developer communities over smaller revenue amounts as they are keen to keep the focus on targeting big enterprises. One solution is to give access to your API for free or at a really low price point with accreditation requirements to provide a mention such as "Service provided by..." in their products and applications. Customers could pay a higher amount to remove this obligation to label their use. Some scoring companies oblige you to mention in any online or mobile publications where the score comes from and forbid you to create a new score that includes their scoring algorithm as a variable, unless you pay a premium plan for white labeling.

Of course, there are other variables that can be applied to set API pricing strategies, but these are the most common ones.

It is important to know that the API and the as-a-service economy favor simple pricing and business models for adoption. Complex models that try to capture maximum value are less self-service and need more sales support to acquire customers than flat, open, and transparent pricing that enables easier self-service onboarding and that give a better estimation of the final price, even if they capture less value per customer on average.

Summary

In this chapter, we introduced the AaaP approach and discussed how you can use it to better design, deploy, and manage your APIs. Adopting this approach means knowing your audience, understanding and solving their problems, and acting on API users' feedback.

The three key concepts we explored in the AaaP space were:

- Using design thinking to make sure you know your audience and understand their problems

- Focusing on customer onboarding as a way to quickly show customers how they can succeed with your product

- Investing in providing a developer experience that manages the post-release lifecycle of your product and gains insights for future modifications

Along the way, we learned how dedication to AaaP principles helped companies like Apple, Amazon, Twilio, and others build not just successful products but also loyal customers. And, regardless of whether your API program is targeting only internal users or both internal and external developers, a loyal user community is critical to the long-term health and success of your APIs.

Now that you have a grasp of the foundational principles of AaaP, we can turn to that common set of skills that we find all successful API programs use to nurture and grow. We call these the "API pillars," and that's what we'll cover in the next chapter.

CHAPTER 4

The Pillars of an API Product

When it's done well, it does look easy. People have no idea how complicated and difficult it really is. When you think of a movie, most people imagine a two-hour finished, polished product. But to get to that two-hour product, it can take hundreds or thousands of people many months of full-time work.

 —George Kennedy

In the previous chapter, we established the perspective of treating the API as a product. Now let's take a look at the work you'll need to do to build and maintain your product. The truth is that it takes a lot of hard work to develop a good API. In Chapter 1, you learned that APIs have three different parts: *interfaces*, *implementations*, and *instances*. To create your API, you'll need to put time and effort into managing all three of those aspects. On top of that, you'll need to keep everything up-to-date as your product continually matures and changes. To help you understand and manage all of that complexity, we've divided this body of work into a set of 10 pillars.

We call them *pillars* because of the way they support your API product. If you don't invest in any pillars, your product is doomed to fall and fail. But that doesn't mean all the pillars need maximum investment for your API to succeed. In this chapter, we've identified 10 pillars. The nice thing about having 10 is that they don't all have to carry the same amount of weight. Some pillars can be stronger than others, and you can even decide that some pillars don't need much investment at all. The important thing is that the combined strength of these pillars raises your API, even as it evolves and changes over time.

Introducing the Pillars

Each of the API pillars forms a boundary for a work domain. Or, putting it another way, each pillar bounds a set of API-related *decisions*. In reality, your work effort can't be categorized this precisely, and some of the pillars will overlap with one another. But that's OK. Our intent isn't to define an irrefutable truth about API work; instead, it's to develop a useful model for examining and talking about the work that goes into producing API products. We'll be building upon this foundational concept of pillars throughout the book as we develop more advanced models for team organization, product maturity, and landscape aspects in future chapters.

The 10 pillars we've defined for API work are as follows:

- Strategy
- Design
- Documentation
- Development
- Testing
- Deployment
- Security
- Monitoring
- Discovery
- Change management

In this chapter, we'll introduce each of these pillars and examine what they are and why they are important for the success of an API product. We'll also describe the decision space for each pillar along with some general guidance on how to strengthen it. We won't be giving you any specific guidance on how to implement any of the pillars in this chapter—after all, a complete discussion of each of these areas of work could fill a book on its own, and we still have many more API management concepts to tackle. However, we'll call out some of the most important decisions in each area from a governance perspective. Let's start by taking a look at the first pillar of an API product: strategy.

Strategy

Great products start with a great strategy, and API products are no different. The API strategy pillar includes two key decision areas: *why* you want to build your API (the goal) and *how* an API will help you to achieve that goal (the tactics). It's important to understand that your strategic goal for the API can't exist in a vacuum. Whatever goal you come up with for your API product needs to bring value to the organization that owns it. Of course, that means you'll need to have some idea of your organization's strategy or business model in the first place. If you're in the dark about your organizational goals, figure that out before you start spinning up new APIs.

Powering your business with APIs

The amount of impact that your API product has on your organizational strategy depends a lot on the context of your business. If your company's main revenue source is selling API access to third-party developers (for example, Twilio's communication APIs or Stripe's payments API), then your API product strategy will be heavily intertwined with your company strategy. If the API does well, the company profits; if the API suffers, the company fails. The API product becomes the primary value channel for your organization, and its architecture and business model will be implicitly aligned with the objectives of the company.

However, most organizations have preexisting, "traditional" businesses that the APIs will support. In these cases, an API will not become the new primary revenue source unless the company makes a major change to its strategy. For example, a bank that has been operating for hundreds of years may open an API to external developers in support of an "open banking" initiative. Narrowly focusing only on the API's business model might lead to adopting a revenue model for the API—one that charges developers for access to API-based banking functions. But thinking about the bigger picture for the bank, this API strategy would be detrimental because it creates a barrier to usage. Instead, the banking API can be offered for free (at a loss) in the hopes of increasing the bank's digital reach, leading to an increase in sales of the core banking products.

API strategy isn't just for APIs that are being offered to the outside world; this is also an important pillar for your internal APIs. That means you'll need to define a product strategy for them as well. The only real difference between internal API strategy and external API strategy is in the users they serve. For both types of APIs, the work of understanding why the API needs to exist and how it can fulfill that need remains the same. No matter what the context is for your API, it's worthwhile to develop a strategic goal for the API that will bring value to your organization.

Once you have a strategic goal for your API product, you'll need to develop a set of tactics that will help you achieve it.

Defining tactics

Achieving a strategic API goal will require you to create a plan for your product that leads you there. You'll need to develop a set of tactics for your work that gives you the best chance of success. Essentially, your strategy guides all of the decision-based work you'll make in the other nine pillars. The challenge is in understanding the link between each of those decision work domains and your goal.

Let's take a look at a few examples:

Goal: increase business-aligned capabilities in your platform

If the focus is on building up a bigger set of business-aligned APIs, your tactics should include some changes to how you design and create your API in the first place. For example, you'll probably want to involve the business stakeholders early in the design stage of your API to make sure that the right capabilities are being exposed through your interface. You'll also probably take their lead in understanding who the primary users are and what the boundaries of the API should be.

Goal: monetize internal assets

A monetization focus requires a set of tactics that help you bring your product to a user community that finds it valuable. It also usually means that you'll be operating in a competitive market, so the developer experience (DX) of using your API becomes very important. Tactically, that means a heavier investment in the design, documentation, and discovery pillars of work. It also means you'll need to do some market research to identify the right audience for your API and make sure you have the right type of product for them.

Goal: harvest business ideas

If the goal is to find innovative ideas from outside your company, you'll need to develop a set of tactics that fosters the use of your API in innovative ways. That will mean marketing the API to the outside world and designing it to be appealing to a user community that provides the most potential innovative value. It also makes sense to invest heavily in the discovery pillar to make sure that you can drive usage as high as possible in order to harvest as many ideas as possible. Equally, you'll need a clear tactic for identifying the best ideas and developing them further.

As we can see from these three examples, you'll need to do the following to develop strong tactics for your API:

- Identify which pillars are essential to success.
- Identify which user communities will drive success.
- Gather contextual data to drive your decision-making work.

Adapting your strategy

While it's important to develop good tactics when you begin building your API, it's also essential that your strategy remains fluid and ready to change. It's no good setting your strategic goal and tactical plan once and then walking away. Instead, you'll need to adjust your strategy based on the results you get from your product. If you aren't making any progress, you'll need to make some changes to your tactics, perhaps adjusting your goal or even scrapping the API and starting again.

Charting your strategic progress means you'll need to have a way of measuring your API results. In fact, it's essential that you have a set of measures for your strategic objectives—otherwise you'll never know how well you are doing. We'll talk more about objectives and measurements for APIs in Chapter 7 when we introduce OKRs and KPIs for APIs. Measurement also depends on having a way of gathering data about the API, so you'll also need to make an investment in the monitoring pillar.

You should also be ready to change your strategy if the context of your API changes: for example, if your organization changes its strategic goal, a new competitor shows up in your market, or the government introduces a new type of regulation. In each of these cases, being quick to adapt can greatly increase the value your API provides. But strategic change is limited by the changeability of your API, so the pillar of change management (discussed later in this chapter) is an essential investment.

Key decisions for strategy governance

What is the API's goal and tactical plan?
> Defining a goal and a plan to achieve it is a core of strategy work. It's important to consider carefully how this decision work should be distributed. You can allow individual teams to define their own goals and tactics to take advantage of local optimization, or you can centralize goal planning to improve system optimization. If you choose to decentralize API strategy work, you'll need to build incentives and controls to prevent any single API from causing irreparable harm. For example, centralizing the authorization step of a goal-setting decision may slow the process down but can prevent unexpected problems.

How is the strategic impact measured?
> The API's goal is a local definition, but you'll also need to govern how well that goal aligns with the organization's interests. That measurement can be decentralized and left to your API teams, or it can be centralized and standardized. For example, you can introduce a consistent process with standardized metrics that teams need to follow for API reports. This gives you the benefit of consistent data for system-level analysis.

When does the strategy change?
> Sometimes goals need to change, but who is allowed to make that decision? The trouble with changing an API's goal is that it tends to be highly impactful, both to the API itself and to the people who depend on it. While you might give your teams the freedom to set the goal of a new API, you'll need to introduce more controls for goal changes, especially once the API has entered a stage of heavy usage.

Design

Design work happens when you make decisions about how something you are creating will look, feel, and be used. Everything you create or change involves design decisions. In fact, all of the decision-making work we describe in the different sections of this chapter can also be thought of as design work. But the pillar of API design we are describing here is special. It's constrained to a specific type of design work: the decisions you make when you are designing the API's *interface*.

We've called out interface design as its own pillar because it has such a big impact on your API. Although it's only one part of what makes an API, the interface is all that your users see when they want to use your product. For them, the interface *is* the API. Because of that, whatever interface design you come up with has a big impact on the decisions you'll make in the other pillars. For example, deciding that your API should have an event-based interface radically changes the implementation, deployment, monitoring, and documentation work you'll need to do.

You'll have lots of decisions to make when you are designing your interface. Here are a few of the important things you'll need to consider:

Vocabularies

What are the words and terms that your users will need to understand? What special characters will they need to know about?

Styles

What protocols, message patterns, and interface styles will the interface adopt? For example, will your API use the CRUD pattern? Or will it use an event style? Or something like the GraphQL query style?

Interactions

How will your API allow users to meet their needs? For example, what calls will they have to make to achieve their goals? How will the status of calls be communicated to them? What kind of controls, filters, and usage hints will you provide to them in the interface?

Safety

What design features will help your users avoid making mistakes? How will you convey errors and problems?

Consistency

What level of familiarity will you provide to your users? Will the API be consistent in terms of other APIs in your organizations or your industry? Will the interface design be similar to other APIs that your users may have used, or will it surprise them with its innovation? Will you adopt ratified industry standards in your design?

That's not an exhaustive list, but as you can see, there is a lot of decision-making ground for you to cover. Designing a good interface is difficult work. But let's be more precise about what the goal is. What is *good design* for an API's interface, and how do you make better design decisions?

What is good design?

If you've done the work of establishing a strategy for your API, then you've already defined a strategic goal for your API. We need to figure out how the design of the interface can help you get closer to that objective. As we saw in "Strategy" on page 84, you can come up with lots of different goals and tactics for an API. But generally speaking, all of them boil down to a choice between two common objectives:

- Acquire more API users.
- Reduce the development costs for API usage.

In practice, you'll need a much more nuanced view of strategy if you want to be effective. But by generalizing the objectives this way, we can make an important observation: good interface design will help you achieve both of these generalized goals. If the overall experience of using the API is good, more users will be willing to use it. Interface design plays a big role in the developer experience of your API, so good interface design should lead to higher user acquisition. Also, a good interface is one that makes it harder to do the wrong things and easier to do the things that solve a user's problems. That translates to a lower development effort for the software that you write when you use a well-designed API.

So, good interface design is worth investing in. But there isn't a concrete set of decisions that makes an interface a "good" one. The quality of your interface depends entirely on the goals of your users. Improving usability and experience is impossible if you don't know who you are designing for. Thankfully, if you've already established *why* you are building this API, it should be a fairly straightforward exercise to figure out *who* you are designing for. Target that user community and make design decisions that will improve their experience of using your API.

Developer Experience (DX)

Throughout this chapter and in this book we'll refer to the *developer experience* of your API. DX is really just the user experience that your API provides, but with the acknowledgment that it is for a very particular type of user—a software developer. An API's DX is the sum of all the interactions that the developer will have with your API product. Interface design is a big part of that, but your documentation, marketing, and support all contribute to the experience you are creating. Ultimately, DX is a measure of how happy or (unhappy) your user base is.

Using a design method

To get the best results from your interface design work, your best bet is to use a method or process. A big part of creating a design is making guesses or assumptions about what you think will work. You have to start somewhere, so you might start by copying an API interface that you like or by following some guidance in a blog post. That's perfectly fine. But if you want to maximize the value that your design interface provides, you'll need a way of testing those assumptions and making sure the decisions you've made are the best ones.

For example, we could decide to adopt the following lightweight process:

1. Come up with a prototype for the interface.
2. Write our own client that uses the prototype.
3. Update the prototype based on what we've learned and try it once more.

A heavier-duty process might look like this:

1. Have an early design meeting with all stakeholders (i.e., users, supporters, and implementers).
2. Codesign a vocabulary for the interface.
3. Conduct surveys with the user community.
4. Create a prototype.
5. Test the prototype with target user communities.
6. Validate the prototype with implementers.
7. Iterate as necessary.

The big difference between these two examples is the amount of investment you'd need to make and the amount of information you'd gather. Deciding how heavily to invest in the design process is a strategic decision. For example, you'll probably scrutinize the interface of an external API being sold in a competitive market more than you would an internal API being used by your own development team. But remember that even a lightweight design process can pay big dividends.

Key decisions for design governance

What are the design boundaries?

An API team with no design constraints can create an interface model that maximizes usability and the experience for their users. But usability is user-centric and comes at the cost of flexibility for users in general. That means there is a system impact to this kind of local optimization. If you are producing many APIs and users will need to use more than one of them, you'll need to introduce some constraints around design decisions. That means you'll need to either centralize the design work or centralize the selection of choices designers have. Some centralized teams publish a "style guide" to document these kinds of design constraints; it can include the vocabularies, styles, and interactions that are officially allowed.

How are interface models shared?

Deciding how the model of an interface should be shared means deciding how the work of API design should be persisted. For example, if you centralize this decision completely, you can decide that all API teams need to provide designs in the OpenAPI description format. This has the drawback of limiting all possible design choices to the options available in the OpenAPI Specification but also makes it easier to share work between teams and use consistent tooling and automation across the system.

Documentation

No matter how well you design the interface of your API, your users won't be able to get started without a little help. For example, you may need to teach users where the API is located on the network, what the vocabulary of the messages and interface is, and in what order they should make calls. The pillar of API documentation captures the work of creating this API learning experience. We call this pillar "API documentation" instead of "API learning" because the most popular API learning experiences are delivered in the form of human-readable documentation.

It's worth providing good documentation for the same reason it's worth designing a good interface: a better developer experience translates into more strategic value. If you don't have good documentation, the API will be more difficult to learn and understand. If it's too difficult to learn how to use, fewer people will use it. If they are forced to use it, the software they write will take longer to develop and is more likely to have bugs. Developing good documentation turns out to be a big part of creating a good developer experience.

Documentation methods

You can deliver API documentation in a lot of different ways: you can provide an encyclopedia-like reference to the resources of your API, you can provide tutorials and conceptual content, and you can even provide highly documented, complex sample applications for users to copy and learn from. There is an incredible amount of variety in the styles, formats, and strategies of technical documentation. To make things easier, we'll split API documentation into two broad, fundamental practices: the *teach don't tell* method and the *tell don't teach* method. In our experience, you'll need to adopt both approaches if you want to create the best learning experience for your users.

The *tell don't teach* approach to documentation focuses on communicating facts about your API that will help users to use it. Documenting the list of your API's error codes and providing a list of message body schemas it uses are both examples of this fact-based approach. This type of documentation gives your users a reference guide for your interface. Because it is highly factual, it is fairly easy to design and develop. In fact, you may be able to use tooling to produce this style of documentation very quickly, especially if the interface design has been serialized in a machine-readable format (see "API Description Formats" on page 91). Overall, this type of factual reporting of interface details and behavior requires less design effort and decision making from your team. The key decisions have to do with choosing which parts of the API need to be documented, rather than how to convey that information in the best way.

Conversely, the *teach don't tell* approach to documentation focuses on designing a learning experience. Instead of just laying out the facts for readers to sift through, this approach provides a tailored learning experience to users. The goal is to help your API users achieve their usability goals while learning how to use your API in a focused, targeted manner. For example, if you own a mapping API, you could write a six-step tutorial that teaches your users how to retrieve GPS information for a street address. This way you can help them accomplish a fairly typical task with a minimum level of effort.

But documentation doesn't have to be passive. References, guides, and tutorials are all helpful to read, but you can also deploy tooling that will help your users learn about your API in a more interactive way. For example, you can provide a web-based API explorer tool that allows your users to send requests to your API in real time. A good API explorer tool is more than a "dumb" network request tool; it guides the learning experience by providing a list of activities, vocabularies, suggestions, and corrections to the user. The big advantage of interactive tooling is that it shortens the feedback loop for users: the cycle of learning something, trying to apply what has been learned, and learning from the results. Without tooling, your users will need to spend time writing code or finding and using external tools, which can result in a much longer loop.

The Developer Portal

In the world of APIs, a developer portal is the place (usually a website) where all the supplementary resources for an API are hosted. You don't have to have a developer portal, but it can really help improve the developer experience for your API by giving users a convenient way to learn about and interact with your product.

Investing in documentation

If you are providing only one type of API documentation, chances are that you are underserving your user community. Different users have different needs, and you'll need to cater to each of them if you care about their learning experience. For example, new users can benefit a lot from the *teach don't tell* approach to documentation because it's prescriptive and easy to follow, but users who are experienced with your API will appreciate your *tell don't teach* documentation because they can quickly navigate to the facts that they need. Similarly, interactive tools can appeal to users who enjoy a live experience, but won't be great for users who prefer to understand and plan—or just have a preference for reading.

In practice, providing all of this documentation for your API can be costly. After all, someone has to design and write all of it—and not just once but over the lifetime of your API. In fact, one of the difficulties of API documentation work is in keeping it synchronized with interface and implementation changes. If the docs are wrong, users can become very unhappy very quickly. So, you'll need to make smart decisions about how much of a documentation effort is sustainable for your API product.

The key factor in making your documentation investment decision should be the value of improving the API's learning experience to your organization. For example, good documentation can help differentiate a public API product from its competitors. It can also be a big help for an internal API that is used by developers who aren't familiar with the API owner's system, business, or industry. The level of documentation investment for a public API operating in a competitive market will usually be higher than for an internal one, and that's OK. Ultimately, you'll need to decide how much documentation is good enough for your API. The good news is that it's always possible to increase that investment as your API grows.

Key decisions for documentation governance

How should the learning experience be designed?

Decisions around learning experience design are often governed separately from the design, implementation, and deployment of an API. If you have lots of APIs, your users will appreciate having a single, consistent learning experience for all of them. But, centralizing this decision carries the usual costs: less innovation and more constraints for API teams as well as a potential bottleneck of centralized technical writing. You'll need to balance the need for consistency against the amount of variety and innovation you need to support. One option is to introduce a hybrid model where most of the APIs have centralized documentation, but teams are allowed to create their own learning experiences if they are trying something new.

When should documentation be written?

There is a surprising amount of variability for when a team should start writing their documentation. Writing early is more expensive because of the likelihood of design and implementation changes, but it can expose usability problems early on, making it worthwhile. You'll need to decide if this is a decision that can be safely decentralized or one that needs more centralized management. For example, does every API regardless of its intended use need to have written documentation before it can be released? Or should teams use their best judgment to make that decision?

Development

The pillar of API development includes all of the decisions that you make when you bring your API to "life." This is the hard work of developing your API's *implementation* in a way that stays true to its *interface* design. The development pillar has an overwhelmingly large decision space. You'll need to decide which technology products and frameworks you want to use to implement the API, what the architecture of the implementation should look like, which programming and configuration languages need to be used, and how the API should behave at runtime. In other words, you'll need to design and develop the software of your API.

The truth is that your API's users don't care how you implement your API. All your implementation decisions about programming languages, tools, databases, and software design are meaningless to them; only the final product matters. As long as the API does what it is supposed to do in the way that it is supposed to do it, your users will be happy. The fact that you do that with a particular database or framework is just a triviality to your users.

But just because your users don't care about your choices doesn't mean that your development decisions aren't important. In fact, development decisions matter a lot, especially for the people who have to build, maintain, and change the API over its lifetime. If you choose technologies that are difficult to use, or esoteric languages that no one in your company understands, the API will be more difficult to maintain. Similarly, if you choose tooling that is too stifling or languages that are just painful to program in, the API will be difficult to change.

When you think about the API development pillar, it's easy to focus just on the choices you'll make to build the first release of the product. That's important, but it's only a small part of the challenge. The more important goal is to make development decisions that improve the quality, scalability, changeability, and maintainability of your API over its entire lifetime. It takes experience and skill to develop software with that perspective, so you'll need to make good investments in people and tools. After all, anyone can write a computer program after a few programming classes, but it takes a real professional to write programs that work at scale, in concurrent use, and that handle all the edge cases that come up in real life while remaining maintainable and changeable by other developers.

There aren't any concrete rules for how you should design and architect your API software, just as there aren't any concrete rules for designing software in general. But there is, of course, plenty of guidance, philosophy, and advice on how you *should* design your software. Generally, you can apply any good practices for server-based development to the API development space. The only thing that is particular to APIs is the healthy ecosystem of API-specific frameworks and tooling for developing instances. Let's take a look at the types of options you have for taking advantage of these helpers.

Using frameworks and tools

A large variety of tools are used in any typical development process, but for API development, we're interested in a specific category of tooling—the kind that helps you offload the API-related decisions and development effort involved in creating a new API release. This includes frameworks that make the job of writing API code easier as well as standalone tools that offer "no-code" or "low-code" implementation.

One tool that is particularly popular in the API management space is the *API gateway*. An API gateway is a server-based tool that is designed to reduce the cost of deploying APIs within a network. They are typically designed to be highly scalable, reliable, and secure—in fact, improving the security of an API implementation is often the primary motivation for introducing a gateway into a system architecture.

They are useful because they can greatly reduce the cost of developing an API instance.

The cost of development goes down when you use a tool like a gateway because it's built to solve most of your problems. In fact, in most cases, these tools require very little programming effort. For example, a decent HTTP API gateway should be ready to listen for requests on an HTTPS port, parse JSON request bodies, and interact with a database right out of the box with only a little bit of configuration required to make it run. Of course, all of this doesn't happen by magic; someone had to program this tool to do all these things. In the end, you're shifting the cost of API development to an outside agency.

When tools work well, they are a godsend. But the cost of using tools like API gateways is that they can do only what they are designed to do. Just like with any piece of machinery, your flexibility is limited to the functions that the machine provides. So, choosing the right tool becomes an important development decision. If your API strategy and interface design take you in a direction of doing lots of nonstandard things, you may need to take on more of the development effort yourself.

The interface and implementation relationship

Supporting the strategy and interface design of your API is really the primary goal for your development work. No matter how great your architecture is and how maintainable your code is, if the API doesn't do what the interface design says it should, you've failed. We can draw two conclusions from this statement:

- Conforming to your *published* interface design is an important quality metric for your implementation.
- You'll have to keep your implementation updated whenever you change the interface.

That means you can't develop your API until you have an interface design. It also means that the people who are doing your development work need a reliable way of understanding what the interface looks like and when it changes. A big risk for your API product is if the design team decides on an interface design that is impractical or impossible to implement properly. If the interface designer and the implementation developer are the same person or on the same team, it's not such a big deal, but if that's not the case, make sure that having the implementation team vet the interface is part of your API design method.

Using API Descriptions Close to the Code

One way to improve your chances of keeping the implementation and interface synchronized is to integrate the interface description into your implementation. For example, if you have an API description format that represents the interface design, you can keep that file in your code repository or even develop an automated test that verifies your adherence to the interface. Taking this further, you can even generate a code skeleton based on the description format—although that's really only effective for the first release.

You can also take the opposite approach: instead of receiving an interface description and using it with your code, you can embed the interface description by hand directly into your code. For example, some frameworks allow you to use annotations that describe an API interface. The combination of your code and the interface annotations can become the "source of truth" for your interface, and you can even use it to generate API documentation. Any of these approaches can be useful in helping to ensure that your implementation doesn't break a promise that your interface design makes.

Key decision for development governance

What can be used for the implementation?

This is the central governance question for implementation. It's a broad question and includes a lot of decisions within it: which databases, programming languages, and system components can you choose from? Which libraries, frameworks, and tools can be used to support the work? Which vendors do you have to work with? Are you allowed to use open source code?

At the time of this writing, there's been a lot of interest in decentralizing these kinds of decisions to improve local optimization. We've heard from lots of companies who've found that their APIs are more efficient, easier to build, and easier to maintain when teams are given more implementation freedom. But decentralization comes with the usual costs: less consistency and fewer opportunities for system optimization. In practice, this means that it can be harder for people to move between teams, and there's less opportunity to gain economies of scale and less visibility over the implementation in general.

In our experience, providing more implementation freedom is worth doing, but you'll need to consider how much decision freedom your system can afford. One way to make it easier to support decentralized implementation decisions is to centralize the selection element, which means centralizing the technology options while decentralizing the team's selection and authority over them.

Testing

If you care at all about the quality of your API, you'll need to expend some effort on testing it. In the pillar of API testing, you'll need to make decisions about both *what* you need to test and *how* you'll test it. In general, API testing is not very different from the typical quality assurance (QA) work that you'd do for a software project. You should be able to apply good software quality practices to the *implementation*, *interface*, and *instances* of your API just like you would for a traditional software application. But as with the development pillar, it's the ecosystem of tools, libraries, and helpers that makes the API domain slightly different from the general testing space.

What needs to be tested?

The primary goal of testing your API is to make sure it can deliver on the strategic goal you should have defined during its creation. But as we've seen throughout this chapter, that strategic goal is enabled by the decision-based work of the 10 pillars. Therefore, the secondary goal of API testing is to ensure that all of the work you've done across our pillars is of sufficient quality to support the strategy. For example, if the usability and learnability of your API are very low, that could impact a strategic goal of acquiring more API users. That means you need to define specific tests to assess the quality of the interface. You also need to test that the work you've done is internally consistent. For example, you'll need to check that the implementation you've developed is consistent with the interface you've designed.

Here is a typical list of test categories that API owners use:

Usability and UX testing
> Identify usability bugs in the interface, documentation, and discovery. For example: provide the API documentation to developers and perform "over the shoulder" observation testing while they try writing client code using it.

Unit testing
> Identify bugs within the implementation at a granular level. For example: run a JUnit test against a Java method in the API implementation's code on every build.

Integration testing
> Identify implementation and interface bugs by making API calls against an instance. For example: run a test script that makes API calls against a running instance of the API in a development environment.

Performance and load testing
> Identify nonfunctional bugs in deployed API instances and instance environments. For example: run a performance test script that simulates a production-level load against a running instance of the API in a production-like test environment.

Security testing
    Identify security vulnerabilities in the interface, implementation, and instance of the API. For example: hire a "tiger team" to find vulnerabilities in a running instance of the API in a secure test environment.

Production testing
    Identify usability, functionality, and performance bugs after the API product has been published in the production environment. For example: perform a multivariate test using the API documentation in which different users are served slightly different versions of content, and improve the usability of the documentation based on the results.

This certainly isn't an exhaustive list, and there are lots of other tests you could do. In fact, even the tests we've described here could be exploded into many more subcategories. The big strategic decision you'll need to make in the testing pillar is how much testing is good enough. Ideally, your API strategy can help guide this decision. If quality and consistency are a high priority, you may find you'll need to spend a lot of time and money testing your API before it can be released. But if your API is experimental, you can adopt a risk-tolerant approach and perform a minimum level of testing. For example, we'd expect the testing policy for an established bank's payments API and a startup's social networking API to be very different in scope.

API testing tools

Testing can be expensive, so it's helpful to adopt process improvements that make it easier to improve your product's quality. For example, some organizations have had success with a "test-driven" method, where tests are written *before* the implementation or interface is created. The goal of this type of approach is to change the culture of a team to be test-centric so that all design decisions result in a more test-friendly implementation. When it works, the net result is an API that is of higher quality because of its implicit testability.

In addition to process and cultural improvements, you can use tooling and automation to reduce the cost of performing tests. The most useful tools in the API testing arsenal are simulators and test doubles, or mocks. That's because the connected nature of API software makes it difficult to test things in isolation, so you'll need some way of simulating other components. In particular, you'll probably need tools to simulate each of these components:

Client
    When you are testing your API, you'll need something that can simulate the requests that will come from your API clients. There are lots of tools available that can do this for you. The good ones will give you enough configurability and variability to come very close to the types of messages and traffic patterns you'll receive in production.

Backend

Chances are your API will have some dependencies of its own. That could be a set of internal APIs, a database, or a third-party, external resource. To perform integration testing, performance testing, and security testing, you'll probably need some way of simulating those dependencies.

Environment

You'll also need some way to simulate your production environment when you are running preproduction tests. Years ago that could mean maintaining and operating a scheduled environment just for that purpose. Nowadays, many organizations use virtualization tools to make it cheaper to re-create environments for testing.

API

Sometimes you'll even need to simulate your own API. That can be the case when you want to test one of your supporting components—for example, an API explorer in a development portal that makes calls against the API—but a simulated version of your API is also a valuable resource that you can give to your API's users. This kind of simulated API is often called a *sandbox*, presumably because it's a place where developers can play with your API and data without any consequences. It's a bit of an investment to make, but it can greatly improve the developer experience for your API.

Make Your Sandbox Feel Like Production

When you release a sandbox for your API's users, make sure that your sandbox reproduces the production environment as closely as possible. You'll have a much happier set of users if the only change they need to make when they finish writing code is to point it at your production instance. Nothing is more frustrating than spending a lot of time and energy troubleshooting an API integration only to find out that the production instance looks and behaves differently.

Key decisions for testing governance

Where should testing happen?

Over the years, testing processes have become more and more decentralized. The big governance decision is to determine how much you want to centralize or decentralize for each of the types of API test stages we've described. Centralizing a testing process gives you more control but comes with the cost of a potential bottleneck. Some of that can be alleviated with automation, but you'll then need to decide who configures and maintains the automated system. Most organizations employ both centralized and decentralized systems. Our advice is to decentralize early test stages for speed and centralize the later stages for safety.

How much testing is enough?

Even if you decide that individual teams can run their own tests, you might want to centralize the decision of the minimum level of testing they need to do. For example, some companies use code coverage tools that provide reports on how much of the code has been tested. In terms of metrics and quality, coverage isn't perfect, but it's quantifiable, and it allows you to set a minimum threshold that all teams need to meet. If you have the right people, you can also decentralize this decision and leave it up to individual API teams to do what's right for their APIs.

Deployment

The *implementation* of an API is what brings the *interface* to life, but that implementation needs to be deployed properly in order to be useful. The pillar of API deployment includes all the work of moving the implementation of an API into an environment where your target users can use it. The deployed API is called an *instance*, and you may need to manage several of these instances to keep your API running properly. The challenge of API deployment work is in making sure that all your instances behave consistently, remain available to your users, and are as easy to change as possible.

The work involved in software deployment is a lot more complicated today than it was in the past. That's mostly because our software architectures have grown increasingly complex, with more interconnected dependencies than ever before. On top of that, companies have pretty high expectations when it comes to the availability and reliability of systems—they expect things to work all the time and every time. Oh, and don't forget, they'll want changes to be released immediately. You'll need to make good decisions about your API deployment system to meet all of those expectations.

Dealing with uncertainty

Improving the quality of an API deployment means making sure that your API instances behave the way users expect them to. Obviously, a lot of the work that goes into making that happen occurs outside the pillar of deployment. You'll need to write good, clean implementation code and test it rigorously if you want to have fewer bugs in production. But sometimes, even when you take all those precautions, bad things happen in production. That's because there is a high level of uncertainty and unpredictability to deal with for a published API.

For example, what happens if there is a sudden spike in demand for your API product? Will your API instances be able to handle the load? Or what if an operator inadvertently deploys an older version of an API instance, or a third-party service your API depends on suddenly becomes unavailable? Uncertainty can pop up in lots of different places: from your users, from human error, from your hardware, and from external dependencies. Increasing deployment safety requires you to take two opposite approaches at the same time: eliminating uncertainty while at the same time accepting it.

A popular method for eliminating uncertainty in API deployments is to apply the principle of *immutability*. Immutability is the quality of being unable to change—in other words, being "read-only." You can apply immutability in lots of ways. For example, if you never allow your operators to change a server's environment variables or install software packages manually, you could say you have an *immutable infrastructure*. Similarly, you could create immutable API deployment packages—that is, a deployable package that can't be modified, only replaced. The principle of immutability improves safety because it helps drive out the uncertainty introduced by human intervention.

However, you'll never be able to eliminate uncertainty completely. You can't predict every eventuality, and you can't test every possibility. So, a big part of your decision work will be in figuring out how to keep your system safe even when the unexpected happens. Some of this work happens at the API implementation level (e.g., writing defensive code), and some of it happens at the landscape level (e.g., designing resilient system architecture), but a lot of work needs to happen at the deployment and operations level. For example, if you can continually monitor the health of your API instances and system resources, you can find problems and fix them before they impact your users.

Designing Resilient Software

One of our favorite resources for improving the safety of a deployed API is Michael Nygard's book *Release It!* (Pragmatic Bookshelf). If you haven't read it yet, make sure you do. It's a treasure trove of implementation and deployment patterns for improving the safety and resiliency of your API product.

One kind of uncertainty that you'll be forced to accept comes in the form of changes to the API. While it would be nice to freeze all changes once you've got your API working reliably, change is an inevitability that you'll need to prepare for. In fact, deploying changes as quickly as possible should be a goal for your deployment work.

Deployment automation

There are really only two ways to make your deployments happen faster: doing less work and doing work more quickly. Sometimes you can do this by making changes to the way you work—for example, by adopting a different way of working or introducing a new type of culture. It's hard, but it can really help. We'll dive into this topic in more detail later, when we talk about people and teams in Chapter 8.

Another way to get faster is to replace human deployment tasks with automation. For example, if you automate the process of testing, building, and deploying your API code, you'll be able to perform releases at the push of a button.

Deployment tooling and automation can be a quick win, but be aware of the long-term costs. Introducing automation in your workflow is like introducing machinery into a factory—it improves efficiency, but it limits your flexibility. Automation also comes with startup and maintenance costs. It's unlikely that it will work right out of the box, and it's unlikely it will adapt on its own to your changing requirements and context. So, when you improve your system with automation, be prepared to pay those costs over time—that means the costs of maintaining that machinery as well as eventually replacing it.

APIOps: DevOps for APIs

A lot of what we've described in this section fits in well with the philosophy of DevOps culture. In fact, there's even an emerging term for applying DevOps practices to API specifically called *APIOps*. We think that DevOps is a good fit for the API domain and worth learning from, no matter what you want to call it.

Key decisions for deployment governance

Who decides when a release can happen?

The question of who gets to release is central to deployment governance. If you have talented people you can trust, an architecture that is fault tolerant, and a business domain that can excuse the occasional failure, you could completely decentralize the decision. Otherwise, you'll need to figure out which parts of this decision need to be centralized. Distribution of this decision is usually nuanced. For example, you could enable "push to release" for trusted team members, or release to a test environment where a centralized team can make a "go/no-go" decision. Distribute in a way that fits your constraints and enables the most speed, with the right level of safety at scale.

How are deployments packaged?

In recent years, the question of how software is packaged and delivered has become enormously important. It's turned out to be the kind of decision that can gradually shift an entire system in another direction. For example, the growing popularity of containerized deployment has made it cheaper and easier to build immutable, cloud-friendly deployments. You'll need to consider who should be making this important decision for your organization. A decentralized, locally optimized decision maker may not understand the impacts to security, compatibility, and scale, but a purely centralized decision maker may not have a solution that fits the variety of implementations and software being deployed. As usual, some type of choice constraint and distribution of the decision is useful.

Beyond just the question of centralization and decentralization, you'll also need to consider which team is best placed to make the highest-quality decision. Should the operations and middleware teams define packaging options? An architecture team? Or should the implementation teams make the decision? Talent distribution is a key factor here: which teams have the people who can make the best assessments?

Security

APIs make it easier to connect software together, but they also introduce new problems. The openness of APIs makes them a potential target and presents a new kind of attack surface. There are more doors to enter, and the treasure is bigger! So, you'll need to spend some time improving the security of your API. The pillar of API security focuses on the decisions you'll need to make to accomplish the following security goals:

- Protecting your system, API clients, and end users from threats
- Keeping your API up and running for legitimate use by legitimate users
- Protecting the privacy of data and resources

These three simple goals hide an enormously complex subject area. In fact, a big mistake that API product owners make is in assuming that securing an API simply means making a few technology decisions. Now, we don't mean to say that technology decisions about security aren't important—of course they are! But if you really want to strengthen your API security pillar, you'll need to broaden the context of security-based decision making.

Taking a holistic approach

To truly improve the security of your API, you'll need to make it part of the decision-making process for all of the pillars we've described in this chapter. A big part of doing that is the work of implementing security features at runtime. For a start, you'll need to extract identities, authenticate clients and end users, authorize usage, and implement rate limits. You can write a lot of this yourself, or you can take the safer and faster approach of implementing tooling and libraries that do it for you.

But API security includes a lot of things that happen outside of the client–API software interaction. Cultural changes can improve security by instilling a security-first mentality in engineers and designers. Processes can be implemented to prevent insecure changes from making it to production or staying in production. Documentation can be reviewed to make sure that it doesn't leak information inadvertently. Sales and support staff can be trained to not inadvertently provide private data or assist in a social engineering attack.

Of course, what we've just described is much bigger than the traditional domain of API security. But the truth is that API security can't exist on its own. It's part of an interconnected system and needs to be considered as one element of a holistic security approach for your company. It doesn't do any good to pretend that it's an island on its own with no connection to your bigger security strategy. The people who want to exploit your system certainly won't be treating it that way.

So, you'll need to make decisions about how to integrate your API work with the security strategy within your company. Sometimes that's pretty easy to do, and other times it's more difficult. One of the big challenges for APIs is in balancing the desire for openness and usability with the desire to lock things down. How far you go either way should be a product of your organizational strategy and the strategic goals of your API.

Key decisions for security governance

Which decisions need to be authorized?
> All of the decisions that people make in your organization have the potential to introduce a security vulnerability, but it's impossible to scrutinize every decision that's being made. You'll need to determine which decisions have the biggest impact to the security of your API and make sure those decisions are the best ones. That's going to depend a lot on your context. Are there "trusted" zones in your architecture that need to have secure "edges"? Are designers and implementers already experienced in good security practice? Is all the work happening in-house or are you working with third-party implementers? All of these contextual factors can change your decision authorization focus.

How much security does an API need?
> A big part of the apparatus of security is the standardization of work decisions to protect the system and its users. For example, you might have rules about where files can be stored or which encryption algorithms should be used. Increased standardization decreases the freedom for teams and people to innovate. In the case of the security context, this is usually justified by the impact of making a single bad decision, but not all APIs necessarily need the same level of scrutiny and protection. For example, an API that is used by external developers for financial transactions will need more of a security investment than an API used for logging performance data. But who makes that decision?

> As usual, context, talent, and strategy are the key considerations. Centralizing this decision allows a security team to make a blanket assessment based on their understanding of the system context. However, sometimes these kinds of generalized rules make it possible for things to slip between the cracks—especially

when API teams are doing new and innovative things that the centralized team couldn't have accounted for. If the decision is distributed, the teams themselves can make an assessment decision, but this requires a decent level of security knowledge within the team itself. Finally, if you are operating in a domain that prioritized security and risk mitigation, you might end up forcing the highest level of security upon everything, regardless of the local context and impact to speed.

> ## The OWASP API Security Project
>
> The OWASP API Security Project (*https://oreil.ly/Vn5YA*) is a fantastic resource for checking that you've done due diligence to secure your API. The Open Web Application Security Project (OWASP) is a nonprofit, community-based foundation that provides guidance on security web applications. In recent years, they've been supporting the community with API-specific material to help address the most common threats that API owners face. If you want to produce better decisions about your API's security, make sure that your team has read and understood the OWASP API security advice *before* design and development begins.

12 API security principles

Derived from Yuri Subach's security checklist applied to APIs, the following is a checklist of the 12 main principles of API security that you can use to guide your team toward safe and secure APIs:

API confidentiality
Limiting access to the information is the first rule of API security. The resource accessible via the API must be available for authorized users only, and protected from unintended recipients during transit, processing, or at rest.

API integrity
Information rendered by the API must always be trustworthy and accurate. The resource must be protected from intentional and unintentional alterations, modifications, or deletions, and unwanted changes must be detected automatically.

API availability
Availability is a guarantee of reliable access to the information by authorized people. Availability comes with its requirements, to the infrastructure and application levels, combined with appropriate engineering processes in the organization.

Economy of mechanism
API design and implementation of the system must be kept as simple as possible. Complex APIs are difficult to inspect and improve, and they are more

error-prone. From the security and usability standpoint, minimalism is a good thing.

Fail-safe API defaults

Access to any API endpoint/resource should be denied by default, and access should be granted only in case of specific permission. A good API security follows the protection scheme "when access should be granted" and does not follow the protection scheme "when access should be restricted."

Complete mediation

Access to all resources of an API should always be validated. Every endpoint must be equipped with an authorization mechanism. This principle brings security considerations to a system-wide level.

Open API design

Good API security design should not be a secret and must be documented and based on defined security standards and open protocols. API security involves all stakeholders of the organization and can also include partners or consumers.

Least API privilege

Every API consumer of the system should operate with minimal API permissions required to do the job. This limits the damage caused by an accident or error related to this specific API consumer.

Psychological acceptability

Effective API security implementation should protect a system but not hamper users of the system to use it properly or discourage them to follow all security requirements. The API security level must be matched to the level of threat. A heavy API security mechanism for nonsensitive resources can be disproportionate in term of efforts for consumers.

Minimize API attack surface area

Limiting surface attack area for an API is the minimization of what can be exploited by malicious users. To reduce the API surface attack area, you can expose only what is needed and limit area damage by limiting scope and rate, throttling the number of API calls before further user validation, and doing due diligence on the use cases.

API defense in depth

Multiple layers of control make it harder to exploit an API. You can limit access to the server to several known IP addresses (white labeling), impose two-factor authentication, and implement many other techniques that increase the depth of your API security practice.

Zero-trust policy

The zero-trust policy means to consider third-party API providers and third-party API consumers unsafe by default, whether external or internal. That means implementing all relevant API security measures for internal and external APIs as if they were all external and nontrustable by default.

Fail APIs securely

All APIs often fail to process transactions due to incorrect input, overload of requests, or other reasons. Any failure inside the API instance should not override security mechanisms and must deny access in case of failure.

Fix API security issues correctly

Once an API security issue has been identified, focus on fixing it properly and avoid "quick fixes" that may do the job in the short term but still don't fix the real cause of the problem. Developers and API security experts need to understand the root cause of the issue, create a test for it, and fix it with a minimal impact to the system. Once the fix is done, the system should be tested in all supported environments and on all platforms. Often API security breaches occur on failures that were identified by the API team but not fixed correctly.

Monitoring

Fostering the quality of observability in your API product is important. You can't properly manage your API unless you have accurate and up-to-date information about how it is performing and how it is being used. The pillar of API monitoring is all about the work you need to do to make that information available, accessible, and useful. Over time and at scale, monitoring API instances turns out to be just as essential to API management as the design of the interface or development of the implementation—if you're in the dark, you can't help but stumble and fall.

There are plenty of things that can be monitored in an API instance:

- Problems (e.g., errors, failures, warnings, and crashes)
- System health (e.g., CPU, memory, I/O, container health)
- API health (e.g., API uptime, API state, and total messages processed)
- Message logs (e.g., request and response message bodies, message headers, and metadata)
- Usage data (e.g., number of requests, endpoint/resource usage, and requests per consumer)

Learning More About Monitoring

With the exception of API and usage monitoring, the types of measurements we've described aren't unique to API-based software components. If you're looking for a good guide to monitoring network-based software components, we encourage you to read Google's *Site Reliability Engineering* (*https://oreil.ly/Il6Iu*) (O'Reilly). It's a great introduction to designing software systems and includes a pretty comprehensive list of the types of things you should be monitoring. Another good resource to take a look at is Weaveworks's RED Method (*https://oreil.ly/qJKtI*), which identifies three categories of metrics for a microservice: rate, errors, and duration.

Each of these groups of metrics will help your API in different ways. Health and problem data will help you detect and deal with faults, ideally reducing the impact of any problems that arise. Message processing data can help you troubleshoot API and system-level issues. Usage metrics can help you improve your API product by helping you understand how your users are actually using your API. But first, you'll need to put in the work of making that data available. Of course, you'll also need to make sure you have a reliable way of gathering all that data and presenting it in a usable way.

The more data you can produce, the more opportunities you'll have to learn and improve your product. So, ideally you'd produce a never-ending stream of data for your API. The costs of data production, harvesting, storage, and analysis can really add up, though, and sometimes those costs are just unbearable; for example, if the round-trip time of your API doubles because it needs to log data, you'll need to pare down some of your logging or find a better way to do it. One of the more important decisions you'll need to make is what you can afford to monitor given the known costs.

Another important decision is how consistent your API monitoring will be. If the way that your API provides monitoring data is consistent with other tools, industry standards, or organizational conventions, it will be much easier to use. Designing the monitoring system is a lot like designing an interface. If your monitoring interface is completely unique, it will take longer to learn how to use it and gather data. That's OK when you have a single API and you are the only one monitoring it, but at the scale of tens or hundreds of APIs, you'll need to reduce that monitoring cost. We'll explore this idea more in Chapter 7.

Key decisions for monitoring governance

What should be monitored?

> The decision of what to monitor is a big one. You can leave it up to individual teams in the beginning, but at scale, you'll benefit if you have consistency in your API monitoring. Consistent data will improve your ability to observe system

impacts and system behavior. That means you'll need to centralize some of this decision making.

How is data collected, analyzed, and communicated?

Centralizing the decisions on monitoring implementation will make it easier to work with API data, but it can inhibit the freedom of API teams. You'll need to decide how much of this decision should be centralized and how much of it should be distributed and decentralized. This becomes especially important when sensitive data is involved that needs to be protected.

Discovery

An API is valuable only if it is being used, but to be used, it first needs to be found. The pillar of API discovery is all about the work it takes to make your APIs easier to find for your target users. This means helping users to easily understand what your API does, how it can help them, how they can get started, and how they can invoke it. Discovery is an important quality of your API's developer experience. It requires good design, documentation, and implementation choices, but you'll also need to do some additional discovery-specific work to really improve the findability of your API product.

In the API world, there are two major types of discovery: *design time* and *runtime*. Design-time discovery focuses on making it easier for API users to learn about your API product. That includes learning about its existence, its functionality, and the use cases that it can solve. Conversely, runtime discovery happens after your API has been deployed. It helps software clients find the network location of your API based on some set of filters or parameters. Design-time discovery targets human users and is primarily a promotion and marketing exercise. Runtime discovery targets machine clients and relies on tooling and automation. Let's take a look at each of them.

Runtime discovery

Runtime discovery is a way of improving the changeability of your API landscape. If you have a good runtime discovery system, then you can change the location of your API instances with very little impact to the API's clients. This is especially useful if there are lots of API instances running at the same time—for example, microservices-style architectures often support runtime discovery to make finding services easier. Most of the work you'll need to do to make this happen is in the development and deployment pillars of an API.

Runtime discovery is a useful pattern for you to know about and is worth implementing if you are managing a complex system of APIs. We won't have time to go into the implementation details of how to make it work, but it does require a technology investment at the landscape, API, and consumer levels. For the most part, when we talk about the discovery pillar in this book, we're talking about design-time discovery.

Design-time discovery

To help people learn about your API at design time, you'll have to make sure you have the right kind of API documentation available. Documentation about what your API does and which problems it solves should be easily available to users who are looking for it. This kind of product marketing "copy" is an essential part of discovery, but it's not the only thing that matters. Helping your users find that information in the first place turns out to be a critical part of this pillar. You'll need to engage with your user community and market to them to be successful. How you do that depends a lot on the context of your user base:

External APIs

If your API is primarily being used by people who don't work in your group or organization, you'll need to invest in getting your message to them. This means marketing your API product in much the same way you'd market a piece of software: search engine optimization, event sponsorship, community engagement, and advertising. Your goal is to make sure that all of your API's potential users understand how your product can help them address their needs. Of course, the specific marketing actions you take will depend a lot on your context, the nature of the API, and the users you are targeting.

For example, if you are developing an SMS API product and competing for developer-users, then you'll advertise in the places you expect your potential users to be: web developer conferences, blogs about two-factor authentication, and telecom conferences. If you are targeting independent developers, you might rely on digital advertising, but if you're aiming for large enterprises, you might invest in a team of salespeople and their network of relationships. If you are competing in a crowded market, you'll probably need to expend a lot of effort to differentiate yourself, but if your product is unique, you may need only a little bit of search engine optimization magic to get people in the door. When it comes to product marketing, context is king.

Internal APIs

If your API is being used by your own developers, you probably have a captive audience. But that doesn't mean you can ignore discoverability for your API. An internal API has to be discovered to be used, and over time if it's too difficult to find, you'll run into problems. If internal developers don't know about it, they won't be able to use it and might even waste time making another API that does the same thing as yours. A competitive market of APIs internally is usually a healthy sign, and reusability is often overvalued in enterprises. But if people in your company are duplicating perfectly good APIs only because they don't know about them, it's a drain on resources.

Internal APIs can be marketed in much the same way as external APIs. Only the marketing ecosystem is different. While you'll probably target the Google search engine with an external API, for an internal API you may just need to get on the corporate spreadsheet that lists the company's APIs. Sponsoring a developer conference can be effective for an external API, but a better strategy for an internal API might be to just visit all the dev teams in the company and teach them about your API.

A big challenge for marketing internal APIs is often the lack of maturity and standardization in the organization. In truth, if you are marketing your APIs in a large enterprise, there is a very good chance that there is more than one API list floating around. To do a good job, you'll need to make sure that your API is on all of the various lists and registries that matter. Similarly, learning about and getting time with all of the development teams in your company may be difficult in practice, but if usage of your API matters to you, it's worth making the investment.

Key decisions for discovery governance

What will the discovery experience look like?
> You'll need to design a good discovery experience for your API's users. That means deciding on discovery tools, user experience, and a target audience. At scale, you'll also need to decide how consistent this experience should be—if you need high consistency, you may need to centralize the design decisions.

When and how are APIs advertised?
> Marketing an API has a time and effort cost, so you'll need to decide who should decide when to market an API. You can leave it up to individual API teams, or you can make that decision centrally. If you're distributing the decision to your teams, you'll need to make sure that any centralized discovery tools and processes don't inhibit them from their discovery goals.

How is the quality of the discovery experience maintained?
> Over time, as APIs change, the information in any discovery system becomes less accurate. Whose job is it to ensure that the discovery system is accurate? Who will make sure that the user experience doesn't degrade at scale and over time?

Change Management

If you never had to change your API, the job of managing an API would be pretty easy. But APIs need to be fixed, updated, and improved, and you'll always need to be ready to change yours. The pillar of change management includes all the planning and management decisions you'll need to make when dealing with change. It's a vitally important and complex domain—in fact, the pillar of change management is what this book is really about.

Generally speaking, there are three goals for change management:

- Choosing the best changes to make
- Implementing those changes as fast as possible
- Making those changes without breaking anything

Choosing the best changes means making changes that enable your API's strategic goals. But it also means learning how to prioritize and schedule change based on costs, contexts, and constraints. That's really the work of managing a product, and it's one of the reasons we introduced the concept of the API as a product in the previous chapter. If you set clear strategic goals and identify your target user community, you can make better decisions about which changes are the most valuable. As you learn more about the work in each of the other nine pillars, you'll get better at understanding the costs. Armed with good information about cost and value, you'll be able to make smart product decisions for your API.

Balancing change safety with change speed is a difficult proposition, but it's what you'll need to do. Each of the decisions you make in the pillars of an API product has an impact on the speed or safety of change. The trick is to try to make decisions that maximize one with a minimum cost to the other. In Chapters 5, 7, and 8, we'll explore this idea further from the perspective of change costs, changes made over time, and the impact of organizations and culture on change. Then, in the last chapters of this book we'll introduce an added complexity: scale. Chapters 9, 10, and 11 address change management for a landscape of APIs instead of just one.

Implementing changes is only half the work of change management. The other half is letting people know that they have more work to do because you've changed something. For example, if you change an interface model, you'll probably need to let your designers, developers, and operations teams know that there is some new work headed their way. Depending on the nature of the change, you'll likely need to let your users know that they may need to update their client software too. The usual way of doing this is by versioning your API. How you version depends a lot on the style of your API and the protocols, formats, and technologies you are using; we'll talk about this more in "Versioning" on page 292.

Key decisions for change management governance

Which releases need to be fast, and which need to be safe?

An important governance decision is how to treat different types of change. If you centralize this decision, you can create a consistent rule that allows for different release processes depending on their impact. Some people call this approach "bimodal" or "two-speed," but we believe there are more than two speeds in a complex organization. You can also decentralize this decision and let individual teams assess impact on their own. The danger of decentralizing is that your teams may not be able to accurately assess the impact on the system, so you'll need to make sure you have a system architecture that is resilient.

Using the Pillars Together

The pillars we've defined in this chapter catalog an enormous expanse of decisions and effort. But we haven't numbered them, prioritized them, or put them in sequence, and that's on purpose. There is massive variation in project and product delivery methods across organizations. So, we wanted to give you a structured way of defining the key decisions and work you'll need to address in a way that's useful to whatever software development method you like to use.

But, one of the problems with compartmentalizing decisions and work into pillars is that they can start to feel like distinct and independent categories of work. In practice, that is almost never the case. In this section, we'll explore some of the most common ways that the API pillars can be used together to accomplish the goals of API product development. We'll take a look at the ways that particular pillars influence one another and the holistic perspective you'll need to adopt when you use them. Later, in Chapter 7, we'll take a look at how investment across pillars changes over the life of an API.

Let's start by taking a look at how API pillars are used together to tackle the challenges of planning and designing an API.

Applying Pillars When Performing Planning

In recent years, the stages of planning and design have gotten a bit of a bad name. Many implementers worry about falling into the trap of "Big Design Up Front" (BDUF) (*https://oreil.ly/0tDY1*), where a team spends a disproportionate amount of time in a design phase, completely disconnected from the practical realities of implementation. As our industry continues to embrace Agile principles, Scrum methods, and Kanban management, there has been a greater emphasis on "doing" and a test and learn approach. We think this is a good thing.

But, we also know that there is immense value in having a clear goal, a coherent strategy, and an articulate blueprint that drives delivery. The need for planning and design is especially important in an API product. That's because changes to any interface always come with a cost. We've all experienced the frustration of having to relearn how to do something when an application changes its user interface. Changes to APIs can be especially costly, because they can easily impact someone else's code or even their entire business model.

That's why, regardless of your delivery methodology, it's worth starting with a clear plan for your API. In our experience, even highly Agile-oriented API teams can benefit from a bit of up-front planning. For API products, it's important to start in the right direction and align the work across pillars with that direction. In particular, we've identified three areas that need focus: design alignment, prototyping, and boundary definition.

Test your strategy and design alignment

As we mentioned in "Design" on page 88, it's important to align your strategy and design work. The work of bringing an API to life across design ("Design" on page 88) and development ("Development" on page 94) involves an incredibly broad number of decisions. We've seen many practitioners struggle when they don't have a clearly defined goal or target to drive toward.

To improve your alignment, it's important to continuously test your design against your strategy. As you make design and implementation decisions, it's easy to lose the strategic perspective of your work. You'll need to recalibrate by testing the decisions against your strategic goals. If you've managed to define KPIs or OKRs, testing your decisions will be much easier.

Comparing Two Strategies: Twitter and Slack

A comparison of the communication applications Twitter and Slack can help illuminate how the decisions we make in strategy can impact all of the decisions we make in other pillars. In "A Tale of 2 API Platforms," Jason Costa emphasizes the impact that a strategic direction (or lack of one) can have on an API product's development. In particular, he highlights how Slack has made purposeful design, development, and change management decisions to fuel their strategic goals.[1] He contrasts this approach with the more organic, volatile strategic direction that Twitter took, which Costa says has resulted in a potentially unrecoverable rift with developers who used their APIs.

His case study highlights an important consideration for any API creator: the decisions we make within a strategic pillar are likely to have an earth-shattering impact on all the other pillars we work within.

Prototype early

Modern software delivery methods emphasize the importance of iterations, sprints, and smaller batches of change. In our experience, this is an essential element to succeeding with an API product. Whenever possible, realize your strategy as soon as possible so you can test its implementability. That means performing work across

---

1 Jason Costa, "A Tale of 2 API Platforms," *Medium*, October 25, 2016, *https://oreil.ly/ZzAlj*.

development ("Development" on page 94) and testing ("Testing" on page 98) even as your strategy is developing.

There are many names for this kind of test and learn activity: proof of concepts, pilots, "steel threads," MVPs, etc. Whatever you call it, the value of early realization is immense. In fact, this idea of continuous improvement is a key theme throughout this book.

API Prototyping Tools

Years ago, prototyping an API meant engaging an engineer to write custom code. But, today there are a wealth of tools that can help. These include frameworks like Spring Boot that accelerate the work discussed in "Development" on page 94, allowing teams to quickly spin up prototyped, testable APIs. Teams can also use interface design tools to quickly bring the documentation pillar ("Documentation" on page 91) work to life. There is a growing ecosystem of web-based and IDE plug-ins that can help you create an API specification quickly. Some tools even allow teams to quickly create APIs from an existing dataset or database. We recommend that you find a tool that helps you focus on the design and usage aspects of your API as early as possible in the design and planning stages.

Defining boundaries

In practice, your API product may actually consist of a collection of individual components. This is especially evident in the "microservice" style of architecture that has become increasingly popular for API implementations. As a result, it's become increasingly important to plan the boundaries for components early so that you can realize your API product strategy.

What Is a Microservice?

There isn't an official, agreed-upon definition for a microservice. Instead, it reflects a style of API-based architecture that has evolved in the 2010s as technologies and organizations have changed. Almost all microservice implementations can be characterized by a decomposition of applications into a set of API-enabled components that are the "right size" to provide value to a business.

In practice, this means that part of your design work for a single API has become defining how that API can be split into multiple pieces. The hard part about getting this right is defining the right set of boundaries for your components. Teams are increasingly doing their initial boundary definition work early so that they can build components that are better aligned with their strategy.

Using the Pillars for Creation

To bring the API strategy to life, we'll need to implement the API product. In Chapter 7, we'll explore what it means to realize an API product from a lifecycle perspective. But, before we do that, it's worth considering how the actual work will get done. So far, we've introduced four pillars that are really important when it comes to building an API: design, documentation, development, and testing. Now, we need to explore how you can use those pillars together in a valuable way.

If you have any software development experience, you'll know that the pillars we've defined for building an API aren't exactly new or novel. All of the software we write nowadays—API or not—goes through the classic stages of designing, developing, documenting, and testing. There are also plenty of software development methodologies that you can use to manage the work across these pillars. For example, Kanban, Scrum, and the Scaled Agile Framework are all enjoying adoption among practitioners as a way of applying Agile principles (*https://oreil.ly/lTAEJ*) to product delivery. We're confident that your organization has an established way of building software and that you'll be able to apply it to your API engineering work.

But, one of the unique things about building APIs is that they encapsulate a lot of different concepts into a single deliverable product. We touched on this earlier in the book, when we introduced the challenge of understanding interfaces, implementation, and instances ("Interface, implementation, and instance" on page 5). You'll need to figure out how to apply the creational pillars of API work in a way that brings those parts together. How do you design, develop, document, and test an API so that the interface *and* the implementation provide the most strategic value?

We're sorry to say there isn't a single silver-bullet approach to unlock that value. But, the good news is that we've managed to identify three approaches that practitioners have been using to succeed: documentation-first, code-first, and test-first. Let's take a look at each of them and understand when they make the most sense.

Documentation-first

When we get into the engineering aspects of APIs, we often focus on their technology elements: the code and configuration that drives the runtime behavior. But, none of that runtime activity happens without a human developer working on the client code that uses the API. That's why some teams take a "documentation-first" approach to their API execution method.

Documentation-first means that the team prioritizes the design of the API's human interface—the documentation. Instead of starting by thinking about the technicalities of implementation in Go, Java, NodeJS, or any other language, they focus on documenting the API before it exists. For example, when building a payments API, we might start by applying the decisions and work in the documentation pillar ("Documentation" on page 91) before we write any code.

One advantage of doing this is that we can test the human interface of the API before we invest in any of the implementation work that goes along with it. For example, if we wrote up a usage and example guide for our new payments API, we could test it with a group of potential developers. Changing the documentation based on their feedback will be much easier than changing an actual API implementation.

But, documentation-first doesn't mean documentation-only. In practice, starting the activities of "Development" on page 94 and "Testing" on page 98 while the specification is being finalized makes sense. You can take this a step further by developing prototypes or "mocks" of the documented API so you can offer a live, invokable product for early testing.

The key to the documentation-first approach is that we key our implementation decisions on the learnability, consumability, and comprehensibility of the API. It's a good technique to use if you want to ensure that your team puts the consumer developer first in the building phase. It's also a nice way to provide early deliverables and assets to nontechnical stakeholders and sponsors.

One of the challenges with the documentation-first approach is that it can lead to products that over-promise and under-deliver. You need to make sure that the interfaces being documented on paper can be realized by the engineering teams that need to build them. In some cases, you may be building on a complex set of downstream capabilities that can't be changed. When the aspirational target state that is documented is significantly different from the reality of the implementer, the cost of building the API can be overwhelming.

Code-first

The code-first approach focuses on the complexity of implementing the internals of the API first. That means the team prioritizes the activities of "Development" on page 94 and "Testing" on page 98 so that they can quickly and efficiently deliver a first release of an API product. This doesn't mean that the team will not provide any API documentation, but it does mean that the documented design will adhere to the decisions made during implementation, rather than the other way around.

The code-first approach is most useful when release speed outweighs consumability and usability for the API. For example, teams building microservices often prioritize engineering work because they don't plan to share their microservice with other teams. In this case, their focus may be on making the code easy to change and release, rather than on consumption.

This approach can also be useful to quickly research and test the implementabilty of an API product as a "proof of concept" or a "technology spike" to check all high-risk elements have been identified or mitigated. For example, an API team may start writing code for a hypermedia or GraphQL API as a first step because they are unfamiliar with that particular API style and need to assess the practicalities of the design.

Code-first teams can (and should) still produce documentation for their interface. Depending on the nature of the project, that documentation may be lighter in nature than a documentation-first team. For example, code-first teams typically document their APIs with machine-readable API description languages such as OpenAPI rather than producing human-readable guides. In some extreme cases, the team will claim that the code *is* the documentation. But, the key aspect of the code-first approach is that the documentation work is focused solely on communicating design decisions that have been made during the coding phase.

As you'd expect, a code-first approach can easily project technical and implementation aspects into the interface design. Making a code-first API easier to consume for outsiders will often require changes to the code or the creation of another API that sits on top of it. It is important to note that if you go beyond immediate team or organization, in a controlled environment, this approach is hard to keep on the long term.

Test-first

A modern variation of the code-first and documentation-first approach is a test-first implementation. In this type of API development, the testability of the API is prioritized above its documentability or implementability. This is an application of Test-Driven Development (TDD) to the API domain.

Test-Driven Development

The concept of Test-Driven Development was popularized by Kent Beck in his book *Test-Driven Development by Example* (*https://oreil.ly/ZP66W*). In practice, TDD is implemented both formally and informally in a number of ways. But, the key ingredient is that production-bound code is designed and engineered so that it can be tested.

A test-first approach means that the API team begins by creating test cases that conform to a desired target state, followed by the work of implementation to make the test case pass. For development (see "Development" on page 94), that usually means writing tests that call the API before the API is written. For example, when developing a payments API, we would write a test case to make a payment via an HTTP request before writing the code to handle and fulfill the request.

Things get more interesting when we consider the pillar of documentation (see "Documentation" on page 91). At the very least, taking a test-driven development approach means that the documentation should reflect the test cases that we develop. In effect, the creation of test cases is the design activity for the interface. But, taking it further, some teams are experimenting with ways to automatically generate documentation and code examples based on the test cases that are being written.

Starting with tests is a fantastic way of improving the testability of an API product. This leads to safer and more predictable future changes, because the team has confidence in their ability to test their deliverables. However, test-first comes with an additional development cost and can delay the time to a first release. In practice, many teams adopt a documentation-first approach to their API product and a test-driven approach to development.

Using the Pillars to Operate and Run

Over the last two decades, there has been an increasing pressure to build software that can be delivered and changed quickly while still performing in a stable, secure, and reliable manner. This has led to changes in the way that software is developed and operated. Organizations are increasingly adopting DevOps cultures, site reliability engineering, and a DevSecOps approach that embeds security within the development process.

Shifting Ops left

Years ago, it was common practice for developers to write an application and then hand it over to an operations team so that they could run and support it. But, today there is an increasing interest in developing apps differently. Teams that embody a DevOps culture bring the worlds of development and operations together so that applications are designed to be operable from the beginning. In many modern development teams, operations has become a first-class citizen in the development process rather than an afterthought.

Applying this approach to API development means that the pillars of design, development, testing, deployment, and monitoring need to be aligned. In practice, this means that teams will need to share the decision making and work that happens across both the creational and the operational pillars. An API team making decisions about tools and frameworks needs to consider both the concerns of writing code as well as the concerns of deployment and run.

In practice, most organizations end up implementing a platform of DevOps automation tools that serve the needs of API development teams. The goal of these tools is to accelerate the time it takes to create and change APIs while also improving their operability. These tools typically enable standardization and automation of testing, deployment, and monitoring tasks.

For example, at the time of this writing, an enterprise organization might roll out a DevOps platform with the following tools:

CI/CD pipelines

A continuous improvement (CI) and continuous delivery[2] (CD) tool automates the process of testing and deploying a software component. In the API space, CI/CD pipelines are often configured to test that an API will not introduce a breaking change before it is deployed into a production environment. This kind of testing and delivery automation can be applied to all deliverables of your API product, including design assets, documentation, and implementations.

Containerization

Today, APIs are often implemented as containers that can be operated as self-contained units of deployment. Adopting containerization can fundamentally change the way that APIs are implemented. Many organizations that start containerizing their APIs end up introducing a "microservices" approach where they break an API product into smaller, independently deployable pieces.

Observability tools

To aid monitoring and troubleshooting, DevOps teams are increasingly implementing tools that aid in aggregation, visualization, and integration of log and monitoring data. For API teams, this means that design and development work needs to adhere to standardized interfaces and formats as determined by DevOps teams. A special case for API products is that observability tools are often extended to external consumers of an API. For example, a developer portal may offer usage and troubleshooting analytics to third parties using a company's API products.

Shifting security left

As we mentioned in the security pillar, APIs present a special kind of attack surface for potential bad actors. In particular, API implementers need to consider threat mitigation across documentation portals, interface design, data storage, and implementation of code. In recent years, three security patterns have emerged that are changing the way that work is done in the API space:

DevSecOps automation

In the same way that Ops-focused tooling has impacted the way that APIs are developed, security-focused tooling is having the same effect. Organizations are increasingly incorporating vulnerability scanners into their CI/CD pipelines so that all changes are inspected quickly and efficiently before they are implemented in production. For example, many enterprise API teams use scanners that check

---

2 Or continuous deployment.

API implementations against OWASP threats. Making this vulnerability scan part of the coding process ensures that teams will address security vulnerabilities early in the development process.

Automated threat detection

Today, organizations are not only passively checking code when scanners are triggered but also actively scanning assets to find vulnerabilities and problems. There is now a healthy ecosystem of tools available to help teams continuously monitor logs, code repositories, databases, and even live APIs. This kind of continuous monitoring for threats helps to change the behavior of API teams so that security concerns are considered early in the development process.

Zero-trust security models

Years ago, most security models depended on creating a secure perimeter so that systems inside the perimeter could be trusted. But, in recent years, Google has helped popularize a "zero-trust" model in which no system should be trusted purely based on its location. This shift is a result of the increasingly decentralized organizational and deployment models associated with modern software engineering. For API teams, "zero trust" means that API creators need to consider how access controls will be enforced as part of their design and development work.

Runtime platforms

Introducing operations and security work across the pillars of design, development, and testing turns out to come with a cost. Teams that traditionally focused on writing code must now understand detailed aspects of operating systems, infrastructure, and security. However, an emerging set of tools and platforms are helping to reduce some of these costs.

API teams are becoming increasingly dependent on the runtime platforms that their software will run on. That's because modern platforms can handle a lot of the complexity that arises from applying the concerns of the operate and run pillars. The specific tools, technologies, and platforms that people use are constantly changing, but at the time of this writing, three technologies stand out as having a big impact: Kubernetes, services meshes, and serverless.

Kubernetes. Standardizing the unit of deployment (e.g., as a "shippable" container) has helped a lot of teams improve the way teams operate and run their APIs. But, running a container safely and resiliently in a production environment still takes a lot of careful planning and management. That's why a lot of teams are incorporating the Kubernetes (*https://kubernetes.io*) container orchestration platform. Kubernetes provides a standardized way of deploying, scaling, running, and monitoring a container workload. It's attractive because it means that you don't need to spend time figuring out the best solution for accomplishing those tasks—it's already done for you. But from a pillar perspective, it's important to understand how this Ops and Run decision impacts all of the other API pillars' work. When you deploy an API component into Kubernetes, you'll need to describe its deployment, routing, and scaling configurations. That means the team that is making decisions in design, development, and testing must also have a good understanding of Kubernetes so that it can build software that works. In theory, making sure that the development team designs and builds for the pillars of operate and run is a good idea and embraces the spirit of DevOps. But, be warned that in practice it can be difficult (and expensive) to find people with such a broad base of knowledge.

Service mesh.   Now that the microservices style has been popularized, there is an increasing number of software products that are composed of smaller, structured software modules and APIs. But, when you decompose an API into smaller pieces, you make the job of wiring those pieces together in an operable way more difficult. There's just more things to manage. To help manage these costs, some teams are incorporating a platform concept called a *service mesh*. A service mesh helps reduce the operational costs of communication between software components over a network. Introducing a service mesh often comes with a high initial complexity cost in the pillars of operate and run because most service mesh tooling is nontrivial to set up, install, and maintain. But a service mesh can offer big dividends across the pillars of design and development—giving your API teams the freedom to build smaller units of deployment in a way that they can be run safely.

Serverless, low-code, and the future.   A common thread in runtime platform innovations for APIs is that they help us build highly scalable and highly resilient software faster and easier. Most of the innovations we've seen do this by both hiding complexity costs and introducing standardization. This trend is continuing with the emerging popularity of "serverless" architectures, hiding all the complexity of running a platform behind a standardized, event-driven interface. Similarly, the trend toward "low-code" architectures hides the complexity of an API-enabled architecture behind a standardized development interface.

The details of serverless, low-code, service meshes, and Kubernetes are beyond the scope of this book. But, from an API management perspective, it is vital that you understand how these platform innovations impact the decisions and work you're managing across the pillars. For example, embracing a serverless platform greatly reduces the cost and scope of your development pillar but introduces a need for serverless expertise in your design, operate, and run pillars.

Summary

In this chapter, we took a tour of the 10 pillars that form the foundation of API product work. In each pillar lies the decisions that have an impact on the final API product. Not all the pillars necessarily require the same amount of work effort, and you'll need to decide how important each pillar is depending on the context and goals for your API. As your landscape of APIs grows, you'll also need to think about how the decisions in each of these pillars should be distributed. We'll say more about that in Chapter 11. We have also seen that some pillars work in groups, with more implications and entanglement of the API practice as a whole. Now is the time to understand how to manage the cost of change of the lifecycle interactions and how to apply the right level of investment with the right level of maturity for your API.

But before we get there, we'll need to explore our 10th pillar, change management, in more detail. What is the cost of making changes to an API? We'll dive into that in the next chapter.

CHAPTER 5

Continuous API Improvement

It is not necessary to change. Survival is not mandatory.
    —W. Edwards Deming

In the previous chapter we introduced the API lifecycle and defined the pillars of work that you'll need to focus on. This lifecycle defines the work that you'll need to do for the initial release of your API. The pillars are also important when dealing with the changes you'll make during the entire lifetime of your published API. Managing API change is a critical element of a successful API management strategy.

Changing your API can have a big impact on your software, products, and user experiences. Shipping a code change that breaks an existing API can have a disastrous ripple effect on all the components that use it. Even changes that don't break the external interface of an API can cause big problems if they alter that API's *behavior* in an unexpected way. Even more to the point, one popular API within your organization can produce a long list of dependencies that might be difficult to document or even see. All this makes change management an important API management consideration.

If you never had to change them, managing your published APIs would be a pretty simple task. But of course, change is an inevitable part of an API in active use. At some point you'll need to fix a bug, improve the developer experience, or optimize the implementation code. Performing these tasks requires intrusive changes to your deployed API.

The job of managing API changes is made more difficult by its large scope. An API product isn't just an interface. Instead, it is a collection of many pieces: interfaces, code, data, documentation, tools, and processes. All these parts of the API product can change, and they must all be carefully managed.

API change management isn't easy, but it is necessary. It's also liberating. If you weren't allowed to change your deployed API, your initial release would be much more difficult. You'd have to build your API the way traditional space agencies design and launch rockets. You'd need BDUF planning and development investment to make sure the API could run for a long time. You'd also need to account for everything that could go wrong and build accordingly.

Thankfully, you don't have to work that way. In fact, embracing changeability as a feature of your API can pay you big dividends. Cheaper and easier change means that you can make more changes more often. That gives you the freedom to take more risks (because you've reduced the time it takes to fix problems), which means you can make more API improvements.

In this chapter we'll introduce a continuous improvement philosophy for APIs that embraces change. You'll learn how a continuous series of small, incremental changes can be the best thing for improving your API product overall. You'll also learn why APIs are difficult to change and what you can do to improve their changeability. To start, let's explore what "managing continuous change" means when applied to the world of APIs.

Managing Change Continuously

While the notion of supporting continuous change for your API may sound like an appealing goal, it is important to keep in mind the *reason* for supporting change. When we apply the AaaP way of thinking from Chapter 3, we can frame change as an attempt to *improve* the API rather than just change for the sake of change. That means that any time we spend on changing the API should be justified. Two key ways to judge this improvement is to focus on (1) improvement to the developer experience and (2) a reduction in maintenance cost for the product's sponsors.

Of course, not every individual change will improve your API product immediately. For example, you might improve the way your API can scale in order to meet future demand—a change that won't pay off until usage grows. A change like this won't lead to an immediate measurable improvement in the developer experience, but it could prevent a degradation of the experience in the future. The point is that any change should be considered in terms of its ability to improve the product, even if the gratification for that investment will be delayed.

In this section of the chapter, we'll focus on two foundational elements for handling change over time: (1) adopting a model for incremental improvement within your organization and (2) increasing the velocity of change in general. To start, let's explore the notion of incrementalism as a change management technique.

Incremental Improvement

If change is the path to improvement of an API product, then a reasonable management goal is to make it as easy as possible to change your API. The best version of your API will come from a continuous cycle of changes or improvements. Some of these changes may offer very little immediate improvement—in fact, some of your attempts at improvement could even cause a temporary degradation to the developer experience for your API. If this happens, you'll need to make another improvement to undo the impact of your failed experiment. Over time, your product and the developer experience will benefit from these continuous incremental efforts to improve the API.

Incremental improvement means that you have an idea of the direction you want to head in but choose to take small steps toward that objective instead of releasing a "big-bang" change that attempts to meet all your future requirements. Applying a series of smaller changes gives the API team an opportunity to react to the results of each change, effectively performing a series of small experiments in order to find the best path toward a goal post that continues to move.

There are lots of ways to approach incremental improvement, and we'll highlight three here: Deming's Plan-Do-Study-Act model, Boyd's OODA Loop, and Goldratt's Theory of Constraints. They each take a slightly different point of view in the way they model the process of continuous improvement.

Plan-Do-Study-Act

The concept of continually making small improvements is a well-established change pattern with foundations in the manufacturing industry. In the 1980s, quality management pioneer W. Edwards Deming articulated his version of this idea with a philosophy he called the "System of Profound Knowledge." Deming's system embraces the complex nature of large organizations of workers and applies a scientific method for improving the way they produce products. One of the cornerstones of his approach is the Plan-Do-Study-Act (PDSA) cycle that defines an iterative, experiment-driven method for improving a process (Figure 5-1).

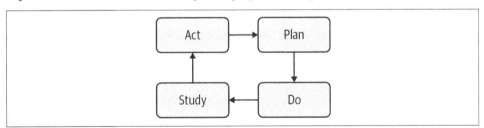

Figure 5-1. Deming's PDSA cycle

The PDSA process defines four steps for applying improvements. First you come up with a *plan*—a theory of how you can improve the system in accordance with a goal, along with the changes you'll need to make to test that theory. Next, you *do*, implementing the changes that you've outlined in your plan. Following that, you *study*, monitoring and measuring the impact of those changes and comparing the results to the plan. Finally, armed with this new information you can *act* by updating the goal, theory, or change actions to further improve the system.

For example, if you wanted to improve the developer experience of your API, you might start with a goal of reducing the time it takes for developers to learn how the interface works. Your plan might be to update the documentation to make it more developer-friendly. You could then "do" the plan by updating the documentation asset, followed by a study of the number of errors that are generated by developers who've viewed the new documentation. With these measurements, you could reassess the type of documentation changes that should be made or even make the decision to perform a more impactful change to the interface model itself.

The PDSA wheel describes an iterative, experiment-based process to improve a system: you make small changes, measure the impact of those changes, and use the knowledge you gain to continue to improve the system. It's a really effective way of dealing with systems that are complex—the kind of system where it's hard to tell exactly what the results of a small change will be.

Deming's PDSA works well for companies that have a high tolerance for experimentation and a well-established culture of post-implementation review and analysis.

Deming's ideas and his PDSA wheel were originally designed for improving the processes for quality management in factories and assembly plants, but the pattern has turned out to be useful wherever there is a need to improve a complex system—including software systems. Software methodologies like Lean, Kaizen, and Agile all share this same principle of continuously improving an identified target. Sometimes that improvement target is a process, other times it's a product, but in all cases it's the continuum of objective-oriented change that leads to agility and success.

Observe-Orient-Decide-Act

Another very popular model for creating a continuous flow of quality decisions is John Boyd's OODA Loop (*https://oreil.ly/M5oeN*). OODA stands for *Observe, Orient, Decide, and Act*. Like the PDSA model, the OODA model is interactive—you keep going through the same steps over and over as you try to continuously improve. In the 1950s, Boyd noticed that US fighter pilots during the Korean War were consistently winning in air battles despite that fact that North Korean pilots were flying more advanced aircraft. Boyd claimed his research rationalized this contradiction, showing that US pilots employed better strategies in air fights—hence the OODA Loop method.

 Boyd's OODA has a colorful backstory and relies on some very interesting "insider" information on how US pilots behave in a battle when making decisions "in real time." In fact, most of Boyd's work focuses on warfare and conflict. In our experience, warfare is not always the proper analogy for IT organizations working to continuously improve their efforts. But OODA continues to be a hot topic in some circles. For more on the implications of OODA Loops in organizations, see Robert Greene's article "OODA and You" (*https://oreil.ly/XqZn8*).

In a nutshell, applying the OODA Loop to your own organization looks like this:

Observe
Select your target issue (scaling, security, some feature set, etc.) and collect as much information as you can from as many points of view that are available. At this stage it is important to include lots of data without any filtering, editing, or analysis.

Orient
This is the step where you apply your experience, knowledge, and data analysis skills to the data you collected. Now is the time to filter out data that "does not apply" and narrow the field down to a few likely options.

Decide
Now is the time to weigh your options, consider costs as well as benefits, and make your best guess about which action to take.

Act
Finally, you execute on the decision by carrying out the planned actions. This, of course, is not the end of the story. Since this is a loop, the results of your actions become the topic of observation, and that puts you back at the start of the OODA Loop.

It is worth pointing out that this model was designed to train pilots who make decisions in split seconds. They iterate through this loop constantly and quickly. In fact, one of the key insights from Boyd's work was that *speed matters*. If you act more quickly than your adversary, you can gain the upper hand, even when you're outmatched technically. For this reason, OODA is often used in cases where market competition is high and—in the case of IT shops—where releasing early and often has a distinct advantage.

Since the OODA Loop is based on making critical decisions and acting quickly, this model works well when you need to get ahead of competition and are already geared for speedy execution based on a rich set of market feedback.

There are, however, lots of situations where speed is not the most important element. In these cases, it can be more helpful to focus on one or two particular problems and solve each one before moving on to the next. One approach that meets this criteria is Goldratt's Theory of Constraints.

Theory of Constraints

The Theory of Constraints (TOC) was described in the 1984 book *The Goal* (*https://oreil.ly/t9Xda*) by Eliyahu M. Goldratt and Jeff Cox. The book is a fictional account of one manager's attempt to "turn around" a failing production plant in 90 days before it is shut down permanently. Through a series of remote consultations with a close friend, the protagonist gains insights and skills and learns to apply the TOC in order to improve the company's operations.

Goldratt and Cox's book continues to be a best seller and widely read. In 2014, a "30th Anniversary Edition" was released. Even though it was focused on physical plant operations in the 1980s, many of the lessons in the book still apply to IT organizations today.

The basics of Goldratt's TOC (*https://oreil.ly/Hl8SS*) center around the notion that the key to success is to identify bottlenecks (or constraints) in the organization and, through a series of steps, to "break the bottleneck." Once this is accomplished, it is time to identify a new bottleneck and start again.

Here are the steps Goldratt and Cox outline in the book:

1. Identify the system's bottlenecks (constraints) and target one of them.
2. Decide how to exploit the constraint (essentially *hack* the system).
3. Subordinate everything else to the previous decision (laser focus).
4. Reduce the bottleneck (fix, replace, or remove the constraint).
5. Once the bottleneck has been "broken," go back to step 1.

In TOC, a constraint is anything that prevents the system (your company) from achieving the goal. For Goldratt and Cox, that goal is making a profit. Also, it is worth noting that, in TOC, the bottleneck might not be something that is "going wrong" at all. It could just be some practice this is inefficient, costly, or unreliable.

Even when things are running smoothly, there is likely a bottleneck somewhere that deserves attention.

In the world of APIs, applying the TOC can be used, for example, to improve developer experience to speed time to market, create better API designs to meet product feature demands, implement more effective and efficient backend services to improve reliability, and so forth.

With its principle of laser focus on a key bottleneck that is preventing the organization from reaching its goal, the TOC approach can be a good fit for companies that are not under a direct threat in the market and want to apply incremental improvements to their operation.

So where is all this going?

We've highlighted a few established approaches to supporting incremental improvements in your organization. But these are not the only ways to introduce continuous improvement, and the ones we have might not fit your company's culture and values. They're provided here as examples and for encouragement as you develop your own strategies for improvement—ones that fit your organizational style. We'll leave it up to you to work out the mechanics, but adopting a continuous cycle of improvements for your API is a key requirement for delivering an API product that can maintain a consistently high quality.

API Change Velocity

If you are going to be making lots of small improvements to your API product, you'll need to make sure those changes can be applied relatively quickly. Otherwise, the cost of making continuous changes will become a big problem. No matter your *current* pace of change, implementing improvements a bit faster will give your API's sponsors a shorter path to innovation and a competitive advantage in the market—but, your changes need to have a reasonable level of quality or you risk damaging the reliability and quality of your API product.

Improving both the speed and quality of change is important whether your API is a public, private, or partner-facing one. If you can't apply quality changes to your interfaces quickly enough, you'll end up slowing down your ability to improve user experiences, launch new products, and improve business capabilities. Optimizing the speed and safety of your API change lifecycle contributes to the overall speed of change for your organization.

But with a finite amount of people, money, and time available, how can you make changes to the API in a way that *optimizes* those resources? As your proposed change goes through each of the stages of the API release lifecycle, how do you make sure you are traveling at maximum velocity?

There are three significant ways to improve the velocity of your API lifecycle without degrading quality: through tools, organizational design, and effort reduction.

Tools and automation

One solution for improving the speed and safety of product changes is to introduce tooling and automation in the place of human effort. Tooling is an attractive option because it can reduce the possibilities of human error while reducing the time it takes to perform a task. For example, CI/CD tools can automate the process of testing and releasing an API implementation, decreasing the cost of deploying an API change significantly.

However, the usefulness of a tool is dependent on its quality and the time you are willing to invest to set it up and configure it. There will always be an up-front initial cost and risk associated with introducing tooling, so if the API product is already well established and in active use (this is a phase of an API that we will later refer to as *realization*), you'll want to do this carefully, on an experimental basis.

All types of API changes can be automated with tooling. At the time of writing, there is a healthy market for API security, documentation, deployment, and configuration tools that facilitate faster and more reliable change processes.

Organizational design and culture

The work we do when we make changes to an API can be classified as knowledge work—the type of work that requires a coordinated process of decision making. If you are building a single API within a small team, the coordination effort is often very small, but at the scale of a large organization with multiple APIs and software components, the higher cost of coordinated decision making quickly becomes a drag on the ability of a single team to perform a change to an API product.

This human element of the change process is usually the biggest bottleneck to achieving high velocity, primarily because it's the most difficult to understand and to change. You can't buy an organizational design or culture in the same way you can buy an API documentation or CI/CD tool.

In Chapter 8, we'll spend more time diving into the organizational aspects of API management, including opportunities for building a decision-making platform that facilitates high-speed, high-quality change.

Eliminating wasted effort

Another way to boost the speed and quality of improvements is by expending less effort on them. If you eliminate the kind of API work that offers the least return on investment to your product goals, you can substantially improve your speed of change. Removing wasted effort also removes opportunities for things to go wrong, resulting in a more reliable net change process.

For example, an API that is built and used by the same development team probably doesn't need the same level of investment in documentation as a public API used by hundreds of third-party developers. There are lots of permutations and variables to consider here. In Chapter 7, when we talk about the API product lifecycle, we'll introduce one set of variables that can give you a starting point for considering the kinds of investments you want to make.

Changing an API

In Chapter 1 we introduced a distinction between the parts that make up an API product: the interface, the implementation, and the instance. After your API is published, you'll need to manage changes to all of these parts. Sometimes you'll need to change all of them together, but you may find yourself changing some of these API elements independently. In this section we'll address the impact of changes that occur in each of these parts. We'll even add a new type of API element called *supporting assets* that includes the parts of the API that are used purely to enhance the developer experience of the API product.

Applying a philosophy of continuous, incremental improvement to your API product (at speed) means designing the process of change purposefully for all four types of API change. These four types of API change will have dependencies on one another, too. They form a stack of dependent change: a change to the interface model will have far-reaching impacts, while a change to supporting assets can easily be done in isolation. You'll get a better understanding of why these dependencies exist as we explore each of the types of change.

The API Release Lifecycle

Your software changes when you apply changes to it. The steps you take to make the right changes, in the shortest time, with the best quality is your release process. Like software, APIs also have a release process—a set of steps you'll follow to effect change. We call this process a lifecycle because of the cyclical nature of changes: as one gets implemented, another is ready to go. Understanding the release lifecycle is important because it has a big impact on the changeability of your API.

Every change you apply to your API will need to be deployed. The release lifecycle is the set of steps that enables this deployment of a change. It defines how a change that starts with an idea becomes an implemented, maintained part of your system. The release lifecycle brings all of the pillars we described in Chapter 4 together in a sequence of coordinated work.

If the release lifecycle is slow, your API's rate of change will diminish. If the release lifecycle lacks quality assurance, changing your API will be riskier. If the release lifecycle deviates from change requirements, your API changes will be less valuable. Getting the release lifecycle right is important. The good news is that the API release lifecycle isn't any different from the software or system delivery lifecycle. That means you can apply the existing guidance for software releases to the components that make up your API. Let's take a quick look at the most popular ones.

One of the most widely known software release lifecycles is the traditional *system development lifecycle* (SDLC). This lifecycle has been around in some form or another since the 1960s, and it defines a set of stages for building and releasing a software system. The actual number and names of stages used vary, but a typical set of stages is the following: initiation, analysis, design, construction, testing, implementation, and maintenance.

If you followed these SDLC steps in sequence, you'd be building software in a *waterfall* style. It's not actually the waterfall model that Winston Royce invented, but it's what people call this type of lifecycle today. It means that each phase of the SDLC has to be complete before the next stage begins. So, your change falls down from the top step to each step after it.

One of the drawbacks of the waterfall cycle is that you'll need to have a lot of certainty about requirements and the problem domain, because it's not great for dealing with lots of changes to the specifications. If that's a problem, you can use a more iterative software development process. An *iterative* approach allows the software team to perform several iterations of releases for a single set of requirements. Each iteration delivers a subset of the requirements, with the goal of meeting all the requirements through consecutive iterations. This iteration model is in line with the approaches we covered in "Incremental Improvement" on page 127.

You can take the iteration idea further and adopt a *spiral* SDLC. In this type of release system, software is designed, constructed, and tested in iterative stages, and each iteration has the potential to shape the original requirements. The spiraling SDLC embodies the spirit of Agile and Scrum methods.

Those are three popular forms of the software lifecycle. Each of them has its own advantages and disadvantages, and you'll need to choose a release lifecycle that makes sense for you. We've tried to write this book in a way that gives you the freedom to use whatever style you want. When we talk about change, we'll refer to your release lifecycle, but we won't tell you what sequence your pillar activities should be in or which software lifecycle you should use. Instead, we'll focus on the product improvements that a release lifecycle can enable. But before we get into that, let's talk a little bit more about the types of API changes your release lifecycle will need to support.

Changing the Interface Model

Every API has an interface model. This is the information that describes the behavior of an API from a *consumer* perspective. It describes a set of abstractions that determine how the API will behave and includes details about communication protocols, messages, and vocabularies. The distinguishing feature of an API model is that it hasn't been implemented—the model is an abstraction and can't actually be used by a computer system to do anything.

Although an interface model can't be invoked by a software program, it can be shared with people. Sharing the model requires it to be persisted or *expressed*. For example, you might express an interface model by drawing boxes and lines on a whiteboard. You can't *invoke* the model you've drawn, but the model as an abstraction will help your team collaborate on the API design.

Interface models aren't limited to being whiteboard drawings and sketches on napkins. They can also be expressed using model-driven languages or even with application code. For example, the OpenAPI specification is a popular standardized language for describing interface models. Using a standardized modeling language gives you the added bonus of inheriting an ecosystem of tooling that can reduce the cost of implementing your model.

You can draw or compose your model however you like: there aren't any rules about the level of detail that a model should provide, or constrains on the format you need to use to communicate it. But keep in mind that whatever method you choose for expressing the model will have a big impact on the level of detail and description you can include. Whiteboards and freehand drawings provide maximum freedom of thought but are constrained in their physical size and implementability. API description languages provide a quicker route to implementation but limit your freedom with heavily defined syntax and vocabularies.

The *design* pillar of our API lifecycle is focused on producing and changing the interface model, so most of the work we are describing fits neatly in there. But the relevance of the interface model isn't limited to this design work. In fact, most of the pillars in the lifecycle are dependent on or impacted by the interface model you define. This is because they are also expressions of your model.

Just as you may have expressed your interface model as a picture on a whiteboard or in the OpenAPI language, you'll also express the model in your application code, API documentation, and data model. When the interface is published and developers begin to write code that uses it, they will also be expressing your model within their implementations. All of these expressions of the model imply a dependency relationship—this is why changes to the model are the most impactful.

Domain-Driven Design

This idea of model-driven software where the implementation exists as an expression of the model comes to us from Eric Evans's domain-driven design (DDD) software design approach. If you haven't yet read his book, *Domain-Driven Design: Tackling Complexity in the Heart of Software* (Addison-Wesley), you should put it on your list!

The best API products have interface models that are consistent across the entire surface. That means developers shouldn't have to reconcile conflicts that arise between the documentation and the published API because the models they've expressed differ in some way. This desire for consistency increases the challenge of making interface model changes, as those changes need to be synchronized across the API product.

Using a consistent model doesn't mean that your implementation code and internal database need to use the same model as your API's interface. In fact, it's usually a bad idea to use the same model for your interface, code, and data—what works best for your interface users is not necessarily what works best inside your own implementation. Instead, using a consistent model means that the internal parts of your API implementation will need to be translated into this consistent interface model before they reach the surface of the API.

Interface model changes are highly impactful, but these changes are inevitable for any API product that is in active use. You may need to add support for a new feature, make a change to improve API usability, or perhaps deprecate part of the interface because your business model has fundamentally changed. Because of all the dependencies involved, interface model changes always have the potential to impact the code that has been written in consuming applications that use the API.

The potential impact of an interface model change to API consumers has a lot to do with the level of coupling that has been introduced between their code and your interface. If you design and implement APIs that provide loose coupling as a feature, you can get away with making bigger interface model changes with less impact. For example, using event-driven or hypermedia-style APIs has the benefit of less coupling between the client code and the API. In the case of an event-driven system, you might be able to change a pattern matching algorithm without making any changes to the component that sends events. A hypermedia API might let you manipulate the required properties for an invocation without changing the client code that makes the call.

Choosing an appropriate style of interface can help you reduce the cost of interface model changes. But that increased changeability for APIs doesn't come for free. You'll need to build the appropriate infrastructure and implementations on both the client and the server side to make them work. Oftentimes the constraints and contexts that you are working in will limit your choices—for example, the developers who are writing client software for your API may not have the expertise to write hypermedia applications. In these cases you'll just have to accept that interface model changes have a high cost.

The best way of reducing the external impact of interface model changes is to make these changes *before* the interface is shared. As Joshua Bloch, designer of the Java Collections API, tells us, "Public APIs, like diamonds, are forever."[1] Once you share that interface for others to use, you'll have a more difficult time making changes to it. The wise API product owner front-loads changes to the interface model in the design stage as much as possible to avoid paying the high price of change after the API is published.

Changing the Implementation

The implementation of the API is the interface model expressed in the components that bring the model to life. The implementation is what allows the interface to actually be used by another software component. An API implementation includes code, configuration, data, infrastructure, and even protocol choices. These implementation components are usually the *private* parts of the product—the things that make the API work but whose details we don't need to share with the consumers who plan to use it.

Your API can't be published without an implementation, and you'll continually need to change that implementation over the life of the API. Because the implementation is an expression of the interface model, you'll find yourself changing the implementation whenever the model changes. But sometimes you'll have an opportunity to change the implementation independently. For example, you may need to fix a bug in the implementation code, reduce the latency time of a poorly performing API, or even completely rewrite the code because you just don't like it anymore.

In these cases, where the implementation change is independent of the model, the impact of the change is hidden behind the interface of the API. This means that consumers won't have to make any changes to take advantage of the improvements you are introducing. This doesn't mean they won't be *impacted*—for example, a performance optimization might have a big effect on the perceived performance for an end user. But it does mean that you can avoid the work of managing changes

---

1 Joshua Bloch, "Joshua Bloch: Bumper-Sticker API Design," *InfoQ*, September 22, 2008, *https://oreil.ly/ibvwF*.

to client software that is dependent on the API. So, implementation changes can be made well after the API has been published and shared without the same rising cost of a change to the interface model.

The risk that comes from an independent implementation change is that it deteriorates the reliability, consistency, or availability of an API product. For example, if a code change breaks a running instance of the API or an implementation behaves differently from the documentation, your client applications will suffer. Changes to the implementation have the potential to impact the instance and supporting assets of the API, so each of these elements has to be updated, tested, and validated accordingly.

Changing the Instance

As we've described earlier, the implementation of an API expresses the model as an invokable, usable interface. But that implementation can't really be used until it's running on a machine on a network that is accessible to consumer applications. The *instance* of an API is a managed, running expression of the interface model that has been made available for your target consumers to use.

Any change to the interface model or the implementation will require a corresponding deployment or change to the API's instances. The API hasn't really been changed until you've updated the instances that its consumer applications use at runtime. However, it's also possible for you to change an API instance independently without altering the model or implementation. This could be the simple case of changing a configuration value, or it could be something more complex like cloning and destroying a running instance of the API. The impact of these types of changes is limited to the runtime properties of a system, with availability, observability, reliability, and perceived performance being the ones that are most often highlighted.

Making independent API instance changes less impactful to the system requires special consideration for the design of the system architecture. We'll discuss the system features and factors that matter the most later in the book when we introduce the API landscape.

Changing the Supporting Assets

If an API is a product, it needs to be more than some code that expresses a model running on a server. In Chapter 1 we learned that supporting the work of developers who have to use our APIs is an important part of the API-as-a-Product philosophy. Creating a better developer experience almost always requires some supporting assets that live outside the implementation of the interface. For example, these assets might include API documentation, developer registration, troubleshooting tools, key material distribution, and even human support staff to help developers resolve problems.

Over the life of your API, the material, processes, and people that support the API product will need to be updated and improved. Oftentimes, this will be a result of a cascading change made to the interface model, implementation, or instance of the API; supporting assets that exist further "downstream" will also be affected when you change any part of your API. This means that the change cost for your API will grow as you develop more supporting assets for the developer experience.

It's also possible to make independent changes to supporting assets. For example, you may want to change the look and feel of your documentation page as part of a modernization effort. These types of changes can have a big impact on the developer experience for your API product, but have no impact on the interface model, implementation, or instance—except in an indirect way as a result of increased usage of and interest in the product.

Changes to supporting assets have the least cascading impact, but they can also produce the highest change costs because they are the most dependent on the other API elements. Lowering the cost of changes to supporting assets can pay big dividends in terms of the overall cost of change for the API product. So, it makes sense to invest in design, tools, and automation to reduce the change effort for these assets.

Improving API Changeability

We've established some good reasons for taking a continuous improvement approach to the API lifecycle. We've shown that performing many small changes at high velocity is an ideal way to improve an API product, and we've delved into the types of changes and improvements that are necessary to get there. But in practice, it's difficult to apply a continuous improvement philosophy to APIs because the cost of change grows as the interface becomes more complicated and it begins being used by other teams.

There are three main costs associated with changing an API that might inhibit changeability: the cost of doing the work, the opportunity cost of a change, and the cost associated with changing dependent components. If you can minimize these three change costs, you'll have more freedom to change the API with greater frequency. More changes means more opportunities to incrementally improve your product.

Effort Costs

The most obvious cost of changing the interface model, implementation, instance, or supporting assets of your API is the time, energy, and money that you'll need to spend as you push a change through the API lifecycle. If you can reduce this basic cost of change, you'll greatly improve your chances of introducing more improvements to the API product.

Earlier (see "API Change Velocity" on page 131), we talked about the need for velocity of change and identified that effort reduction, tooling, and organizational change can help lower some of this work cost for an API. But in truth, improving the velocity of change is a complex problem.

The amount of resources required to make an API change is a product of at least the following factors: the complexity of the problem, the experience and talent of the people doing the work, the change process design, and the complexity and quality of the implementation. That's a substantial list, and it isn't exhaustive. Fortunately, reducing work costs is a core goal of professional software development, and there is a mountain of research, advice, and opinion available to help—and the things that work for changes to software generally work for API products as well.

Identifying the specific change methodologies, quality management processes, architectures, implementations, and automation tools you can use to reduce your work effort is beyond the scope of this book. We've tried to introduce a few core strategies, patterns, and philosophies that will give you the best chance of achieving velocity of change, but you'll need to do the hard work of turning that general advice into something that works for your organization.

Opportunity Costs

Another kind of cost that might inhibit change is the desire to refrain from changing the API because you want to gather more information first. Losing the opportunity to gather more information becomes a cost for changing the API. Tom and Mary Poppendieck, creators of the Lean software development approach, describe this activity as waiting until the *last responsible moment* to make a critical decision.

To make things more complicated, you must also consider the cost of *not* making a change and the associated missed opportunities to both improve your product and gather feedback about the change. In a lot of situations, it's better to ignore the "last responsible moment" principle so that you don't muddy your thinking with the fear that you should wait until you know more. Making small code changes to a published software component is an example where you might deem the decision not critical enough to worry about this type of opportunity cost. This is particularly true if you have immediate feedback about a mistake and the time to recover from the problem is small.

A lot of the typical changes to API products fit these characteristics of being noncritical and easy to recover from. For example, changing the look and feel of human-readable API documentation provides fast feedback in terms of its successful implementation and is easy enough to reverse if it turns out to be problematic. But some types of API changes are difficult to recover from and will require you to tread carefully—for example, changing the interface model of your API, which can have far-reaching consequences. These types of changes need to be managed appropriately, and the cost of changing without sufficient information should always be considered.

One way to reduce the opportunity cost of making a change is to do a better job of gathering information in the first place. In Chapter 9 we'll introduce the system quality of *visibility*, which can greatly reduce the opportunity cost of making API changes.

Coupling Costs

When it comes to APIs, and especially when it comes to the *interface model* of an API, the biggest blocker to free and easy change is the *coupling* that we create between the API and its consumers. There are lots of different styles of APIs, but no matter which one you choose, you'll always end up introducing some type of dependency or coupling between the senders and receivers of messages. This coupling has a big impact on what you can change about the API and when you are free to change it.

APIs are just vessels for communication and conversation between software modules. When humans communicate, they use a shared understanding of vocabulary, gestures, and signals to facilitate a meaningful conversation. Software components also need to have a shared knowledge in order to have a conversation. For example, shared knowledge of message vocabularies, interface signatures, and data structures are all useful in building a meaningful interoperation between two components. The important changeability factor for APIs is how many of these conversational rules are hardcoded into the released component's code. When the semantics of an API are defined at design time, the cost of changing the interface rises.

This coupling is unavoidable and can exist in all kinds of places in many different forms. In fact, when you hear people talk about a particular API being "tightly coupled" or "loosely coupled," it often takes a bit of detective work to understand exactly what they mean. Do they mean that the network address of the API has been hardcoded somewhere? Are they talking about the changeability of the semantics and vocabulary of messages? Or maybe they are referring to how easily they can create new API instances without impacting the API consumers.

For example, event-driven architectures (EDAs) are often described as offering loose coupling between event senders and receivers. But, on closer examination, it turns out that the loose coupling only pertains to the knowledge that a message sender has about which components are receiving its messages. In fact, the structure, format, or vocabulary of event messages can introduce tight coupling and be the source breakage for message consuming components. See Chapter 6 for more on how API style choices affect coupling.

Some API styles in particular are very prescriptive in what they define at design time. If you are building an RPC-style interface, you'll almost certainly use some kind of *interface definition language* that documents the interface model with high precision. The nice thing about having a highly specific interface model is that the code becomes easier to write—in fact, RPC-style APIs often have ample tooling to make it as easy as possible to get started.

The problem with the highly specified interface model becomes apparent when you want to make changes to that interface. If you adopt a continuous improvement model, you may find that there are lots of small improvement opportunities for your interface. However, because the semantics of the API are hardcoded in the client's released code, changing the interface model will require a corresponding change in the code of all the API consumers.

Generally, we want to avoid breaking clients that are dependent on our APIs. But in practice, you may find that you care less about the reliability of some clients than others. For example, an API change that will break a little-used, third-party application is more justifiable than a change that would break your organization's customer-facing mobile application.

There isn't a black-and-white answer to how much coupling is appropriate for your API and when you should be willing to make changes. If loose coupling was free, we would all do it, but long-term value comes with short-term costs and building APIs that handle change very well requires up-front effort. You'll need to make a decision pretty early on about the cost of change and what type of API you think you'll need.

Keep in mind that a low degree of changeability combined with a high cost of code change means that continuous improvement of the API's model isn't a realistic strategy. In the best case, it means that your continuous improvements will be limited to interface model changes that don't break clients. In this scenario, it's a good idea to start with a BDUF approach to the interface model before it gets used heavily.

Isn't All This Just BDUF?

If you are familiar with the Agile Manifesto, you may be wondering if what we've described in this section is an example of the BDUF antipattern that Agile practitioners try to avoid. The short answer is "yes and no." First, we certainly understand the value of limiting the planning effort (in time and resources) when you're engineering software. As the Agile Manifesto (*https://oreil.ly/khE1R*) points out, while there is value in "following a plan," it makes sense to favor "responding to change." And that's the key takeaway here from a change *management* point of view: there is value in following a plan.

When it comes to APIs, it can be difficult to introduce changes because of the ripple effect that change has on the application code that uses it—especially API consumer code written by teams that are in control of the API service code. A great example of this is a third-party API that your organization consumes. You don't have control over that API's design or implementation, and yet you rely on that interface to be stable and reliable both now and into the future.

It makes sense to consider your own APIs as "third-party APIs" for other teams within your company. When it is time to change those APIs—interface promises that you need to keep over time—you need be sure to maintain stability and reliability. You also need sufficient planning in place to ensure you understand the target audience of the API, have properly stated its purpose, and have a general idea of the direction the design needs to follow in order to meet the needs (purpose) of the target audience. However, as we pointed out in "Incremental Improvement" on page 127, you do not need to map out *all* the detail before you begin. You need to keep the long-term goal in mind while you iterate along the assumed path to reach it.

It is also important to keep in mind that, by reducing the *cost* of change in general, you also reduce the need for BDUF practices. Often, the extended "planning" activities are focused on quantifying and mitigating the risk of change itself. This effort to reduce the cost of change can easily overshadow the work of carefully exploring, documenting, and defining the new features that are the purported subject of the change. That's why small iterations are so valuable in your change management efforts. The smaller the change, the fewer potential risks and the easier it is to "undo" the change when you run into unexpected problems.

In our experience, the companies that do well are the ones that have a clear and persistent vision of where they are headed. At the same time, they manage progress one step at a time and are constantly on the lookout for new evidence that can help them adjust their short-term expectations. An organization that successfully engages in continuous change has a set of built-in practices like the ones we've called out in this chapter.

Summary

In this chapter we introduced the continuous improvement model of change and identified why it's a good approach to use for your APIs. We also outlined the four types of API changes: changes to the interface model, implementation, instances, and supporting assets. To make it all work, we underscored the importance of achieving change velocity and walked through the main blockers for API changeability, including the coupling between client code and an API.

In the next chapter, we'll introduce a maturity model that can help you frame your continuous changes within the context of an ever-evolving API product.

CHAPTER 6

API Styles

Design depends largely on constraints.
—Charles Eames

APIs are a necessary design element in any infrastructure that interconnects components digitally. APIs allow various components to communicate, and looking at it this way shows what general pattern APIs actually are. When we say "pattern" here, we refer to the general communication interactions that APIs support. Note that this is at a higher abstraction level than specific technologies that define concrete ways of implementing patterns.

Since APIs are such a general pattern, the question arises whether there is one right way to design APIs. But unsurprisingly, the world is a little bit more complicated.

A good example is the "REST versus GraphQL" debate, which has been happening for several years in various forms. If we look past the strange debate that one API approach is generally better than another, it doesn't take long to see that this question compares things on a different level. Let's briefly look at these levels because they give us a great way to distinguish patterns (which we call API styles) from technologies.

REST is a pattern, meaning that there is no "REST technology" or "REST protocol." HTTP is a useful foundation for implementing that pattern, but it also takes media types (the web's term for the payloads being exchanged via APIs) to end up with a RESTful architecture that can be implemented.

On the other hand, GraphQL is a technology that defines how clients can query into a data model managed on the server. It defines everything that is necessary to use GraphQL APIs, which most importantly are exchange formats, and the semantics of how exchanging them makes a GraphQL API work. GraphQL is not the only way how the query pattern can be turned into a specific technology, but currently it's the most visible. Other technologies based on this query pattern are OData in the space of enterprise IT and SPARQL with a more research-oriented slant.

What this shows us is that it is helpful to distinguish between the general design pattern that an API is using and a specific technology that is a way to implement this design pattern. That way, we can have more focused discussions either about the general design approach that an API is taking, or about a specific technology that is then used for the concrete API design.

We call these different design approaches *API styles*. In the following section, we will look at the five fundamental styles in the API space and what their properties and typical application areas are. Looking back at the comparison from earlier, these are based on two out of the five styles; the first once focuses on resources as the most fundamental API abstraction, while the second one focuses on query capabilities as an API's main abstraction.

APIs Are Languages

Before we dive into the styles, let's take a step back and look at what APIs really are. They are nothing but a language that defines how various applications can communicate. Like any other language, API languages need two key elements to work. API languages need ways for how individual messages can be exchanged (you can think of this as sentences when you look at human languages). API languages also need ways of how the exchange of messages turns into a meaningful conversation (you can think of this as the shared goal of having a meaningful conversation when you look at human languages).

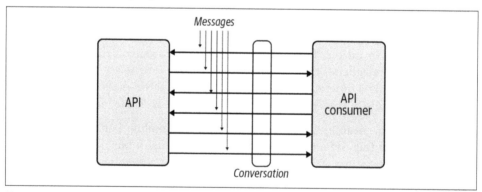

Figure 6-1. APIs are languages: messages and conversations

Because APIs are languages in the IT space, it also is important to think about the main abstractions they are based on. These main abstractions manifest themselves in the communication patterns and in the communicated elements (the exchanged messages).

In the following discussion of the five API styles, we take a close look at the main abstraction that an API style is built on (the "first principle" of the API style), and at the fundamental interaction patterns. In all these cases, we look at how this presents itself for the API consumer (who "sees" only the API and not the implementation) and for the API developers (who have to develop the code that implements the API).

Let's look at two simple real-world examples of how the problem being solved can be important in determining an appropriate solution.

For an API that allows things to be submitted, such as an order, it can make a lot of sense to use an API with a rather traditional control flow. If an API supports a purchase process, there is probably a workflow of requesting product information, supplying purchasing information, receiving the purchase confirmation, and supplying shipping information. All of this works well in traditional request/response APIs, and styles using this pattern may be particularly well suited to representing the act of purchasing something as a guided process.

For an API that notifies consumers of certain events, it may be useful to look at an API style with a different interaction pattern. For example, if an API can notify consumers when a customer's address has changed, it would be useful if the API triggered an event, and consumers would be listening for that and get notified when it happens. This way, consumers don't have to do any kind of polling, and these events can be propagated and processed in a fast and efficient way.

It is important to keep in mind that all styles can be used to design and implement working APIs for both of these scenarios. It is simply that the problem addressed by an API is an important constraint when it comes to deciding which style and technology to pick. As the saying goes, "If the only tool you have is a hammer, every problem looks like a nail." When you consider styles as being tools in your API toolbox, then the more APIs you are working with, the more likely it is that having more than one "style tool" can help you to solve problems in a better way.

There are other important constraints, of course. These include the API landscape, the expected audience of the API (private/partner/public), knowledge about consumer preferences, and more. We will discuss these additional constraints in more detail in "How to Decide on API Style and Technology" on page 156, but first we will discuss the individual styles.

The Five API Styles

API styles are *API interaction patterns*, based on the interaction model and the main abstractions upon which an API is built. Being an interaction pattern means that the API style will determine how an API is designed and how this design will be implemented in a specific technology.

One of the most important aspects of API styles is that, ideally, an API's design constraints, the choice of style, and technology for implementation should be aligned. If that's not the case, this misalignment may lead to poor designs (when the design constraints and the style do not align) or poor implementations (when the style and the technology are not aligned).

The five styles presented here have been selected based on interaction patterns and technologies that have been or are popular in the API space. It certainly would be possible to come up with a different list of styles, but the ones we present here have worked well for us in our API practice, and they provide a useful framework for better understanding the many API technologies that are in existence.

For each of the styles, the most important aspects are the interaction model and the main abstractions, and these are the topics we focus on when describing the styles. As we will discuss after a description of the styles, none of them is inherently "better" or "worse" than the other ones; they all have specific histories and motivations. Their suitability depends on the constraints of a given API design task.

For each of the styles, we show a figure that illustrates the main properties of the style, i.e., the interaction model and the main abstractions. We also describe how that style maps into technologies and will give some well-known examples.

Tunnel Style

The tunnel style has its roots in mostly thinking about how to expose existing capabilities from an IT perspective. It goes back to ideas such as remote procedure call (RPC), which looks at designing distributed systems in a way that they mostly "feel" like a local system. The idea is that an API is defined for existing "procedures" (or whatever the name is that a programming environment is using to call a named code unit). APIs then become a simple extension of what in a local programming scenario would be simply calling a named procedure.

The tunnel style is convenient from a developer's point of view because it can take very little effort to create APIs. The main abstractions of this style are procedures, and often they already exist. Tools can be used to expose procedures as APIs, in which case a lot of the task of "creating the API" can be automated. There still should be some management layer for securing the APIs, but that can be addressed with using a component such as an API gateway.

Figure 6-2 shows this simple model: APIs are exposed by implementations, and typically each implementation has its one "endpoint" where all exposed procedures are available as APIs. All calls of these procedures are "tunneled" through that endpoint, where the style's name originates. If consumers are using APIs exposed in different implementations, they have to use their individual endpoints.

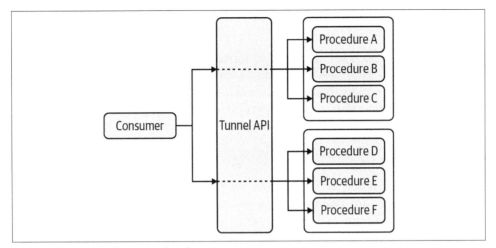

Figure 6-2. API styles: tunnel style

One problem is that the "API endpoint" has little to do with the actual API it is exposing. It is simply a technical access path (the "tunnel") that all calls have to go through. This can make it slightly complicated to manage security and other issues at the network level. Accessing the APIs behind the endpoint looks identical, meaning that it is harder to manage APIs with components that are not embedded into the implementation.

While the API management issue may be seen as a purely technical issue, there is a deeper problem with the tunnel style: it is very much focused on exposing implementations, meaning that there is no step where an API is first considered from the consumer perspective, then designed with that perspective in mind, and eventually implemented so that the API meets the needs of consumers.

The tunnel style was the style of choice for the first wave of "web services" (in the late 1990s and early 2000s) that used SOAP, an XML-based protocol for remotely calling procedures. There probably isn't just a single reason why SOAP did not end up delivering the promises that most people were looking for. But it certainly did not help with adoption rates that most SOAP endpoints directly exposed implementation details that were often hard to understand and use for potential API consumers.

SOAP (and other tunnel-style protocols) use HTTP as a simple transport protocol to "tunnel" to the endpoint. This was one of the main reasons why the design ended up this way, because it was relatively easy to add these endpoints to HTTP firewall configurations, and thus it was assumed that this design would help with adoption.

Another advantage of the "tunnel" approach is that SOAP and similar protocols could be tunneled through different "transport protocols." That way, IT and specifically security teams were able to gradually transition between various transport protocols while they were making sure that the transport protocol was robust and secure to use as a tunnel.

However, a second wave of "web services" started looking at HTTP in a different way. They asserted that HTTP was designed to interact with individual resources (on the web, these would be pages, images, and similar resources) and that an API style more in line with the web would be a more appropriate way to design and implement APIs. This is how the *resource style* came into existence.

Resource Style

In contrast to the tunnel style, the resource style starts with a consumer-oriented focus. The focus is on which resources to expose to consumers so that they can interact with these resources. The word *resource* in this context should be interpreted loosely and in fact can be assumed to be similar in scope to what you would have in resources as web pages when designing a web site. There can be resources for persistent concepts such as products, product categories, and customer information. But there also can be resources for process-oriented concepts such as ordering products or selecting a shipping option. In short, everything that is a concept worth identifying because it is used in interactions between the provider, and the consumer is turned into a resource.

As shown in Figure 6-3, the general structure is not all that different from the tunnel style. But that's really just looking at it from a very high level. The big difference is how the components in the diagram are created. While the procedures in the tunnel style are simply exposing what is defined in the implementation, the resources now create a model that has been derived from a consumer perspective.

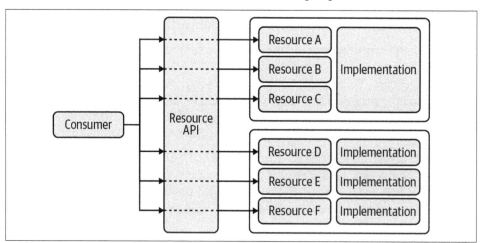

Figure 6-3. API styles: resource style

For example, the implementation of an ordering process may have a variety of resources to work through. These might very well resemble the web pages that you go through on many shopping websites: make product selections by browsing products and potentially adding them to your cart, proceed to the checkout, make your payment, and finally provide your shipping information. Every step along that path is a resource that you are interacting with, and designing a shopping website to a large degree means mapping the various aspects of the overall shopping process to resources.

In a well-designed resource-oriented shopping API, these steps will be represented by individual resources. They probably need some information to link up the individual steps (such as a shopping cart identifier and later an order identifier), and we will discuss in "Hypermedia Style" on page 151 how this can be handled in a more elegant way. But apart from this, the API consumer will use the API based on how the API's function was decomposed in individual resources, much like these processes in real life also are a sequence of well-defined interactions.

The idea of resources gives us a great way to expose the relevant aspects of an API's functionality and at the same time allows us to hide implementation details behind the resources. However, what this style lacks is the ability to better represent the fact that, oftentimes, there are workflows across these resources. If all that matters is exposing resources, then maybe this is not such an issue. But oftentimes there are processes (or other kinds of relationships) across the resources, and if that's the case, then the hypermedia style adds a crucial element to the resource style to address those concerns.

Hypermedia Style

The *hypermedia style* takes the resource style and adds the web's essential ingredient: links between resources. Just as on the web, the most important paths across resources can be navigated by simply using links between them (instead of having to know each resource individually and enter its URI in the browser's address bar); the hypermedia style does the same but for the resources of an API.

This means that on the surface, the hypermedia style looks similar to the resource style. The main abstractions of a hypermedia API are its linked resources, and the resources themselves are exposed in a similar way as in the resource style. But as an essential difference, in the hypermedia style, another fundamental abstraction is that of links between resources, as shown in Figure 6-4.

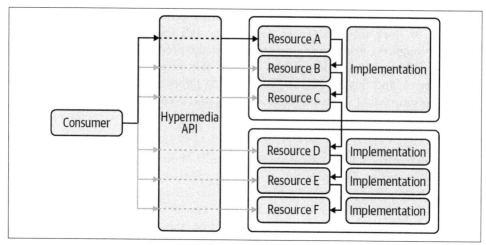

Figure 6-4. API styles: hypermedia style

Since we mention the web as a well-known example of a hypermedia system, it's worth pointing out a crucial difference with APIs: on the web, humans read pages and then decide which link to follow. For hypermedia APIs, this decision is usually made by a machine. This means that links need to have machine-readable labels so that machines can identify the available options and then make a choice. These labels are conceptually similar to the text of a link that humans click on web pages, but the labels are represented in the machine-readable representation of resources, which nowadays in many cases will be JSON.

In the same way as on the web, where you can "navigate" with your browser by using links, the same can be done in a hypermedia API, where you can "navigate" across resources using the links between them. To understand the crucial difference to the resource style, just imagine a web without links: it wouldn't be the same at all, would it?

There are two main advantages of hypermedia APIs over resource APIs, and they both are a direct result of the added links.

Links help with scenarios that have "main workflows," because consuming the API then becomes a question of following the right links to get the job done. A well-designed hypermedia API will always provide all the links necessary to choose the available next step. Some of these links can depend on context. For example, in a shopping API, the part of the workflow where shipping information is necessary might provide different options, depending on the identity of the customer and other contexts such as ordered goods and shipping destination. Designing these options into the API results in a good developer experience (DX) because it is immediately apparent which possible next step a workflow provides.

Links span resources, and it doesn't matter whether these resources are provided by one API or several APIs. This means that hypermedia is a great way to provide a unified and easy-to-use experience across resources, even if these are provided by various APIs. As we will discuss in Chapter 9, API design and good DX do not just apply to individual APIs; they also are important across an API landscape. Because hypermedia can link across APIs, it becomes easier for developers to work with several APIs when these are providing links interconnecting resources across APIs.

All of this sounds very positive, and it certainly is true that the success of the web as a very large and very scalable information system indicates that hypermedia may be a good pattern to follow. Some popular APIs are using the hypermedia style, but it still is much less frequently used than the resource style.

One reason is that for developers, working with hypermedia can be challenging initially. As software developers, the traditional mindset is that the code we're writing *is* the control flow and that we're using functions ("Tunnel Style" on page 148) or resources ("Resource Style" on page 150) along the way. Being steered by data that we receive requires a change in mindset and programming practice, and this may be one reason why the hypermedia style is only slowly gaining momentum.

Like everything in technology, there is no single solution that is best for all problems, and the same is true for API styles. While hypermedia does have some useful attributes, it can also lead to "chatty" APIs that require a number of interactions to access all required information. If an API consumer from the very beginning just knows what they want, wouldn't it be more efficient to let them say what they want? This is the idea behind the query style covered in the next section, which builds on a model where the API provides access to a potentially complex set of resources and allows a consumer to write a query to get exactly what they want.

Query Style

The *query style* is rather different from the resource and hypermedia styles, because it provides a single entry point to access a potentially large set of resources. The idea of the query style is that these resources are managed in a structured form by the API provider. This structure can be queried, and the response contains the query results. At some level, this can be seen as similar to how databases work. They have an underlying data model for the data they store, and a query language that can be used to select and retrieve parts of that data, as shown in Figure 6-5.

As with databases, the choice of the data model and the query language can differ based on the technology. But the important aspect is that each API request becomes a specific query to be interpreted and resolved by the API, and as such the model is rather different from the resource and hypermedia models where resources have rather fixed representations that can be retrieved by API requests.

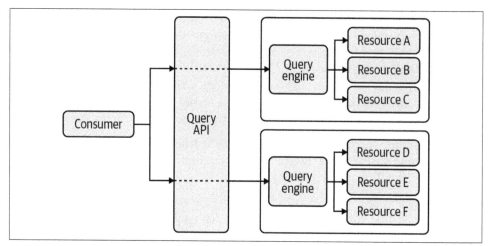

Figure 6-5. API styles: query style

One advantage of the query style is that each consumer can request exactly what they want. This means that with a well-constructed query, it may be possible to combine results that would have required numerous requests in resource/hypermedia APIs. However, for this to work, consumers need to have a good understanding of the underlying data and query models (so that they know how to use the query API properly and effectively) as well as a good understanding of the API's domain model (so that they know what to query for in the potentially complex domain model provided by the API).

As mentioned earlier, there is no "one best style for an API" without taking constraints around the API into account. Given today's trends in API technologies, it seems that query-style APIs are particularly successful when it comes to building single-page applications (SPAs). These applications use private APIs that are often just used within the same organization by the backend team and frontend developers, working on mobile or web apps, for example. In this scenario, shared domain knowledge is very good, changes to the data model can be coordinated across teams, and generally speaking the higher efficiency is worth the higher coordination effort.

All styles described so far (in "Tunnel Style" on page 148, "Resource Style" on page 150, "Hypermedia Style" on page 151, and "Query Style" on page 153) share one fundamental assumption: the API is used in a request/response manner in which the consumer sends a request and expects a response. This is a useful pattern when the consumer is the starting point of an interaction, but how about scenarios where something happens on the server side and the API consumer would like to be notified? This is a scenario where the fifth and last style, the event-based style, is a good fit.

Event-Based Style

In contrast to the styles discussed so far, the fundamental idea of the *event-based style* is to reverse the interaction pattern. Instead of consumers requesting something from the provider, the provider creates events that are then delivered to consumers of the API. This interaction pattern immediately raises the question: how is this delivery done, and how is it even known that a consumer is interested in receiving certain types of events?

This fundamental issue can be resolved only by introducing some form of infrastructure, which can be done in a variety of ways. Sometimes this infrastructure takes the form of a Publish/Subscribe (PubSub) pattern, and sometimes it is a more decoupled layer that manages events by types and then allows events to be produced and consumed based on these types. In either case, this general pattern is shown in Figure 6-6.

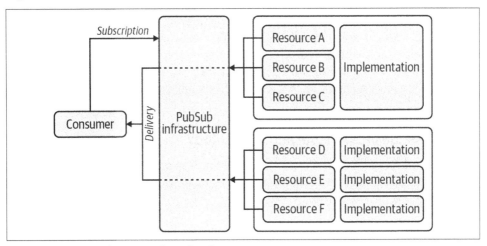

Figure 6-6. API styles: event-based style

Generally speaking, the idea of the event-based style is that interactions are triggered by events, and therefore the idea of an API is based on events as the main abstraction. There are two general cases of how this is being achieved in specific architectures.

One approach is that event consumers (*clients* in the usual API terminology) are directly connected to event producers, and the stream of events that these producers are generating is delivered to the consumers. This sometimes can be as low-level as getting a stream of measurements from some device, where each event represents a measurement that the device has taken. In this case, subscription means getting an event stream from that source.

Another approach is that event consumers connect to a delivery fabric (sometimes referred to as *message broker*) that decouples them from event producers. The fabric takes care of managing events, and consumers must subscribe to certain event types so that the fabric can make sure that events of this type are delivered to subscribers. In this case, the architecture is much more centered around the delivery fabric, and all event producers and consumers are connected to this fabric.

As in the other styles, the main abstractions are procedures ("Tunnel Style" on page 148), resources ("Resource Style" on page 150 and "Hypermedia Style" on page 151), and schemas/queries ("Query Style" on page 153). This means that when using the event-based style, everything should be driven from events. AsyncAPI is a description language that focuses on events (which it calls *messages*) and that has gained some popularity recently.

One interesting difference of the event-based style is the underlying architecture. All the other styles are inherently decentralized because they assume synchronous interactions between consumers and producers. In most cases where the event-based style is used today, it uses the delivery fabric (the message broker) mentioned earlier and thus relies on a centralized infrastructure that everybody interacts with. While modern products such as Kafka are highly scalable and resilient, this is a remarkable difference when compared to the decentralized approaches that other styles are based on.

How to Decide on API Style and Technology

After going through these five styles, the question is how to choose among them and then how to settle on a technology that implements that style. We'll look at these questions in the next two sections.

Picking a Style

As is usual in all design and engineering work, there is no "single best style" that can be picked among the five styles that we have discussed. It all depends on the constraints, and these constraints can be largely grouped into three categories:

Problem
As discussed in the individual styles, each style has a certain focus and certain strengths. Thus, it is important to think about the problem that is addressed with an API. Is it one that's mostly centered on providing access to structured and possible complex data? Maybe the query style is a good fit. Is it a problem that exposes processes that consumers should be able to navigate through? Maybe the hypermedia style is a good fit. Or is it a problem where things happen that consumers want to learn about? Maybe the event style is a good fit.

Consumers

Every API is built for consumption, and thus an API's consumers always should be an important design aspect. Since APIs ideally are reused, it's not always possible to plan for all consumers and their constraints, but it makes sense to design with at least *some* consumers in mind and to make assumptions about others. Consumer input can be in the shape of preferred styles or technologies, but it also can be a question of how easy an API should be able to understand or use and what kind of scenarios will drive the adoption of the API.

Context

Most APIs are part of an API landscape. That landscape can have a different audience and scope, depending on whether the API is meant for private, partner, or public consumption. But in all of these cases, it is important to take that bigger context into account. In the end, the goal of an API should be to be a good API *in the context of how it is consumed*. For this reason, if an API landscape does favor a certain style, this definitely is an argument in favor of using that style for a new API that is designed within that landscape.

In the end, it is important to think about picking a style as one part of the API process, and "Design Thinking" on page 50 tells us to always be mindful about consumers. Before jumping into designing the actual API, it is therefore important to first think whether the style will fit the needs of the consumer, and then of course pick a technology corresponding with that has to be seen the same way.

Choosing a Technology for a Style

Once you're done picking a style, the next task is to pick a technology that works well for the style. As previously mentioned, each of the styles has various choices that you can make.

For example, for the resource style, there is REST as an architectural pattern, but that doesn't mean that REST gives you concrete technologies. For REST, choosing HTTP as a protocol is a popular choice, and for the representation format it's probably safe to say that JSON by far overshadows any other representation (such as the XML that was popular before JSON).

For the query style, it's probably fair to say that GraphQL by now is by far the most popular choice. There are alternatives such as SPARQL, which is typically used in scenarios that center around technologies that are part of the Resource Description Framework (RDF) technology stack. The big advantage that GraphQL has is that it plugs into a JSON-based ecosystem. While GraphQL does not use JSON for queries, it returns results in JSON that make it easy to process in JSON-focused environments.

For the event-based style, there is currently some momentum behind implementing *all* of an organization's APIs that way. As we'll discuss in the following section, that's not the only way of approaching this, but it is an idea that does have some momentum, and whenever this approach is discussed, Kafka is often mentioned. While in that case Kafka often turns into a crucial and central piece of an organization's API strategy, it also is possible to treat events more on a per-API basis. In that case, specific protocols such as Server-Sent Events (SSE) or WebSockets can be used to send events to browser-based applications, for example.

Avoid Painting Yourself into a Style Corner

Like many things in architecture, there is rarely a single best way of approaching all problems in a design space. The same is true with API styles. There is no "best" API style. They all have strengths and weaknesses that depend on the problem that is being addressed.

In this book, one of the goals we have is to not just look at individual problems and solutions. This means that we don't want to focus on looking at just one API and recommending how to decide which style (and technology) to use for this API. We always want to "zoom out" and look at the bigger picture, as we'll discuss in Chapter 9.

The reality of the bigger picture is that APIs are constantly evolving and changing, and designing the landscape for change is an important consideration. In the past, we have seen approaches that were sometimes rather rigid on styles and technologies. There were SOAP-focused landscapes (based on the tunnel style), HTTP-focused landscapes (based on the resource style or, less frequently, on the hypermedia style), and in recent years there has been quite a bit of momentum toward GraphQL-focused landscapes (based on the query style). The most recent wave seems to be in the form of EDA, often in conjunction with Kafka, which is using the event-based style.

One approach to take is to not "pick" one of the styles (and a technology) as the single design to go with, but instead to embrace diversity and to make sure that the API landscape has some diversity. This is a topic often discussed in the context of Chapter 2, where one of the goals is to find a balance between bringing some order and organization to the API landscape, but without the landscape restricting things too far. This is a tricky balance to get right and would warrant a whole book in itself.

But, coming back to the styles that we have discussed in this chapter (and to the opening quote that "design depends largely on constraints"): for large organizations, it rarely is a good choice to be too restrictive and to try to solve every problem with one style. Instead, treating API styles (and technologies) as a function of the problem that an API is addressing will make it easier to cultivate an API landscape with a better balance of diversity and coherence.

All too often, our classical IT background may lead us down the road of thinking that in order to achieve interoperability and economies of scale, we must tightly control technologies. Instead, what can lead to more resilient and flexible landscape is to acknowledge the fact that there is no best API style and that for now we are embracing more than one style being used in our API landscape.

Summary

In summary, API styles are a way to look at API design that focuses less on specific technical details and focuses on general interaction patterns for APIs. We have discussed five API styles along with their main abstractions and scenarios where they tend to be good fits. We also discussed how to pick a style matching your problem and how to then move on to picking a technology that matches the style.

Finally, we briefly discussed the relationship of API styles and diversity in your API landscape. If there is one important takeaway from this section, it's to have a more nuanced view of the sometimes passionate debates around API technologies. APIs may be used to expose very different capabilities and may be intended and designed for very different consumers. Not painting yourself into a style corner is an important consideration and will only become more important with your API landscape evolving and growing over time.

CHAPTER 7

The API Product Lifecycle

Growing old is mandatory; growing up is optional.
   —Attributed to Chili Davis

When it comes to API management, understanding the impact of changes is vital. As we discussed in the previous chapter, there are different types of costs associated with changes to your API: work costs, opportunity costs, and coupling costs. The overall cost of change depends upon the part of the API you are changing.

What's more, the costs of change for an API aren't static—as the context of the API changes, so do the costs associated with changing it. For example, the coupling cost of an unused API is near zero, but the coupling cost for the same API with hundreds of consumer applications depending on it would be massive by comparison.

In truth, the reality of API change management is even more complex than that example suggests. What if your API has only a single consumer that happens to be owned by a major partner of your business? What if you have hundreds of registered developers, but none of them is driving revenue to your core products? What if you are managing an API that is profitable but doesn't fit your business model anymore? In each of these cases, the cost of change is completely different. In fact, there are probably thousands of contextual permutations to consider. All this variation makes it difficult to create a blanket assessment of API maturity for all API products.

Although it's a challenging prospect, it would still be nice to have a universally applicable model of API maturity. First, it would give us a generic way of measuring the success of the API. Second, it could give us a framework for managing an API in each stage of its life, particularly in terms of its changeability costs. So, we'll try our best to come up with a model that works for everyone.

In this chapter, we'll introduce an API product lifecycle that provides you with a maturity model for APIs. We'll describe the five stages of maturity that are relevant to all APIs. To make it fit your context, we'll also introduce a method for defining milestones that match your own business and product strategies. Finally, we'll explore how each lifecycle stage impacts the pillars of work you perform on your APIs. But before we dive into the product lifecycle, we need to define a method for measuring API products.

Measurements and Milestones

The API product lifecycle that we've promised to introduce in this chapter has five stages, each of which is delineated by a milestone. The lifecycle stage's milestone defines the entry criteria for an API. As your API matures from creation to value generation to retirement, it will progress through these milestone gates. To define your product milestones, you'll need a way to measure and monitor your API.

In Chapter 4 we introduced the API management pillar of monitoring. Establishing a data gathering system is an important first step for measuring the progress of an API product. You can't chart your progress if you don't know where you are. Gathering the data is a technical challenge that can be overcome with good design and good tooling, but identifying the right set of data for product lifecycle measurements requires a different type of approach.

You'll need to define product milestones that make sense for your API, your strategy, and your business. If you define your own milestones, we can build a generic set of lifecycle stages that can be applied to your unique context. To build those milestones, you'll have to define a set of objectives and measurements that make sense for your product. In this section, we'll introduce two tools that can help you with these definitions: OKRs and KPIs.

OKRs and KPIs

Throughout the book we'll use the term *key performance indicator* (KPI) when we talk about measuring the value or quality of something. A KPI isn't magic—it's just a fancy term for describing a specific kind of data collection. A KPI describes how well a measured target is performing. The hard part about this is identifying the smallest number of measurements that provide the most insight. That is why these measures are called *key* performance indicators.

KPIs are useful because they represent purposeful measurement. In contrast to generic data collection, KPI data is carefully selected. KPIs should provide insight for the management team about a team or product. They provide clarity about the performance of the thing they are measuring, to aid in optimization. For example, two KPIs for a call-center team might be the number of abandoned calls and the average wait time for callers. Frequent evaluation of these call-center metrics, combined with a desire to improve them, would have a big impact on management decisions.

If management decisions are heavily influenced by performance indicators, then careful data selection is vital. Poor measures will lead to poor decisions, so selecting the right set of KPIs is important. This means that someone has to identify the most critical success factors for the organization and develop metrics accordingly. But how does this happen?

Some companies use *OKRs* to identify their *objectives* and the *key results* needed to achieve them. OKRs force management teams to answer "Where do we want to go?" and "What will it take to get there?" Depending on whom you listen to, OKRs either have a strong relationship with KPIs or are meant to replace them entirely. Either way, OKRs are useful because they represent a purposeful attempt to marry cascading objectives in an organization with the results and performance needed for progress.

OKRs at LinkedIn

Some organizations have found OKRs to be incredibly helpful in their drive to succeed. For example, LinkedIn CEO Jeff Weiner credits OKRs as being an important tool for aligning team and individual strategies with organizational objectives. He holds that OKRs should be about "something you want to accomplish over a specific period of time that leans toward a stretch goal rather than a stated plan. It's something where you want to create greater urgency, greater mindshare."[1] For Weiner, OKRs are useful only when the objectives are thoughtfully crafted and continuously broadcast, cascaded, and reinforced.

When we use these terms in the book, our intention isn't to create an OKR or KPI requirement. You don't need to hire a KPI or OKR consultant in order to successfully manage your API. OKRs and KPIs are useful tools, but it's the culture and perspective of objective setting and performance measurement that are most important. We chose to use these specific terms because we know that they represent the keys to a wealth of information, advice, and tooling for those of you who want to dive deeper. But the most important thing is to have clear objectives and measurable data to chart your product's progress.

---

1 "The Management Framework that Propelled LinkedIn to a $20 Billion Company," *First Round Review*, February 7, 2015, *https://oreil.ly/yDkkd*.

Further Reading

If you want to learn more about KPIs and OKRs, we suggest starting with Andy Grove's *High Output Management* (Vintage), the book that started the OKR movement. If you want something more instructive, take a look at *Objectives and Key Results* (Wiley) by Ben Lamorte and Paul R. Niven.

Defining an API Objective

The objective that you set for an individual API needs to reflect the strategic goals of your team and organization. Your API's objective doesn't need to be exactly the same as your organization's overall goal, but it should be aligned with it. That means realizing your API's goal will also help your organization move closer to its goal. If your API fulfills its promised value, the organization should benefit. This relationship between your API's goal and the organization's goals should be clear and easy to understand.

Achieving this kind of goal alignment requires that you understand something about your organization's strategy. Ideally you do; if not, that should be your first step. In the OKR world, objectives can be cascaded down, with each part of the company defining objectives that align with a greater goal. For example, the CEO's team sets a strategic objective and identifies the key results, which allows a business unit to create objectives that foster those results; within the business unit the divisions can create objectives aligned with the identified results, and so on, down the line. In this way, OKRs can cascade through various teams and individuals in the company.

OKRs aren't the only way to achieve this kind of goal alignment. For example, Robert Kaplan and David Norton's "balanced scorecard" system (*https://oreil.ly/HYlns*) has a similar method of cascading performance objectives; it and other systems like it (*https://oreil.ly/fp9fA*) have been in use since at least the 1960s. We'll leave it to you to determine how to align your API objectives with the wider organization. The most important thing is for the objectives to exist and for this definition of success to provide value to your company and sponsors.

There are no rules about what can or can't be a goal for an API, but Table 7-1 provides examples of some common API goal types.

Table 7-1. Examples of API objectives

Goal type	Description
API usage	Reach a number of invocations per period.
API registration	Reach a number of new or total registrations.
Consumer type	Attract a specific type of consumer (e.g., a bank).
Impact	Produce a positive business impact driven by the API (e.g., % increase of product purchases).

Goal type	Description
Ideation	Harvest a number of new business ideas/models from third-party API users.
Revenue	New revenues directly associated with API business models.
App ecosystem	Number of applications consuming the API and completing the product.
Internal reuse	Number of internal departments or business units reusing an internal API.

You can also mix and match these goals—for example, you may want to set objectives for both usage and consumer types—but keep in mind that adding more objectives reduces your ability to optimize the design for a specific goal. The API's goal drives the work that you'll perform for it, but that doesn't mean it will never change. You'll need to reevaluate your objective if the organizational goals change or if it turns out your goal isn't providing real value.

Identifying Measurable Results

A goal is useful only if you have an accurate measure for it. Otherwise, it's not a good goal; at best it's an aspiration. Managing an API means establishing a clear set of measurable goals and adjusting your strategy based on your progress toward them. Achieving this requires thoughtful design of the measurements or KPIs of the API.

Good measures should enable good objectives. This means that our measurable results are the results that will enable the objectives we've defined already. Defining clear, measurable objectives makes it much easier to determine the key results or key progress indicators. But even with this direction, you'll still need to define those measurements.

If you are at all interested in defining good data measurements, you should read Douglas Hubbard's book *How to Measure Anything* (Wiley). It's a great starting point for understanding the whys and hows of measuring. Hubbard tells us that the goal of measurement is to aid in decision making in domains of uncertainty. That's certainly the sort of thing that we are after—we may know what our objective is but remain uncertain about our progress toward it or how to measure the desired results.

In his book, Hubbard defines a set of questions that you can ask yourself to figure out what type of measurement "instrument" you need. Let's use those questions and apply them to the API measurement domain:

"What are the parts of the thing we're uncertain about?"
> Most things can be decomposed into smaller pieces. Hubbard tells us that there is a big benefit to decomposing measurement targets. When the thing you want to measure has a high level of uncertainty, look for ways to decompose it into smaller, easier-to-measure pieces. For example, you may want to measure developer satisfaction for your API. That is a measure that is full of uncertainty—but can it be decomposed into smaller, more measurable pieces? It probably can:

support requests, referrals, and product ratings are all quantifiable measurements that could be used to determine happiness levels.

"How has this (or its decomposed parts) been measured by others?"
Whenever possible, learn from the measurements done by others. If you are lucky and the problem domain is the same, you may be able to lift and replicate those measurements—but even if you can't do that, seeing how others have done measurements is highly instructive and will help you with your own. A good place to start is with API strategist John Musser's "KPIs for APIs" talk (*https://oreil.ly/t70nQ*), but unfortunately there aren't many API measurement examples in the public domain.

However, most of the measures that apply to APIs have equivalent measures in other fields. Any measures for developer experience can draw inspiration from the general domain of user experience measurement. Measures for business impact can draw from the OKR and KPI world generally. Measures for registration, usage, and activity have parallels in the product management world. So, it shouldn't be difficult to find how others have solved similar problems.

"How do the observables identified lend themselves to measurement?"
After decomposition and identification of secondary sources, you should have a better idea of *what* you want to measure. To answer this question, you'll need to determine *how* you should measure it. For example, measuring support requests would require you to track all the channels that support requests are made in: email, social media, telephone, and face-to-face interaction. This is the step where you begin designing the data gathering system.

"How much do we really need to measure it?"
With an unlimited budget, your data collection system could be perfect. But does it need to be? Hubbard wants us to consider how important perfect information is for our API product decision making. Context is king here. How important is this API to your business? How impactful will the management decisions be to the organization? For example, if you are developing an API only for yourself to use, you may care very little about managing it carefully, and your investment in accurate measurements will be small.

"What are the sources of error?"
At this point you should consider how misleading these measurements might be. Are there biases and inconsistencies? Does the method of observation influence the results? The goal here is to identify potential problems and try to address them. In the API domain, problems can arise from technical challenges (are the tools reporting data correctly?), missing data (are we tracking all of the support requests?), and flawed decompositions (are these the right measures for developer happiness?).

"What instrument do we select?"

When Hubbard talks about an "instrument," he means a process or system for continuously gathering measurement data. In our API domain, this means the type of KPI that should be measured along with the monitoring implementation that you will have developed for it.

Armed with the answers to these questions, along with examples from secondary sources, you should be able to define the right measurements. With the measurements defined and the work we described in Chapter 4 for the monitoring pillar done, you are ready to build KPIs for the product lifecycle.

The API Product Lifecycle

A general model for understanding the maturity of a product already exists. It's called the *product lifecycle*, and it defines the four stages of development, growth, maturity, and decline that all products go through from a market demand perspective. We've taken the concept of the *product lifecycle* and applied it to APIs in order to come up with an *API product lifecycle*. It consists of five stages: *create, publish, realize, maintain,* and *retire* (Figure 7-1).

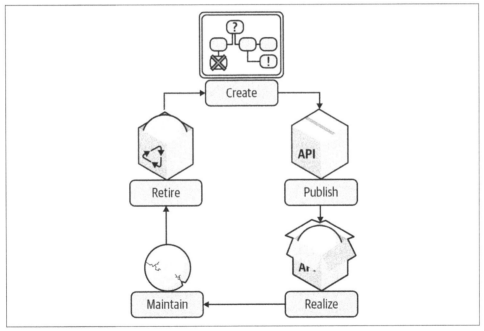

Figure 7-1. The API product lifecycle

As we mentioned at the beginning of this chapter, the API product lifecycle is a model that can help you chart the progress of your API and adapt your management as it matures.

In Chapter 5 we described the release lifecycle of an API. The product lifecycle is a superset of those releases. Each stage of the API product lifecycle may contain many individual releases. Releases or changes don't cause the API product to reach the next stage of maturity, but those incremental improvements will indirectly help the API to mature to the next stage.

In the following sections, we'll go through each of the product lifecycle stages in detail. We'll identify what happens during each stage and the kinds of milestones you'll need to define to reach it.

Stage 1: Create

An API in the *create* stage has the following characteristics:

- It is a new API or a replacement for an API that no longer exists.
- It has not been deployed in a production environment.
- It has not been made available for reliable use.

Every API starts with an inception point—somehow, someone, somewhere in the organization decides that an API should be published when the right API doesn't exist already. There are many reasons to build APIs, but in this stage it's critical to pin down exactly what those drivers are. Are you hoping to sell access to the API? Will it enable faster application development? Is it just a dumb pipe for data access? Getting a better understanding of why your company needs this particular API is essential to identifying the goals, values, and audience for it.

When APIs are in this early inception stage, they have a high degree of changeability. As we learned in Chapter 5, the interface model becomes more difficult to change when applications are actively using it. When your API is in the create stage, you have an opportunity to make intensive changes without having to worry too much about coupling costs. Your effort costs can also be minimized at this early stage, since there is little impact when bugs or defects are introduced.

A hidden cost of work in the create stage, however, is the rising opportunity cost of not progressing your API product to the next maturity stage. This can happen when you avoid publishing your API to users because you want to spend more time working on design aspects while it is safe to make changes. But if there are other teams, organizations, or people depending on your API in order to perform their own work, the absence of that published API can become a real problem. It often turns out that publishing a good API today is better for your business than publishing a great API tomorrow.

The length of time your API spends in the create stage becomes an important product management decision. You'll need to weigh the value of design freedom and its rising opportunity cost against the increased coupling and effort costs that are associated with later product stages. A good rule of thumb is to sort out those parts of the API that offer the least changeability first. For example, if you are building a CRUD-style HTTP API, you'll want to design, test, and improve the interface model as much as possible in the create stage because, if the model is not robustly designed for extensibility, which often occurs, the coupling costs grow so high later on.

The create stage of your API product is also the time when you'll need to put the team together that will help the API mature. You can always add and remove people as the product grows in complexity, but designing the initial product team is an important foundational step for your API. As we'll discuss in Chapter 8, the size, quality, and culture of your team will have a big impact on the product you create. It's important to get these qualities as correct as possible early on in the life of your product.

Milestones for the create stage

Every API begins life as a new creation, but you'll need to decide when exactly that creation point happens. How do you define the beginning of an API product journey? Of course, all of this can happen organically. It's perfectly fine to decentralize the creation decision and let individual teams create competitive API products. But you may still want to define some minimum level of diligence before API product work can begin.

For example, you could decide that every API product needs to have a strategic goal defined before design and development work can commence. This would require some form of centralized decision distribution, probably in the form of centralized authorization. Or you could make a rule that anyone in the organization can invent an API product, but work can begin only if they find three other people willing to invest three months of effort.

How you define the creation milestone depends a lot on your context, but it's important to have a shared understanding of what it takes to kick off an API product lifecycle. That will help to avoid wasted investment in products that aren't worth the effort.

Methodology: Creating APIs including citizen developers

Most of the API design methodologies are tech driven, involving only tech stakeholders, developers, and architects. But as more and more businesspeople are involved in API programs and projects, a new concept has emerged in the API design process to now include not only developers but also the business stakeholders, whom we can call *citizen developers*.

An interesting methodology has been developed by Arnaud Lauret in his book *The Design Of Web APIs* (Manning).

This method involves encouraging all stakeholders in the API design process in the create phase. It consists of asking questions to all stakeholders and engaging in the discussion. The business stakeholders define the business needs in plain English in a pattern that is easy transcribed into technical terms:

Who	What	How	Inputs? (source)	Outputs (usage)	Goal
Who is the user?	What can they do?	How do they do it?	What do they need? Where do they come from?	What do they get? What's their usage?	What is the end goal?

By answering the following questions as a team, with all business and technical stakeholders participating, a richer understanding of the whole API value chain will be developed:

Who	What	How	Inputs? (source)	Outputs (usage)	Goal
Banking app user	Buy a financial product	Search for a financial product to subscribe	Financial product marketplace	Product (apply to subscribe)	Search a financial product by exploring the marketplace
Internal developer	Update products offer	Add a product in marketplace	Product description, features, icon, name provided by product manager	Product description in marketplace	Add a product in the marketplace

In this way, business stakeholders can participate in the design specification of the API and give useful insights for tech stakeholders to align with machine-readable API specifications.

When you think about it, for REST APIs:

- "What" represents the resource that will be manipulated and its path.
- "Who" represents the user role and authorization and access management features of the APIs.
- "How" represents the HTTPs verbs to manipulate the resources (GET, POST, PUT, PATCH, DELETE, LINK).
- "Inputs" represents the API fields to send as parameters or body.
- "Outputs" represents the API response.
- "Goal" represents the API user story to be featured.

With this methodology, you will be the able to create APIs and keep developers and citizen developers in constant communication. Together, team members specifying the API in business terms and those able to translate this into technical terms work together to create an API that aligns all goals.

Of course, this is not the only methodology. Other methodologies involve API design like the APIOps Request and Responses Canvas and its API Design with Events Canvas, targeted to create event-driven APIs.

Stage 2: Publish

An API in the *publish* stage has the following characteristics:

- An API instance has been deployed to a production environment.
- It has been made available to one or more developer communities.
- The strategic value of the API is not yet being realized.

Publishing your API is an important product milestone and represents the entry point into the second stage of API product maturity. Your API has been published when you've made an instance of it available to consumers. This is the point at which you have officially opened the doors to the API and are welcoming interested users.

Publishing can't happen without deployment—the act of moving the API implementation into one or more instances—but deployment alone doesn't automatically qualify as publishing. For example, you can deploy a prototype of your API design in the *create* stage without declaring it ready for real use. Publishing happens when you signal to your API's user community that the API is open for business and ready to use.

If you are building a public-facing API for third-party developers, this is the stage at which you make the API discoverable and usable by developers who have needs that your API fills. For an internal API, this could be the point at which your interface is added to an enterprise catalog and made available for other project teams to use. For an API that supports a single application, this might be the stage where you email the development team and let them know the API is stable and ready to be used in their code.

Making the API available to consumer applications is the first step toward realizing its strategic value. But in the publish stage of an API product, this is only a *potential* value, not an actual realized one. Using the metaphor of a shop, it means you've opened up your doors, but you haven't sold your profitable items yet. You can't realize the value of an API without publishing it, but publishing doesn't guarantee you'll get value from the API. Building it doesn't mean that your target audience will come.

The distance between publishing an API and realizing its value depends on the API's strategy. If the realization goal for the API is unrealistic, it will languish in the publish stage. If the goal is trivial, it might be realized on its first use. Context is also a big factor. If you are developing the API for your own application, you have greater control over its fate, while a public API developed for third-party developers requires patience and investment. But no matter the factors, your goal should be to move the API into the *realize* stage as soon as possible.

One caveat to the principle of realizing value as quickly as possible is the changeability impact for a published API product. While you have the potential to impact dependent consumer applications at this stage, these are consumers who are not yet returning realization value to your business. This means there will be no short-term loss of value if you introduce an impactful change. For some organizations this is seen as an opportunity to perform more experiments, gather data, and take bigger risks.

However, you'll need to temper your desire to make changes in the publish stage with awareness of the long-term effects these changes might have. Existing consumers may have the potential to deliver value with continued use, but too many changes might drive them away before that can happen. If your API product exists in a competitive market, it may also hurt your ability to attract the types of consumers who are most desirable for your realization target.

The API is generally changeable at this point because your primary users have not been activated. But keep in mind that changing the quality of the API at this stage can have unintended consequences and prevent you from acquiring the level of investment you want from your target user base. An API instance that is frequently out of service or often changes its interface model in ways that break clients will send a strong (and not positive) signal to a prospective user base.

The degree to which you change your API in the publish stage should be governed by your APIs, core changeability, the scope of its availability (public, private, or partner-facing), and the types of users you are trying to reach.

Milestones for the publish stage

The milestones you define for the publish stage should identify when the API is ready for active usage. You'll need to decide what kind of trigger constitutes being ready for real use. Here are some examples:

- The API has been promoted to a production environment.
- The API website has gone live.
- The API has been registered in the corporate registry.
- API availability has been announced by email.

In addition, you may want to define some measures that indicate if the API is actually being used. This will help you determine the potential impact of changes that you want to make early in the publish stage. For example, user registrations, API invocations, and documentation views may be helpful metrics.

Methodology: API user stories for client application end users

You may be already familiar with the concept of user stories. In agile methodologies, user stories are a small, self-contained unit of development work, represented by a simple description of a feature told from the perspective of the person who desires the new capability, usually a customer of the system. It describes how to accomplish a specific goal within a product and follows this format: "As [a user persona], I want [to perform this action] so that [I can accomplish this goal]."

API user stories could take the same approach but focus on API goals, that is, that they align with more than one end-user story. According to the design outlined in the create phase, the goal is to achieve a level of minimalism in the number of endpoints. This ensures a level of simplicity and consistency and makes sure that APIs can support more than one user story outlined for the client application. A general rule should be that you have fewer API endpoint user stories than client application user stories.

Internal APIs. If you consume your own APIs, you will probably know the end-user client application stories you want to accomplish and have a full list of these. In this case, the API user stories you publish need to cover all of the needs and features of the end-user stories for client-consuming applications. This is a good way to know if the publish phase is meeting the internal usage requirement.

One API user story, one user story. A simple way to write your API user stories would be to match them with every feature you want to enable in the client applications consuming them:

API user story	User story
As a developer, I want to access users' LinkedIn accounts so I can sign them up.	As a user, I want to be able connect with a contact via their LinkedIn profile details.
As a developer, I want to enable users to upload a photo so I can display it in the profile UI.	As a user, I want to be able to choose my profile photo so I am recognizable in the app.

A common problem to watch out for is that your APIs will be too granular and too coupled with the final UI of the end-user applications. This prevents the opportunity to cultivate simplicity and the reusability of the APIs.

One API user story, many user stories. The real goal is to keep a simplicity and consistency of API endpoints, but also to maximize their reuse across all production-ready internal client applications. While you may start with one API story for each client end-user story, when it is possible, and when it makes sense, aim for one API story to refer to multiple end-user stories:

API user story	User story
As a developer, I want to access a user's LinkedIn account so I can ask for authorization with OAuth2.0.	As a user, I want to be able connect with LinkedIn so I can sign up in two clicks.
Same as above	As a user, I want to be able to import my LinkedIn posts to my profile.
As a developer, I want to enable users to upload a photo so I can display it in the profile UI.	As a user, I want to be able to choose my profile photo so I am recognizable in the app.
Same as above	As a user, I want to be able to update my profile photo so I can keep people in my contacts engaged with my profile.

Open API to third parties. If you already have an internal API that you want to publish to others or if you are building an open API for access by partners in an ecosystem, a second step is needed. A new set of client application stories needs to be defined. Indeed, ecosystem partners, your external API consumers, and third-party developers may want to use your API to build different types of features (and different applications) than your core client application. A new set of ecosystem user stories will need to be documented for the API. It is only at this publish phase that you will be able to really dig in and discover these features from the external users (via user interviews and other outreach activities that gauge the needs in your ecosystem).

The API user stories will often need to be redefined to match these new external client application stories.

Let's see an example:

API user story	User story
As a developer, I want to access a user's LinkedIn account so I can ask for authorization with OAuth2.0.	As a user, I want to be able connect with LinkedIn so I can sign up in two clicks.
Same as above	As a user, I want to be able to import my LinkedIn posts to my profile.
As a Developer, I want to enable users to upload a photo so I can display it in the profile UI.	As a user, I want to be able to choose my profile photo so I am recognizable in the app.
Same as above	As a user, I want to be able to update my profile photo so I can keep people in my contacts engaged with my profile.
As a third-party fintech app developer, I want to access the photo of the user for identity verification.	As a third-party fintech app user, I want to be able to validate my identity so I can create an account.
As a third-party social network app developer, I want to access the photo of the user for filling in profile information.	As a third-party social network app user, I want to be able to validate my identity so I can create an account faster.

Again, this isn't the only methodology that can be employed, but it is a grounded, practical technique you can use to learn about your users in the publish phase, which will help you mature enough to go on to the next phase.

As an API publisher, you will be able to complete user stories that document user needs by discovering new features and product ideas from internal and external sources and unlock, little by little, their value.

Stage 3: Realize

An API in the *realize* stage has the following characteristics:

- A published API instance exists and is available.
- It is being used in a way that realizes its objective, business or technical.
- Its realized value is generally trending upward.
- Breaking this API will have an impact on users' operational efficiency.

Thinking of your API as a product means continually improving it in support of a business objective. Up until this point, your API product has offered a *potential* to provide value. But when the target audience actually begins using the API in a way that meets your strategic objective, you can finally consider its value to be *realized*.

Realizing the value of the API is the ultimate goal of operation efficiency. Getting to the *realize* stage as quickly as possible and continuing to realize value for as long as possible is the hallmark of a high-value API. The challenge for the API owner is to decide what realization means. This is a difficult stage to create a measure for because it requires the API product owner to have a good understanding of the objectives of the API.

Properly defining the objectives for an API becomes the critical step in realizing value—or at least in being able to measure and manage your ability to produce a valuable API. The visibility and observability of the products you are creating are essential to managing a group of APIs together, so this realization measure is important.

For example, a payments API that is being marketed to third-party developers as a pay-to-use API product may define an objective of processing 10,000 paid payments per month as a realization goal. From this measure, an API product owner can clearly identify that even with 6,000 developers registered to use the API, a measure of 5,000 payment requests per month means the value of the API has not been realized.

However, an API that is used only by internal groups in an organization would have a vastly different realization target. For example, a payments API used internally within a bank's software architecture might have a realization goal of processing online banking payments in production. In this example, as soon as the online banking system begins using the API for payment processing, the API is considered realized, regardless of the actual volume of requests.

To make things more complicated, not only should the realization goal reflect the context of the API, but it must also continually be reviewed and revised as that context changes. For example, the payments API that you release for profit to third-party developers will need to change its realization target if the underlying business strategy changes—say, if you decide that long-term sustainability requires you to market primarily to the enterprise market. The corresponding milestone objective for realization could then change to something like "handle 500 payment requests for a Fortune 500 organization."

Milestones for the realize stage

To build a KPI that identifies when you've reached this stage, you'll need to have a good idea of who you are building the API for. The audience for your API should be pretty easy to identify if you've been able to define your objectives with a reasonable level of clarity. That doesn't mean your target API user will necessarily be a specific user persona—lots of APIs are launched to be as flexible as possible with the goal of serving anyone and everyone. The important thing is to be certain about the type of user access that means you've realized the API.

At this point it's also useful to measure the level of engagement that users have with your API. In fact, the primary goal for your API at this stage is to build engagement levels to the point that the API is being used legitimately—whatever that may mean in your case.

When an API enters the stage of realization, your job isn't done. The best success will come from continuing to reap value from this product. That means having a set of measures that help you track progress and make product management decisions accordingly. The kinds of OKRs and KPIs we discussed earlier in the chapter have their greatest applicability for APIs in this stage.

Methodology: Value Proposition Interface Canvas

In their book *API Product Management* (Leanpub), Andrea Zulian and Amancio Bouza push the concept of thinking about your API design in terms of its value proposition rather than as just a technical interface. Inspired by Osterwalder's Value Proposition Canvas, they created the Value Proposition Interface Canvas that can help you to understand if you have achieved your realized value.

It consists of a method of working to define the real value your API is providing, how it matches the users' pains, and how it enables users to create gains. In this method you have two components: the customer profile and the value proposition map.

Customer Profile

The customer profile outlines the jobs that the customer wants to get done as well as the derived gains and pains that facilitate or hinder getting the job done.

Value Proposition Interface Map

This is the map of your company's relevant apps, products and services, data, and business processes. Based on this map, it is possible to derive the pain relievers and gain creators, which are related to the customer's pains and gains, respectively. Pain relievers solve a customer's pain and gain creators facilitate a customer's gain. Generally, the pain relievers and gain creators shape the value proposition. The interface represents the Value Proposition Interface (VPI), which is an API. The VPI describes the interface to the value proposition and how the customer can use them.

By walking through the following two cycles, you will put yourself in the user's shoes and evaluate, one at a time, the pain and the gain the API provides. First, you will answer from the PAIN point of view:

Customer jobs

Describe the jobs the customer needs to get done.

Customer pains

Be clear about why those jobs are painful. Validate those pains with the customer.

Value sources

List relevant data sources, apps, business processes, and other products and services involved.

Pain relievers

List the features of your API product that will relieve their pain.

Value Proposition Interface

Translate the product features to API features. More precisely, describe the API's resources and methods.

Second, answer these same five steps from the GAIN point of view:

Customer jobs

Describe the jobs the customer needs to get done (same as before).

Customer gains

Be clear about what can provide gains. Validate those gains with the customer.

Value sources

List relevant data sources, apps, business processes, and other products and services involved.

Gain creators
    List the features of your API product that will create gain.

Value Proposition Interface
    Translate the product features to API features. More precisely, describe the API's resources and methods.

As Zulian and Bouza explain, it is important to be sure that the gains are not just the positive side of the pains but are real gains and opportunities provided by the new API.

This methodology can help you sharpen the value proposition of the API and maximize its realized value.

Stage 4: Maintain

An API in the *maintain* stage has the following characteristics:

- It's being actively used by one or more consuming applications.
- Its realized value is stagnant or downward-trending.
- It is no longer actively being improved.

While an API is generating realized value, it stays in the *realize* stage of its lifecycle. But eventually the pace of growth will subside and the API will enter into a steady phase, or even experience a decline in value-generating usage. When this happens, the API is in the *maintain* stage.

An API in this stage will still need to have a degree of changeability, but the goal of change in the maintain stage is slightly different from in the realize stage. Now changes are being made to keep the API in its steady state for as long as possible. These may include bug fixes, modernization improvements, and changes due to compliance, but very few changes will be made with the goal of acquiring new users.

Making changes in the maintain stage requires special care, because you'll need to ensure that the consumers of the API who are still providing value will not be negatively impacted by the changes you make. It's best to be risk averse with regard to the types of changes that are applied to APIs in this stage. If a large, impactful change is required, the API may need to transition back to the publish stage and try again to realize value that has been lost (this is sometimes done by releasing a new version of the API).

Milestones for the maintain stage

The milestones for the maintain stage will be dependent on the milestones for the realize stage and are primarily trend-based. For example, if you already have a measure for user growth defined for the realize stage, a corresponding measure of growth over the last six months might help for maintenance. If growth stagnates or declines, this could be an indication that the API has entered into the maintain stage. You'll need to define which measures are the key indicators, what the period should be, and what the threshold for stagnation is.

Methodology for the maintain phase: Self-servicing and automation

At the maintain phase, the API has realized its productized value and is solving user problems internally or externally. When it is about maintaining this value for as long as possible, the goal will be to diminish required ongoing costs while maintaining the value being created from the API product. This is done by empowering more self-service on the consumer side and integrating as much automation into business processes as possible.

On the consumer side, the self-service approach will be about maximizing the autonomy of API consumers. For instance, with a great developer experience, developers will be able to sign up, safely share their credentials, read the documentation, test the API, provision their environment, and follow use-case-based step-by-step tutorials without the need for a human to assist them. For API companies with the top developer experience, more than 90% of API users integrate successfully without any need for one-on-one support.

On the provider side, the goal will be to reduce the operational cost of keeping the API up and running properly. This can come with mutualization and with automation. At this stage, the API is now part of a portfolio under the management of the API owner or API product manager who handles multiple APIs (where in the realized phase, it is more often one product manager for one API).

Alongside this approach is a growing focus on automating actions. For instance, by leveraging a DevOps approach for APIs, or an APIOps approach, you can test the design, documentation, development, and deployment via an automated APIOps toolchain that reduces the need for manual work to fix bugs, apply security patches, and install updates.

In the maintenance phase, the goal is to keep the API running at its maximum value/cost ratio. Self-service on the user side and automating workflows on the provider side can enable you to stay in that maturity phase as long as possible, before the API's maintenance costs are higher than the value being generated. When that inversion has been reached, it is time for the API to be retired.

Stage 5: Retire

An API in the *retire* stage has the following characteristics:

- A published API instance exists and is available.
- Its realization value is no longer enough to justify continued maintenance.
- An end-of-life decision has been made.

Everything has to end, and chances are that your API product will eventually need to be retired. There are many reasons why an API might enter the retire stage, including loss of demand, changes to operational costs, the rise of newer and better alternatives, and shifts in objectives and goals for the business. All of these scenarios can be summarized as either an inability to sustain a realized value or a fundamental change in the objective for the API product.

When an API enters the retire stage of product maturity, it is an indication that it *needs to be removed*, not that it is already gone. The API product team must plan and perform the work of removing the API from the team's offering of live, available API products. The product team can decide what retirement for an API actually means, but the goal is usually to eliminate as much of the cost associated with the product to be retired as is possible. In some cases, this may mean removing all API instances from production servers, while in others it may mean simply marking the API as "deprecated" and refusing to make any further changes or offer any support for it.

This decision about what retirement means is often driven by the cost associated with the retirement stage, including taking away something useful from the people who were using the API product. Removing an API that others depend on can be a difficult decision to execute. For APIs that are used internally within an organization's technical architecture, the API owner might be forbidden from removing the instance for fear of the unplanned work that will arise from its removal. In the case of a public API, an organization may be wary of damage to its brand and its credibility with the user community if it removes a function that previously existed.

From an API product perspective, retirement of an API should not be deemed a failure or a mistake. Product retirement is a natural part of the cycle of continuous improvement in the overall landscape of your APIs.

Milestones for the retire stage

Just like the other stages of API maturity, it is important for the API product team to define the milestones that would indicate that the API is in the retire stage. These milestones might be performance-related (for example, the number of API messages processed over a timespan) or cost-related (for example, the estimated cost of improving an API to meet some future business objectives).

Google is famous for retiring products and projects that don't meet specific measurable targets within a given amount of time. At Google, those targets could be active user numbers in the hundreds of thousands, and the expectations of user growth can be quite aggressive. These types of measures make sense for a product strategy that seeks massive user growth, but wouldn't be great for an internal user authentication API.

Milestones for the retire stage represent either a floor or ceiling threshold. For example, you may set a minimum number of requests that an API in the maintain stage must serve, or you could set a maximum cost level before the product enters the retire stage. The cost of retiring a product varies wildly based on the type of applications it supports and the scale of developer users. So, you'll need to set these limits based on your API's unique situational context.

Methodology: Retiring APIs without breaking applications using API metrics

Breaking changes, sunsetting APIs…anything that means a developer needs to get back into the code to keep the application running properly is scary. So for your developer users, retiring an API can definitely cause some dread and anguish. As the API provider, there are some anxiety-reducing, respectful ways that you can do it. It is possible to do it without any notice, for whatever reason you need and without communication, but it is far better to keep the goodwill and trust you have generated with your users and do it in a way that is respectful. If done well, you can even avoid breaking any applications that rely on your API.

Deprecation and sunsetting policies.   A good practice is to alert your users in advance about your deprecation policy. What will you do when the API will stop being provided? Your API users want to know now. *Deprecation* means declaring an API not recommended to use or implement anymore. It happens often when a new API has been created as a replacement, so we deprecate the one users should not use anymore. *Sunsetting* means officially retiring and shutting down an API and its instance.

Often it starts with an announcement that the API will be deprecated on a certain date, giving valid reasons and explaining how to replace the functionality with a newer version. This communication gives time for technical and business teams to know what to do and make their plans. A roadmap is often shared announcing how the sunsetting will happen.

For instance, a first milestone may be that meeting the SLA will be stopped, or that customer support for low-tier paying customers will be stopped. A warning banner will be placed on the API documentation portal to inform visitors that "this API will be deprecated," and they will be referred to a resource link with the new version or replacement solution.

A second milestone will be to stop support for all customers. Some companies even place warning messages directly into API responses in the documentation to be sure that developers are alerted via their code of what will happen.

Then comes the actual sunsetting milestone: the official shutdown of the API, and the API is fully retired.

Tracking usage with API metrics for a "write once, run forever policy".   Some companies are able to promote that they will never break APIs nor retire APIs, like Stripe or Salesforce. They call this a "write once, run forever policy" that promises developers that they will have to write code once and only once to have an application consuming the API working forever. What can we learn from them about retiring APIs? The main way to manage this policy is to keep all versions live. And they actually do! But not all companies can handle the support charge, so there is another option.

Using API management analytics, you are indeed capable of knowing which user and application is consuming which version of your APIs. With this insight, when you intend to deprecate an API version, you can anticipate the impact it will have and for whom. Is it affecting your biggest customers? Is it affecting critical internal applications?

Once you have mapped these impacts, you can manage the relationship in a human way. Talk directly to the stakeholders who will be impacted and discuss your roadmap and the alternatives.

If people are informed well in advance and new versions or replacement solutions proposed, over time you will see more and more users of the soon-to-be retired API migrating to your newer version. With a little luck and good enough incentives, by the sunsetting milestone date, you may not have any API users of the version to be retired. If you still have some API users who will not upgrade to the new version, you will have to manage it. Your first solution is that you can continue your retiring deadline and accept that this will break the applications of these consumers. But that may not be the most diplomatic option.

For external APIs, an option is to augment the price of support for that API (in a similar way to how Microsoft used to increase support for older versions of Windows for corporate customers). This creates financial incentives for companies to migrate to your newer version.

For internal APIs, this can be done by technical means, such as ending SLA commitments, or via a managerial decision to impose the upgrade on internal API consumers.

Applying the Product Lifecycle to the Pillars

The API product lifecycle that we've just described is a useful way of understanding the maturity of your API product. This understanding can be helpful for thinking about the changeability cost of the API in each stage. The product lifecycle can also help you manage the work you need to do for your API. In this section, we will use the ten pillars of API product development that we introduced in Chapter 4 to highlight how your work might change depending on the lifecycle stage of your product.

The pillars of API management work we've defined will have significance in every lifecycle stage (see Table 7-2). You'll never be able to unreservedly ignore any of them. However, some of the pillars hold more importance in certain stages than others. These are the pillars that deserve more of your focus and possibly more investment during specific stages of the API product lifecycle.

Table 7-2. Pillar impact by lifecycle stage

	Create	Publish	Realize	Maintain	Retire
Strategy	✓				✓
Design	✓	✓			
Development	✓	✓			
Deployment		✓	✓		
Documentation		✓	✓		
Testing	✓		✓		
Security	✓				
Monitoring		✓		✓	
Discovery		✓	✓		
Change management			✓		✓

Working on the Pillars

The pillars that we highlight in these sections aren't the only aspects you need to work on. You'll be making changes and improvements to your API throughout its lifecycle. Chances are that you'll be doing work across all of the pillars in every stage of life for your API. Our goal is to show you which pillars have the biggest impact in each stage so you can plan your investment of time and effort accordingly.

Create

In the *create* stage, the focus is on developing the best API model before you take on active users. That will require a special focus on strategy, design, development, testing, and security work.

Strategy

The create lifecycle stage is when the strategy needs to be developed in the first place. Once it's established, there will be very little real feedback about actual API product usage, since most of the work in this stage will be design and implementation effort. This lack of data about the strategy means that you should expect very little change to the strategy during this stage. One exception to this is when the cost of executing your strategy is too high. For example, you might find that it's impractical to create a design and implementation that aligns well with your strategic goal. If that's the case, you'll need to make some strategic changes.

In the create stage, you:

- Design your initial strategy.
- Test it for design and implementation practicality.
- Update your goals and tactics based on feasibility.

Design

In Chapter 5 we described how API interface models become harder to change when the API gets actively used. This is why interface model design work is so important in the early stages of an API product's lifecycle. If you can come up with the best design during an API's create stage, you'll have the greatest freedom to increment, improve, and innovate early.

A big challenge to designing in the create stage is that you'll be making a lot of assumptions. You'll be assuming that the design decisions you've made for the interface model are the ones that make sense for developers. You'll also be assuming that your design will be practical to implement. Unfortunately, these types of assumptions are often wrong.

To get the best interface design this early in the life of the product, you'll end up having to perform some validation of your model. You'll need to get feedback from the implementation team that the design you've come up with is feasible—ideally this validation includes the development of prototypes that can be called. You'll also need some feedback from developers who represent your target audience.

In the create stage, you:

- Design the initial interface model.
- Test the design from a user perspective.
- Validate the implementability of the interface model.

Development

In the create stage, development work is focused on implementing an interface model to be published. As we described earlier, that work can also include prototype development for testing the design. The primary development goal in this first stage of life is to create an implementation that works and that provides all the functionality described in the interface model. But to really get long-term value from development, the implementation should also be designed to reduce the maintenance and changeability costs of the code, data, and infrastructure.

In the create stage, you:

- Develop prototypes.
- Test the interface design from an implementation perspective.
- Develop an initial implementation of the API.

Testing

In the create stage you'll need to test the interface design and initial implementation. This is your chance to expose usability problems and improve the design of the API early in its life. Like with all quality assurance, the cost of usability testing can vary. A high-investment version could involve lab-based usability tests, focus groups, surveys, and interviews. A low-investment version could be as simple as writing code for your API.

The right investment level will be determined by the value you'll get from improving quality. If you are operating in a highly competitive API market and your audience has many product choices, investing in better usability quality might make sense. If you are designing the API only for yourself, you'll probably perform only enough testing to validate your design assumptions. But in all cases, testing those design assumptions is necessary to avoid the rising cost of interface model change.

You'll want to test the implementation too, but in the create stage the implementation quality isn't as vital. The API hasn't been published for use yet, so you can afford to defer an implementation testing investment to later. That doesn't mean testing your code in the create stage is a bad thing. In fact, adopting practices like test-driven development will probably improve the quality of your implementation in the long run. The point here is just that it's a decision you can make based on your own context.

In the create stage, you:

- Define and execute a testing strategy for the interface model.
- Define a testing strategy for the implementation.

Security

When it comes to security work, the safe play is to invest in it heavily throughout the life of the API. The amount of actual diligence required will be dependent on the constraints imposed on you by your industry, government, and competitive marketplace, but it's difficult to imagine a scenario where no security work is required at all. You will always need to do some work to protect yourself, your system, and your users.

A lot of this work needs to happen *before* the API is published. It's no good to open up the doors to your API instances and only then consider how to keep things safe. That's why we've identified the create stage as the most significant one for the pillar of API security. That might seem counterintuitive, but we believe that the security work you perform during this stage is the most significant and gives you the best chance of success. Security is most relevant for a live API instance, but the foundations for security are laid while it is first being designed and implemented.

During the create stage, your security work should be focused on applying security policies to your proposed design. If your industry or organization doesn't have any defined requirements, you'll need to come up with some yourself. At this stage it is important to make security a first-class concern within the interface design and implementation.

The implementation work in the create stage should include designing and building an appropriately secure infrastructure for your API. That includes access control functions as well as a design for handling overuse that might take your service away from legitimate users. No API is too small or unimportant enough to risk being vulnerable. In fact, great exploitation targets in any large system are those components that were deemed trivial and not worth the investment of a secure implementation.

In the create stage, you:

- Define your security requirements.
- Validate the interface model against your security requirements.
- Define a strategy for securing the initial implementation and instances.

Publish

The *publish* stage is the "door opening" moment for your API product—it marks the point where you officially open your API up for use. In this stage, other people will begin to depend on your API and will write code based on the interface model you've advertised. The pillars that matter the most in this stage are design, development, deployment, documentation, monitoring, and discovery.

Design

Although most of the design work will happen in the create stage, interface design work remains important in the publish stage. That's because this is your opportunity to improve the design of your interface based on actual usage. When you publish your API, you'll find out if the assumptions you made about the design are correct. Some of that will come out during testing in the create stage, but you'll learn a lot of new lessons once users get their hands on your API for real.

In truth, you'll be making changes to the interface throughout its lifetime. Whenever you need to add a new feature, enhance an existing operation, or improve usability, you'll be changing the interface model. But those changes will be easier to make during the create and publish stages. The publish stage is your last opportunity to make invasive design changes with a minimal amount of harm, or at least without impacting users who are delivering realized value.

In the publish stage, you:

- Analyze the usability of the interface.
- Test design assumptions you made in the create stage.
- Improve the interface model based on your findings.

Development

If you change the interface, you'll end up having to make changes to the implementation. But that's not the interesting part of the development pillar in the publish stage. We are highlighting this pillar because the publish stage is the best time to optimize the implementation independent of the interface model. It's your chance to improve the implementation such that it is more performant and easier to change and scale.

You can certainly do this kind of work during the create stage, but the publish stage gives you the benefit of having real usage to base your optimization on. Unlike the interface model, you have the freedom to change the implementation in small, iterative steps. In this way, you can avoid having to do too much big design of the code up front. Instead, you can optimize it in small pieces as you learn more about what needs to be improved. In truth, you'll continue to optimize your implementation throughout the life of the API, but the publish stage presents a great opportunity to do the most with the least risk.

In the publish stage, you:

- Optimize the implementation for scalability and performance.
- Optimize the implementation for changeability.
- Make these optimizations based on observed usage.

Deployment

An API can't be considered published if an instance hasn't been deployed. So, deployment is a core pillar for the publish stage. At the very least you need to make sure an instance is available to users, but it's a good idea to start building a deployment infrastructure that will support later growth. This is especially important if your API's strategic goal involves increased usage. For example, reaching a revenue or innovation target will probably need a deployment architecture that can handle a lot of demand.

One aspect of deployment work is to develop a release pipeline that will allow you to make changes to the API (recall that it's important to achieve velocity for your API changes). The work of designing and constructing this pipeline should ideally start during the create stage of the product, but the publish stage is when it becomes more urgent to get one in place.

Another aspect of deployment is the work of operationalizing your API instances. This means building and maintaining a system that will address scale, availability, and changeability requirements for your product. A good operations system will keep your API available and performant even as the demand on system resources grows. Keeping your API instances in good health is an essential part of building a good developer experience. An API that is frequently unavailable or unreasonably slow will have trouble moving to the realize stage.

In the publish stage, you:

- Deploy the API instance.
- Focus on making the API available.
- Plan and design your deployment for future demand.

Documentation

You'll need to perform documentation work throughout the lifecycle of your API, but the documentation pillar becomes particularly important during the publish and realize stages of the API product lifecycle. During the publish stage you'll be trying to increase the realized value of the API by attracting the right kind of usage. This is your chance to experiment with the documentation design and come up with something that helps you get the usage you want.

That means you can start with a low level of documentation maturity and keep building it up as you learn more about your API's usage. For example, you might start by offering only a technical reference, but add tutorials and examples based on observed usage. In particular, this allows you to focus the documentation on the trouble spots or learning gaps of your API. You can find those by investing in user testing during the create stage or in the publish stage from the questions that your users will ask.

In the publish stage, you:

- Publish documentation.
- Improve documentation based on actual usage.

Monitoring

Getting product feedback is most important in the publish and realize stages of the API lifecycle. In the publish stage, you need good measurements to determine if you've hit your realization milestone. In the realize stage, you'll need data to ensure that your API is still trending upward in terms of demand and realized value. Monitoring is useful throughout the entire product lifecycle, but it's essential for these particular stages. You'll usually use the same metrics in both the publish and realize stages, so if you invest in good monitoring here, you can reuse that solution later.

In the publish stage, you:

- Design and implement strategic measures for your API.
- Design and implement system monitoring for your API.
- Build a monitoring system that can be used during realization.

Discovery

Discovery is the most situationally dependent of our ten pillars. The work of discovery is the effort you expend to promote the API product, engage with developers, and generally increase the traction your API has with your target audience. If you are developing an API for your own team, discovery can be as simple as sending an email. If you are building an API for a large enterprise, discovery could mean following an intake and registration process for new services. If you are building an API for the general public, it could mean hiring a team of ten people to build and implement a marketing strategy. That's quite a wide spectrum of effort and investment.

But in all of these cases, regardless of the effort expended, the value of discovery is highest during the *publish* stage of the API's life. This is when you'll want to maximize engagement with your API, because you have instances available to use, and the right usage can help you generate realized value from your product. But as we said earlier, how you do this discovery and how much you invest is highly dependent on your context.

In the publish stage, you invest in marketing, engagement, and findability for the API.

Realize

Getting to the *realize* stage is the goal of any API product. The main objective now is to increase the value you get from the API and avoid impacting the users who are helping you the most. The most impactful pillars in this stage are deployment, documentation, testing, discovery, and change management.

Deployment

When the value of your API is realized, it's imperative that you keep the system available and running for your users. That means that your deployment architecture becomes very important. While you will have performed your initial deployment design during the publish stage, in the realize stage you'll focus on maintaining and improving it. That means taking the necessary steps to keep your service running even as the demand profile changes in unexpected ways. Making these kinds of changes may even require you to redesign the implementation. That's perfectly fine as long as you can protect your high-value users from being negatively impacted.

In the realize stage, you:

- Make sure that the API's instances remain available.
- Continually improve and optimize the deployment architecture.
- Improve the implementation as necessary.

Documentation

The realize stage is your opportunity to continue to improve the developer experience of your product. In particular that means improving the documentation and learning experience. While it becomes more difficult to change the interface model at this point, changing the documentation is much less impactful. Humans are much better at adapting to change than software is, so you have some freedom to experiment with new formats, styles, tools, and presentation. The goal here is to continue to drive realized usage by reducing the learning gap for new users.

In the realize stage, you:

- Continue to improve the documentation.
- Experiment with additional supporting assets (e.g., API explorers, client libraries, books, and videos).
- Drive new usage by reducing the learning gap.

Testing

In the realize stage, testing work prevents changes to any part of the API from having a negative impact on users. At this stage, usage of your API is directly contributing to the value of your product. Changes will be necessary, but you need to mitigate the risk that changes will cause undesirable effects. The level of investment you make in this type of testing work should be based on the impact of things going wrong.

Ideally, the kinds of tests you run in the realize stage already should have been created in the publish and create stages of the API lifestyle. But as your API approaches and enters the realize stage, your testing strategy should be evaluated to make sure it is giving you the best levels of risk mitigation. As the API matures into maintenance and eventually retirement, the demand on testing will decrease. During these stages you should be able to leverage the assets you've already created.

In the realize stage, you:

- Implement a testing strategy for interface, implementation, and instance changes.
- Continually improve your testing solution.
- Build a testing solution that can be used in future stages.

Discovery

Discovery in the realize stage is broadly similar to the discovery work from the publish stage. The only difference is that the discovery work here can be more precise. You'll have a better idea of which user communities provide the most value, so you can invest more in fostering those.

In the realize stage, you:

- Continue to invest in API marketability, engagement, and findability.
- Invest more in high-value user communities.

Change management

The heart of the API product lifecycle is the evolving impact of changes to the API. In fact, we've been describing change management throughout this section, for each of the other pillars of the API product. But in general, when it comes to change management as a work pillar itself, it becomes most important during the realize stage of a product's life.

In Chapter 5 we described the four types of changes that you'll need to manage with an API product: changes to the interface model, implementation, instances, and supporting assets. Within each pillar, you'll find yourself making changes to many of these API parts, often at the same time. All these changes need to be managed to reduce their impact, but this impact reduction is most important when you have active, realized usage. This is when a good change management system and versioning strategy will provide the most value.

In the realize stage, you:

- Design and implement a change management system.
- Carefully communicate changes to users, maintainers, and sponsors.
- Support change activities with a goal of minimizing impact to realized value.

Maintain

In the maintain stage you aren't getting new value, but you don't want to harm the usage you already have. The goal here is to keep the engine running and maintain it. There's a lot of work involved in doing that, but we think the most important is the work involved in the monitoring pillar.

Monitoring

If your API is in a state of maintenance, your only objective is to keep the status quo. That means less emphasis on design, development, or change and more emphasis on support and availability. You may not need to make monitoring improvements at this point, since a lot of that work will have taken place during the publish and realize stages. But it's still the most important pillar in the maintain stage, so you'll need to invest some time and energy to make sure you are getting the right kind of system- and product-level data.

One objective is to have a system that lets you know when something out of the ordinary happens. That will be an indication that you have some work to do. Another goal of monitoring in the maintain stage is to keep an eye on the value that your API is providing. When it drops too low, it may be time for the API to be retired.

In the maintain stage, you:

- Ensure that the monitoring system is operational.
- Identify patterns that will require special care.
- Observe metrics that could trigger a retirement decision.

Retire

While this is the final lifecycle stage, remember that an API in the retire stage isn't gone yet. This is the stage where you've identified that an API product needs to be deprecated. The most important pillars in this stage are strategy and change management.

Strategy

When it's time to retire your API, you'll need to address a special set of strategy issues. How will existing users be supported, compensated, or placated? Is there a new API that users should be migrated to? What is the timeline and set of steps that will need to be in place for the API to be retired? How will the impending retirement be communicated to the user base? Regardless of the scale, context, and constraints of your API, you'll need to form some type of retirement strategy, even if it's a minimal, informal one.

That means forming new goals, new tactics, and a new set of actions. The original goal of your API that you have set in the create stage is no longer your target. Instead, you need a goal that fits the retirement of your product. For example, you may have a goal to minimize the number of users you'll lose if you want them to migrate to a new API. Or your goal might be to eliminate the cost of supporting the API as soon as possible. These two very different goals will each require a tactical plan and set of actions to enable them.

In the retire stage, you:

- Define a retirement (or transition) strategy.
- Identify a new goal, tactical plan, and set of actions.
- Measure progress toward this retirement goal.

Change management

Managing change in the retire stage means managing the impact of retiring the product. This isn't the time to introduce enhancements or improvements to the API, so the focus here isn't on versioning or managing a big rollout. Instead, the work here involves assessing the impact to your users, brand, and organization of an impending deprecation and managing that change effectively. This work should align with your retirement strategy.

In the retire stage, you:

- Assess the impact of retiring your API.
- Design and implement a plan of communication and deprecation.
- Manage implementation and instance changes to support that deprecation.

Summary

In this chapter we introduced an API product lifecycle that describes the five life stages of a successful API product. We also described how well-designed objectives and measures are needed to determine your API's maturity level. Finally, we described how the work of managing a single API product is impacted by its lifecycle stage. In the next chapter, we'll take a look at the API product lifecycle from the perspective of the people and teams that do the work.

CHAPTER 8

API Teams

Great things in business are never done by one person. They're done by a team of people.
—Steve Jobs

You may have noticed that we've put off discussion about how you create, populate, and manage teams for your API program. While this is an important topic, it turns out to be quite a challenge to collect and reflect general information about such a personal and organization-dependent topic. Each company has its own way of managing people, its own boundaries within the organization (divisions, products, services, sections, teams, etc.), and its own way of creating some form of hierarchy to manage its people. All these variables make it hard for us to come up with just one set of recommended practices for building successful API teams.

However, by talking with several companies, we have been able to identify some general patterns and practices that we can share. In our observations, organizations all use some form of teams, titles, and job roles to describe the work they need to get done and assign that work to the people responsible for doing it. We don't find much consistency in the *titles* companies use for the members of teams, but what we do find that is fairly consistent across companies is a set of *roles* for handling tasks within a team. In other words, no matter what titles people have, the same kinds of work need to be done.

This idea of focusing on roles rather than titles is echoed by software architect, author, and trainer Simon Brown. When referring to software architecture in particular, he says, "Becoming a software architect isn't something that simply happens overnight or with a promotion. It's a role, not a rank."[1]

---

1 Simon Brown, "Are You a Software Architect?" *InfoQ*, February 9, 2010, *https://oreil.ly/GEznF*.

In our experience this sentiment applies to all the roles on an API team. For that reason, we'll start this chapter with what we call a common set of API roles. Similar to the way we presented the API pillars (see Chapter 4), we see these roles as representing common tasks and responsibilities—ones that *someone* in your organization needs to take on. For that reason, we'll also spend time discussing how the API pillars match up to the API roles we define here.

We also find that, in some cases, the exact makeup of the API team can vary based on the maturity of the API they are working on. For example, in the early create stage (see "Stage 1: Create" on page 168), you don't need to focus on testing or DevOps, and in the maintain stage (see "Stage 4: Maintain" on page 178), there is usually not much work for frontend or backend developers. So, we'll review the mix of API roles you can expect to need as each of your APIs travels through its lifecycle.

Another important aspect to all this is how API teams interact with one another. Most of the companies we work with offer some coordinating body or "team of teams" that helps all the teams (no matter where their APIs are in their lifecycle) keep up with one another, manages interoperability, and encourages collaboration. This additional process of "engineering the engineers" will be covered in depth in the next few chapters as we introduce our notion of the API landscape.

Finally, a big part of making teams work well together falls under the name *company culture.* This is another area we find successful companies invest time and resources into managing. As was discussed in Chapter 2, one of the ways to scale up API governance is to distribute some of the decision making. One way to ensure consistency in decision making in this distributed environment is to pay close attention to the company culture and—where needed—learn to nudge that culture in positive directions. In the last section of this chapter we'll spend time on some key concepts we see organizations use to help them identify, monitor, and influence company culture in order to improve the overall effectiveness of their API programs.

But to start out, let's identify the set of common roles we find in most API teams and how these roles can be applied to make sure you cover the API pillars we talked about in Chapter 4.

API Roles

Just as we showed you a set of common *skills* for dealing with the aforementioned API pillars, we have also put together a set of common *roles* for dealing with APIs. In this chapter, the roles are presented as a set of job titles. However, our experience is that titles for API positions are not very standardized across companies. An API program manager in one company is called the API owner in another company, the API architect at company B is called the product architect at company Z, and so forth.

For that reason, the titles we're using here may not correspond to the titles in your company. However, we're pretty sure the actual roles do exist somewhere in your organization—or at least they *should*. That's because, just as we stated that the API pillars were all skills that are common to successful API programs, the roles we're describing here are the ones you'll need to make sure *someone* on the team is responsible for.

That means while you are reading this list of API roles (and the titles we gave them), you can do the work of associating them with their equivalents in your own organization. That's a really good exercise, by the way. If you go through your list of job titles and descriptions and find that one or more of *our* roles isn't represented, that's a pretty good indication that you have an opportunity to enhance your organization's job descriptions to make sure all the responsibilities we list here are covered somewhere in your list of API-related jobs.

Scope of Responsibility

It is also important to keep in mind that these roles each represent a defined scope of responsibility. When someone takes on a role, they take on the responsibility for all the tasks within the scope of that role. And most of the tasks involve decision making with a particular skill set (designing, development, deployment, etc.).

With that explanation as a backdrop, let's go through our list of API roles to establish a basic understanding of the kind of responsibilities involved in a healthy API program. You'll notice that we've divided the list up into two parts:

- Business roles
- Technical roles

This division may seem a bit arbitrary, and it might not track with the way your company arranges job titles and responsibilities. But we think it can help to point out which roles tend to lean more toward meeting business objectives (OKRs) and which roles tend more toward meeting technical objectives (KPIs). We talked how these two relate to each other and their use in managing your APIs in "OKRs and KPIs" on page 162.

A Reminder About Roles and Titles

Remember, the job titles we list in this book were invented for the purpose of reinforcing the connection between *API roles* and the *API pillars* from Chapter 4. The roles and job titles within your own company will likely be different from the ones we use here; however, the API pillars we covered earlier are all skills and responsibilities your company will need to cover. How you associate the pillars with your own job roles and titles is an exercise we leave to you, the reader.

Business Roles

The first group of roles we'll review are the ones we call *business roles*. The people who take on these roles are primarily focused on the business side of the APIs. They often have the responsibility of speaking in the customer's voice, aligning the product with clear strategic goals (e.g., promoting new products, improving sell-through, etc.), and matching APIs with company-wide OKRs. Sometimes the people fulfilling these roles will come from the business or product parts of your company. Other times, they will come from within the IT ranks. The important difference between these roles and the *technical roles* we'll cover next is that business roles focus first on business objectives.

We've defined five business roles to represent the decision-making responsibilities we see in healthy API programs:

API product manager

> The product manager (PM)—sometimes called the product owner—is the main point of contact for the API. This is in keeping with the API-as-a-Product (AaaP) approach we covered in Chapter 3. They are responsible for making sure the API has clear OKRs and KPIs and that the other members of the team are in place to support the needed API pillars (Chapter 4). The PM is also responsible for monitoring the API and shepherding it successfully through the full API lifecycle (Chapter 7). The API PM role is in charge of defining and describing to the rest of the team the *what* of the API (or jobs-to-be-done). It will be the technical roles on the team that will be responsible for the *how*. PMs are also responsible for ensuring that the expected developer experience (design, onboarding, and ongoing relationship) meets the needs of the API consumers. The PM's role is to make sure all the moving parts come together as expected.

API designer

> The API designer is responsible for all aspects of the design. This includes making sure the physical interface is functional, is usable, and offers a positive experience for developers. The designer also needs to make sure the API helps the team to achieve the identified business OKRs. In some cases, the designer

will work with the technical roles to make sure the design helps the team meet the technical KPIs, too. Often the designer is the first line of contact for API consumers and may be responsible for taking on the "voice of the consumer" when helping the team make decisions about the look and feel of the API. Finally, the designer may be called upon to make sure the overall design matches established company-wide style guidelines.

API technical writer

The API tech writer is responsible for writing the API documentation for all stakeholders connected with the API product. This includes not just the API consumers (e.g., the developers using the end product) but also the internal team members as well as other stakeholders from the business community (e.g., the CIO, CTO, etc.). Most tech writers will come from a technical background and have some programming experience, but this is not always the case, nor is it always required. It is important for tech writers to be effective communicators as well as effective researchers and interviewers, since they often need to understand the point of view of both the API providers and the API consumers. For this reason, tech writers often work closely with the API designer and product manager to make sure the documentation is accurate, up-to-date, and in keeping with the company's design and style guidelines.

API evangelist

The API evangelist is responsible for promoting and supporting the API practice and culture within the company. This is especially true in large organizations where internal users do not have easy access to the original API team that created the product. Evangelists make sure all internal developers using the API understand it and can accomplish their goals with it. Evangelists are also responsible for listening to API consumers and passing their feedback on to the rest of the product team. In some cases, evangelists may be responsible for creating samples, demos, training materials, and other support activities in order to maximize the developer experience for those using the product.

Developer relations

The developer relations role, sometimes called the developer advocate or DevRel role, is usually focused on external use of the API (i.e., outside the company that created it). Like the API evangelists, DevRel staff are responsible for creating samples, demos, training materials, and other assets to help promote the use of the product. And like evangelists, DevRels are often the ones responsible for listening to API consumers and helping turn their feedback into fixes or features that the API team can deal with. However, unlike internal evangelists, DevRels are also often tasked with "selling" the API product to a wider audience, and as such may participate in customer on-sites, presales activities, and ongoing product support for key customers. Additional duties can include speaking at public events, writing blog posts or articles on how to use the product, as well as other brand-awareness activities in order to help the team reach their stated business goals.

While these five roles are often aligned with business goals and strategies, as you can see from the descriptions, most of the roles still rely on some level of technical knowledge and skill in order to meet their objectives. The next set of roles we'll review are focused directly on the technical aspects of creating, deploying, and maintaining the API product.

Technical Roles

The second set of roles we defined are what we call *technical roles*. These roles are focused on the technical details of actually implementing the API's design, testing and deploying it, and maintaining it in a healthy, usable state throughout its active life. Typically these roles are responsible for speaking in the voice of the IT department, including advocating for safe, scalable, and secure implementations that can be properly maintained over time. Often, the technical staff are responsible for achieving important KPIs as well as helping the business staff reach their OKRs.

Even though we've divided our list of roles into two distinct groups, there are some parallels between the business roles and the technical roles. For example, the business role of product manager has a parallel in the lead API engineer on the technical side. And both groups of API roles have, as their ultimate goal, the creation and deployment of a technically stable and economically viable API product.

We've defined six technical roles to represent the key decision making involved in the work of implementing, deploying, and maintaining successful APIs:

Lead API engineer
> The lead API engineer is the key point of contact for all the work related to the development, testing, monitoring, and deployment of the API product. This role is the technical equivalent of the product manager business role. Just as the PM is responsible for the *what* of the API, meaning the design and business goals, the API lead engineer is responsible for the *how* of the API, meaning the technical details of what it takes to build, deploy, and maintain the API. The lead engineer is the one with the responsibility to coordinate the other technical members of the team.

API architect
> The API architect is responsible for the architectural design details for the API product itself as well as making sure that the API can easily interact with required system resources, including APIs from other teams. It is the responsibility of the API architect to advocate for the overall software and system architecture of the entire organization. This includes supporting the security considerations, stability and reliability metrics, protocol and format selections, and other so-called

nonfunctional elements that have been established for the company's software systems.

Frontend developer

The frontend API developer (FE) is responsible for making sure the API offers a quality consumer experience. That means helping to implement the company's API registry, consumer portal, and any other activities related to the frontend or consumer end of the API. Similar to the designer role on the business side, the FE has the job of advocating for API consumers, but from the technical point of view.

Backend developer

The backend developer (BE) is responsible for the details of implementing the actual interface of the API, implementing data storage, connecting it to any other services it needs to complete its work, and generally faithfully executing on the vision of the PM and API designer's description of what the API should do and how it should do it. It is the responsibility of the BE to make sure the API is reliable, stable, and consistent once it is placed into production.

Test/QA engineer

The API test/quality assurance (QA) engineer is responsible for everything related to validating the API design and testing its functionality, safety, and stability. Typically the test/QA role is charged with writing (or helping the FE/BE write) the actual tests and making sure they run effectively and efficiently. Often this testing goes beyond simple bench tests and behavior testing and includes making sure there are tests for interoperability, scalability, security, and capacity. Typically this involves the use of testing frameworks and tooling selected by the test/QA community within the company.

DevOps engineer

The DevOps role is responsible for every aspect of the building and deployment of the API. This includes monitoring the API's performance to make sure it is in line with the stated technical KPIs and is properly contributing to the business-level OKRs. This usually means working the delivery pipeline tooling, authoring build scripts (or teaching others how to do this), managing the release schedule, archiving the build artifacts, and supporting any rollbacks of broken releases, if needed. The DevOps role is also responsible for maintaining a dashboard showing real-time monitoring data as well as storing and, when needed, mining offline API logs to aid in the review, diagnosis, and repair of any problems identified while the API is in production. Depending on the company's production hosting options, DevOps staffs will need to support several environments, including desktop, build, test, staging, and production. This may include both on-premise and cloud systems.

In this section, we introduced the idea of thinking about the work to be done over the life of your API as a set of roles, or scopes, of responsibility. To make things a bit easier for our discussion, we came up with two sets of roles (business and technical) and gave these roles names that look like typical job titles.

As we mentioned at the start of this section, the roles are just that—they identify areas of expertise that need to be covered within your API programs. We'll look at this aspect of team composition next.

API Teams

In the previous section, we identified 11 roles that represent scopes of responsibility. Teams need people to fill these roles to cover all the important aspects of managing APIs throughout their lifecycle. However, a role is different from an actual person on a team. You might not need every role on the team represented by a unique person. Some people may be able to cover more than one role. For example, in many organizations, both the API evangelist and the developer relations role can be handled by the same person. Another example is that some small teams may rely on a single person to fulfill both the test/QA and DevOps roles.

People Can Belong to Multiple Teams

Although we are going to describe some specific teams in this section, it's up to you to decide how you want to distribute people among these teams. It's perfectly fine to fill each API team with full-time, dedicated members, but it's also fine to allow people to be members of multiple teams at the same time. Later in this chapter, we'll share the story of Spotify's "squads, tribes, chapters, and guilds" model that takes a matrix approach to team membership.

Also, your team may not need to cover *all* the roles throughout all the API maturity stages (see Chapter 7). For example, in the maintain phase of the API lifecycle, you usually do not need much help from frontend and backend developers. And for some organizations, some of the roles are not hosted directly in the team but are filled by "floating" staff shared within the company. For example, the role of designer might be filled by one of the business-side product design people who works in an on-demand basis for any API team that needs design work.

Teams and API Maturity

In Chapter 7, we described how an API changes over its lifetime. It's important to understand how the focus of your team and your team members will change along with it so that you can plan your teams accordingly. In each stage of the API product lifecycle, some roles play a primary role, and some play only a secondary or supporting role. Primary roles are the ones that make the biggest impact with their decisions. For example, in the create stage, almost everyone on the team has important responsibilities, but the designer's decisions about the interface design strongly influence all of the other work.

Primary roles are also the ones responsible for the work that must be done in an API. For example, in the publish stage, the API can't be deployed unless someone takes on the DevOps role and builds a deployment architecture.

As you can see, team population is greatly affected by the API's maturity and the roles needed at any one time. With that in mind, let's go through the API lifecycle stages from Chapter 7 and identify the primary and secondary roles in each, along with the types of activities that each of these roles will be responsible for.

Stage 1: Create

Primary roles
    Product manager, designer, API lead

Secondary roles
    API evangelist, DevOps, API architect, backend developer

The create stage is your opportunity to come up with a foundational strategy and the best interface design at a time when you won't impact real users. To come up with the best API strategy, you'll need someone with a good understanding of the organizational context and the API product domain, as well as the ability to set the best course of action. That person is usually the product manager. A good API product manager will have enough experience to identify an API goal that can help the sponsoring organization as well as the tactical plan that will enable it.

The designer role is a natural fit for the work of designing an interface. A good API designer will be able to make high-quality decisions about the interface model's design based on their experience. That means making decisions about how the model should look and also decisions about how the design assumptions should be tested and validated. Most importantly, a good designer will have a sense of how much design *investment* is needed based on the context of the situation.

In addition to the work of designing the interface, someone will need to design, architect, and engineer the implementation of the API. Some of that work will be experimental and exploratory in nature. This is the implementation that will eventually be released to the public in the subsequent publish stage. This development work involves a team with cross-functional talent but is orchestrated by the API architect and API lead roles.

Tables 8-1 and 8-2 identify the primary and supplementary activities in the create stage.

Table 8-1. Primary activities in the create stage

Activity	Roles
Develop the strategy	Product manager
Design the interface model	Designer
Engineer the implementation	API architect, API lead, developer

Table 8-2. Supplementary activities in the create stage

Activity	Roles
Develop prototypes	API lead, backend developer
Test the implementability of the design	API architect, API lead, backend developer, technical writer
Test the security of the design and implementation	API architect, test/QA engineer
Test the marketability of the design	API evangelist, DevRel
Test the usability of the design	Designer
Plan and execute a testing strategy for the implementation	API lead, test/QA engineer

Stage 2: Publish

Primary roles

Product manager, API technical writer, DevOps

Secondary roles

Frontend developer, designer, backend developer, API evangelist, DevRel

Reaching the publish stage means you're ready to let users have access to your product. To get this work going, you'll need people with expertise in deployment, documentation, and discovery activities. There are also a host of supplementary activities that you'll want to cover if the API is valuable and you have the bandwidth to do it.

Getting an initial set of documentation published is an important piece of work in this stage, so you'll need someone who can handle the role of technical writer to do the work of writing and publishing the docs. The technical writer is a key role in the publish stage. A good writer will make it easier for prospective users to get started and for existing users to work faster. That's something that you'll definitely want in this stage because it will help you reach the realize stage faster.

Getting the API published means that instances of the API will need to be deployed. That's typically the job of the DevOps engineer role. The DevOps engineer's responsibility in this stage includes designing the deployment process, monitoring solutions, and deploying architecture for the API instance.

Finally, the product manager will need to trigger the publishing event. Publishing an API will have a special meaning for you and your target audience based on the context of your product. It could mean registering the API in an internal service catalog, sending an email to your prospective users, or something else. However it's done, it's the PM's responsibility to make sure that it happens.

Beyond these primary activities are a set supplementary activities that will improve the quality of the API product. The documentation and other supporting assets are going to need to live somewhere, so lots of organizations implement a developer portal at this stage. Once the API is actively used, you'll be able to improve the design and implementation based on the usage data (the monitoring pillar). It's also a good idea to continue to drive usage by performing marketing and discovery work.

Tables 8-3 and 8-4 identify the primary and supplementary activities in the publish stage.

Table 8-3. Primary activities in the publish stage

Activity	Roles
Write and publish documentation	Technical writer
Design the deployment architecture and deploy instances	DevOps
Publish the API (i.e., make it officially discoverable)	Product manager

Table 8-4. Supplementary activities in the publish stage

Activity	Roles
Design and implement a portal	Frontend developer
Market the API	API evangelist, DevRel
Gather design feedback from users	API evangelist, DevRel
Improve the interface design	Designer
Collect usage information from deployed instances	API lead, DevOps
Improve and optimize the implementation	API lead, backend developer
Test the security of the implementation and deployment	API architect, test/QA engineer

Stage 3: Realize

Primary roles
> DevOps, product manager

Secondary roles
> Designer, test/QA engineer, API architect, API lead, backend developer, frontend developer, technical writer, DevRel, API evangelist

When the API is realized, the stakes are raised. Now, it's important to have people involved who can make sure that the API stays available for your high-value users. That's why the primary activities are the management of changes and improvement of the deployment architecture.

Even though the API is realized, there's still going to be a great deal of change happening to the interface, implementation, and instances. A good product manager should be able to manage all of that change in a way that will keep driving realized value without negatively impacting existing users. How exactly this should be done depends a lot on the people involved, the strategic priorities, and the culture of the organization.

While the product manager is managing change, the DevOps engineer is focusing on improving the resilience, observability, scalability, and performance of the deployment architecture. A good DevOps engineer will be able to apply the right set of tools and practices based on the situational aspects of the API. The goal is to prevent any diminishment of quality for established, high-value users.

To continue to drive realized value, it makes sense to continue to enhance and market your offering. That's why a similar set of analysis, implementation, and discovery supplementary activities have been defined for this stage as for the previous stage. You don't have to do these things, but without constant improvement your API may pass quickly into the maintain stage before you have a chance to recoup a good return on any investment you've made.

Tables 8-5 and 8-6 identify the primary and supplementary activities in the realize stage.

Table 8-5. Primary activities in the realize stage

Activity	Role
Improve and optimize the deployment architecture	DevOps
Manage and prioritize changes	Product manager

Table 8-6. Supplementary activities in the realize stage

Activity	Roles
Improve the interface design	Designer
Improve and optimize tests	Test/QA engineer
Improve and optimize the implementation	API architect, API lead, backend developer
Test the security of the implementation and deployment	API architect, test/QA engineer
Improve and optimize the onboarding and learning experience	Frontend developer, technical writer, DevRel
Market the API	API evangelist, DevRel

Stage 4: Maintain

Primary roles

DevOps, DevRel, API architect

Secondary roles

Product manager, API lead, backend developer

In the maintain stage, the goal is to keep the API running. That means the key role is that of the DevOps engineer, who must monitor and maintain the deployed instances. In addition to this basic maintenance work, it's important to have an eye on what may change in the system and how that might create new work for the API team. A good API architect will be tuned into potentially impactful changes and will be able to identify the kinds of changes needed in the API to accommodate them and keep the product running.

You'll need also to have some level of engagement and support for existing users, even if the API is no longer being actively shopped around. The DevRel role is best placed to provide this kind of support and can help the product to continue to deliver value to new and existing users, even as the rate of realization stagnates.

Finally, to support this maintenance work, the product manager and technical team will need to be ready to make any necessary changes. Although the rate of enhancements and improvements will have dropped drastically, there is still a need to make changes in support of issues that the API architect or DevRel have identified from their respective domains.

Tables 8-7 and 8-8 identify the primary and supplementary activities in the maintain stage.

Table 8-7. Primary activities in the maintain stage

Activity	Role
Improve and optimize the monitoring system	DevOps
Support existing users	DevRel
Identify system changes that will deteriorate API quality	API architect

Table 8-8. Supplementary activities in the maintain stage

Activity	Roles
Plan and schedule implementation changes	Product manager
Make required implementation changes	API lead, backend developer
Make required deployment changes	DevOps, backend developer

Stage 5: Retire

Primary role
    Product manager

Secondary roles
    DevRel, API evangelist, API architect, DevOps, API lead

The primary work of the retirement stage is strategic, so the product manager plays the key role. A good PM will be able to identify a deprecation strategy that works best for the given circumstances. In the same way that they have the experience to develop a tactical plan for a new API, they should have sufficient experience to build one for retirement.

Enabling this strategy means doing the work of removing the deployed instance from the deployment architecture and supporting users through the time of transition. The DevOps engineer is responsible for deprecating the API in the deployment domain, and the DevRel is responsible for deprecating the API in the user domain.

There also may be a need to form a technical plan to enable the product manager's strategic plan. For example, it might make sense to return response messages indicating that deprecation is imminent or choose specific response headers that indicate the retirement state of the API. This plan needs to be developed by someone with technical expertise, so it is usually handled by the API architect or API lead.

Tables 8-9 and 8-10 identify the primary and supplementary activities in the retire stage.

Table 8-9. Primary activities in the retire stage

Activity	Role
Develop a retirement strategy	Product manager

Table 8-10. Supplementary activities in the retire stage

Activity	Roles
Communicate the retirement plan and help users transition	DevRel, API evangelist, technical writer
Design a technical retirement strategy	API architect, API lead
Update the deployment architecture and remove instances gracefully	DevOps, API lead

In this section we've talked about how the lifecycle stage of any single API product affects the composition of its team and the primary and secondary roles that make up that team. We've learned that, as an API changes over time, so does the complexion of the team that owns that API.

Another important aspect of API teams is scaling *across* teams. In most companies with a healthy API program there is more than one API team. How do the teams work together? What tactics can you use to make sure teams are not working at cross purposes or contradicting one another? And how do you ensure consistency in execution across a collection of teams? These kinds of considerations are the last thing we'll cover in this section.

Scaling Up Your Teams

Understanding that roles are the essential building blocks of teams and that team composition requirements are affected by the maturity stage of the API product is just the start of the challenges of governing API teams. Another big element is dealing with *many* teams. Often each API has a team, but there is more than one API. Working in a community of teams (a team of teams?) brings a whole new level of complication.

It is a good idea to treat each API team as an independent group—that means they can solve their own problems with minimal dependencies on other teams. But reality is not quite the same as theory. Theoretically, teams don't need one another. Actually, teams can't work well without one another! So how does that work? There is a constant push/pull between maintaining independence and working well with others. It is important to build more than a single team strategy. It is also important to have a larger view of how the various parts (teams) fit together as a whole.

In his book *Team of Teams*, General Stanley McChrystal talks about a different way of thinking about how large organizations succeed: "As the world grows faster and more interdependent, we need to figure out ways to scale the fluidity of teams across entire organizations."[2] That means understanding how to get teams to work together without forcing them to become dependent upon one another.

One organization that has built a reputation for being able to scale up its team system is the digital music company Spotify. Spotify's 2012 whitepaper on the topic is an often-quoted reference to thinking about ways to improve the effectiveness of both individual teams and cross-team communications. Even though the paper is a bit dated (six years is a long time in internet terms!), we find many other organizations using similar approaches to those outlined in that Spotify paper—so much so that we think it is still valuable to understand the key lessons from Spotify and explore how you can apply them in your company.

Teams and Roles at Spotify

In 2012, Agile coaches Henrik Kniberg and Anders Ivarsson published the paper "Scaling Agile @ Spotify." Its opening line acknowledges, "Dealing with multiple teams in a product development organization is always a challenge!"[3] Kniberg and

---

2 Stanley McChrystal et al., *Team of Teams* (New York: Portfolio, 2015).

Ivarsson then go on to explain how Spotify designed its team management model to help maximize information sharing without jeopardizing team independence. This model (or some variation of it) is now something we see at many companies.

The Spotify team model has four key elements or groupings:

- Squad
- Tribe
- Chapter
- Guild

Squads are small, self-contained teams of five to seven members, similar to a Scrum team. They are the basic unit of work at Spotify. A squad has all the skills needed to do its assigned work, from design to deployment, just like the teams we've been talking about here. At Spotify, each squad has a mission or job *within* a larger product group. For example, for the Android music player, one squad might "own" the playback experience, another might own the search experience, and so forth. The squads get the work done.

In Spotify's model, the *tribe* represents a larger product scope, such as the aforementioned Android music player, the website, or the backend storage service used by all other client products. In this way tribes are collections of squads. At Spotify, they try to keep the total number of people in a tribe to around 100. This is considered large enough that there is enough diversity in the group to get things done, but not so large that it gets too hard to maintain healthy relationships.

Dunbar's Numbers

The maximum squad size (7) and tribe size (100) are based on the work of British socioanthropologist Robin Dunbar. We'll cover Dunbar in more detail in "Leveraging Dunbar's Numbers" on page 216.

With squads and tribes, Spotify is able to build an effective strategy for creating and maintaining its products and services. However, that's only one-half of the challenge. It is also important to enable some level of efficiency in this community. That means some kind of inter-squad and inter-team communication to share knowledge and ensure consistency across teams and products—and that's where Spotify's chapters and guilds come into play.

---

3 Henrik Kniberg and Anders Ivarsson, "Scaling Agile @ Spotify," October 2012, *https://oreil.ly/TcVDp*.

Since each team is self-contained, each team is likely to have a designer or backend developer, product manager, etc. Each person fulfilling these roles has their own challenges and learning experiences. However, often these experiences are similar to those of others in the same role on other teams. For example, what it takes to be a good product manager for a squad in the infrastructure tribe is a set of skills all product managers share, even if their exact approaches are not the same. It therefore makes sense for product managers in the same tribe to get together once in a while and share their experiences and knowledge with one another. In the Spotify model, this is what a *chapter* is about—people with the same roles within a single tribe (e.g., the same product group) getting together and sharing knowledge.

Guilds, on the other hand, are a way to share knowledge across multiple product groups. For example, getting some of the product managers from all areas of the company together (from customer-facing products to internal-facing systems) offers an additional level of knowledge sharing. In your company, a guild might represent a collection of team leaders from across the globe who get together once a year to share what they are working on in their various divisions.

The model of squads, tribes, chapters, and guilds provides a mix of self-contained teams without creating isolated groups of people who don't talk to one another. This approach to scaling teams helps Spotify balance independence with cooperation.

Factors for Your Scaling Approach

After Spotify shared their story, many large organizations scrambled to adopt the Spotify model with the hope of emulating the company's agility and product culture. The companies that seemed to succeed in gaining agility were the ones that adapted and evolved the model to their own context. In practice, simply copying the Spotify model provides little value, except as a safe, proven starting point. A testament to this is that "Spotify themselves have continued to improve and evolve" (*https://oreil.ly/dQJUt*) their ways of working, beyond the point of time that is described in their paper.

The right way to scale your API teams will depend on your organization's context and constraints. What works at Spotify may not work at Google. What works in a retail chain may not work in a government space agency. Context matters.

We've identified three factors that have the biggest impact on the scaling model for your teams: organizational value, prioritized goals, and distribution of talent.

Organizational value

Different organizations do different things—and this has a big impact on how their teams are scaled. While the technology that drives an API is likely to be similar, the value that comes from the work is often vastly different. We recommend that you identify the core types of APIs that provide the most value from extra investment. This will help you understand how your scaling model should work.

On the surface, most private companies have broadly similar goals: increased revenue, reduced costs, and employee happiness. But, beneath this general approach, most companies have more opinionated strategies. It's important that you understand what your organization prioritizes the most—and what it is willing to de-prioritize to get there.

For example, a technology company may focus on creating a differentiating set of APIs that they offer to other developers to purchase and use. This may require a big investment in infrastructure and engineering to compete with other technology solutions. Conversely, a retailer might focus on the differentiating value that comes from changing their customer experience as quickly and often as possible—while using commoditized technology platforms.

Understanding the type of work that benefits your organization the most should guide your decision making around the types of teams (and APIs) you'll need to put together. This includes shaping the level of investment in roles such as developer relations, product management, and developer for teams within your organization.

Organizational scale

APIs and their teams can grow pretty quickly once they get started. So, it's important that you consider how the decisions that you make in the API world will integrate within the wider company and its people. In particular, you need to pay attention to your organization's size, scale, and complexity. Is it a large, globally distributed organization? Is it split into multiple divisions? Does it have clear, authoritative decision makers?

If you want your API teams to move fast in a big company, you'll need to figure out how they can stay connected with all of the stakeholders, overseers, and authorities that they'll need to interact with. Alternatively, if you're managing APIs in a small, fast-moving startup, you'll need to devise a scaling strategy that doesn't create a bottleneck for the organization.

Distribution of expertise

The biggest danger that comes from "copying and pasting" a team scaling approach is that talent often varies wildly from company to company. This is largely due to differences in organizational value and organizational scale. A mid-tier bank is unlikely to have the same quantity of API and technology experts as a large software company. That's because that kind of people investment wouldn't make sense for their business model or their size.

But this has a big impact on how you scale your API teams. If you have fewer people who can make important decisions, you'll need to centralize them or find a way to distribute their expertise.

The Spotify approach to scaling teams represents a decentralized point of view. Scaling is built into the working model itself. Another way we see companies scaling their teams is by employing a central team designed to collect information from all the other teams and share it through whitepapers, standards documents, and best-practice training.[4]

These aren't the only factors you'll need to consider when you're scaling your teams, but we think they are the biggest. Considering your organization in terms of its value, scale, and expertise will help you adapt a scaling model to your context. And that leads us to the last section of this chapter, which is about company culture. The way team members work together and the way teams collaborate with one another is greatly influenced by the culture and values that already exist within an organization. For that reason, it is important to invest time in learning about and crafting your own company's culture.

Culture and Teams

Company culture can act as an implicit form of governance for your organization. In Chapter 2, we introduced the idea of centralized and decentralized decisions. To review, when decisions are centralized, you need to use authority to make sure people implement them properly. However, when you decentralize a decision, using authority as a means of compliance and validation does not work. That's where culture comes in. Culture is like an invisible hand that shapes decision making within teams and throughout the company, without the need for extensive authority mechanisms such as processes, standards, or common tooling. Essentially, with the "right" culture and people, you can safely decentralize more of your decisions while still maintaining a consistency of outcomes. That is why investing in crafting company culture can pay off in big ways. A consistent culture can ensure consistent outcomes, even when you are working to distribute decision making and scale up responsibility.

The process of making the right decisions involves more than just knowing what needs to be changed and how to go about distributing the responsibility for making those changes. Company culture is another important element in all of this. This is an area some people in the IT space are not comfortable talking about, but the culture of the organization is a thing that deserves attention.

---

4 We'll talk more about this team in "The Center for Enablement" on page 254.

The concept of company culture made its first appearance in print in the book *The Changing Culture of a Factory* (Psychology Press). Dr. Elliott Jaques defined it as follows:

> The culture of the factory is its customary and traditional way of thinking and doing of things, which is shared to a greater or lesser degree by all its members, and which new members must learn.

The acknowledgment that an organization even *has* a culture leads to the possibility of actually affecting the existing culture, of steering it in some direction. And that leads to notions of how to recognize what kind of culture is operating within your company and what it would take to modify it.

The 1970s and '80s gave way to a wave of books and theories on how to identify, categorize, and manage corporate culture. One important book from that era is Gareth Morgan's *Images of Organization* (Sage). Morgan put forward the idea that corporate culture can be characterized using simple metaphors such as machines, organisms, brains, and so forth. These metaphors can then help you think about how your company culture operates and how you can identify ways in which you can change the organization's culture.

We won't try to review the last 70 years of scholarship on corporate culture here, but we note that many companies we work with are actively working to understand their company culture and how they can improve and direct corporate culture in meaningful ways. To that end, we will share three topics that come up often when we visit with companies working to create and manage APIs and services in an IT environment. They are:

- Mel Conway's observations on how group *interactions* affect output
- Robin Dunbar's theories on how team *size* affects communication
- Christopher Alexander's observations about how *variety* affects productivity

We'll also touch on the role of experimentation in company culture and how it affects teams.

Recognizing Conway's Law

In the last several years, Mel Conway's 1967 paper "How Do Committees Invent?" has become an almost *required* topic in presentations about microservices as well as APIs in general. This paper is the source of what Fred Brooks dubbed "Conway's law" in his 1975 book *Mythical Man-Month* (Addison-Wesley). Conway's law states:[5]

---

5 Melvin E. Conway, "How Do Committees Invent?" *Datamation*, April 1968, *https://oreil.ly/PXGIt*.

> Organizations which design systems...are constrained to produce designs which are copies of the communication structures of these organizations.

This "law" is an observation about how the way groups are organized affects the output they produce. An often-cited supporting observation comes from Eric S. Raymond, author of *The Cathedral & the Bazaar* (O'Reilly), who states, "If you have four groups working on a compiler, you'll get a 4-pass compiler."[6] Boiled down to its essence, Conway's law tells us that, when it comes to producing working software, the organizational boundaries you have will determine the applications you get. This is both good and bad news.

As we mentioned at the start of this chapter, the software we write is "dumb"—it does only (and precisely) what humans tell it to do. Conway reminds us that the way we arrange people into groups—where we place the boundaries between teams—*determines* the results. For this reason some IT consultants talk about implementing a "reverse Conway." They encourage setting up your teams and boundaries *first* in order to get the results you want. This can work to some extent but has its own problems. In the same 1967 paper, Conway warns us about getting too aggressive with our organizational scalpels:

> [Conway's law] creates problems because the need to communicate at any time depends on the system in effect at that time. Because the design which occurs first is almost never the best possible, the prevailing system may need to change. Therefore, flexibility of organization is important to effective design.

Essentially, you can't "out-Conway" Conway's law! There is a trade-off here. It's important to point out that the notion of organizational structure is key to influencing company culture. Companies that seem to do well in managing culture have at least two things in common: they work to make boundaries both clear and flexible over time.

It is fine to establish clear boundaries between teams early in the project. This helps sort out responsibilities *within* teams and delineate interfaces *between* teams. However, it is also important to keep Conway's warning in mind: "The design which occurs first is almost never the best possible." Therefore, as you move forward with your API and component projects, it is important to adjust boundaries based on real-world discoveries. This is a normal part of the work.

---

6 Paul Logan, "Conway's Law: How to Dissolve Communication Barriers in Your API Development Organization," *Medium*, August 24, 2018, *https://oreil.ly/PassA*.

Model-Driven Design

A useful way to align your team model and your APIs is to embrace a model-driven design approach as described by Eric Evans in his book *Domain-Driven Design*. That means you create and maintain a set of models that are *expressed* as APIs in your architecture and as teams in your organizational design. When you update the model, you update your teams and architecture—and vice versa. This enables you to continually improve your teams and system design over time.

A good example of this type of approach is Matthew Skelton and Manuel Pais's *Team Topologies* (*https://oreil.ly/wmJZY*). Their model helps to design teams that are bounded to APIs and software components. You can use Team Topologies along with domain-driven design and software architecture models to evolve a design that incorporates Conway's law, instead of fighting it.

Just like so many other aspects of the API management space, managing the culture is *continuous*. Conway gives us hints on what we can do to effect change (e.g., focus on the boundaries between teams) and warns us that our first attempts are rarely the best possible option ("the prevailing system may need to change"). That leads to questions about how teams and team size can affect the corporate culture. And this leads us to the work of Robin Dunbar.

Leveraging Dunbar's Numbers

Conway tells us about how teams and boundaries affect the output of any endeavor. So, a logical question is what makes up a team and, more directly, what is an optimal team size? Many of the customers we work with rely on the 1990s research of Dr. Robin Dunbar for the answer. In popular social science writings, his theories on how the brain affects group size are best known through what's called *Dunbar's number* (*https://oreil.ly/WE3aO*), which posits that we can successfully keep track of and maintain useful relationships with, at maximum, about 150 people. Any group larger than that taxes most brains' abilities to lead and manage the group. Essentially, once the group grows past this number, keeping the members coordinated, on-task, and working together gets much tougher.

There are many confirmations of the power of 150 when it comes to communicating with groups. William "Bill" Gore, founder and chairman of the W. L. Gore company from 1970 to 1986, established a rule that once a single factory contained more than 150 people, the group should be split up and a new building built (sometimes right next to the existing one).[7] Netflix's Patty McCord calls this the "stand-on-a-chair"

---

7 Robin Dunbar, "Friends to Count On," *Guardian*, April 25, 2011, *https://oreil.ly/lYNzp*.

number: once you get past 150, a team leader can't easily just stand on a chair to address the entire group.[8]

While Dunbar's 150 is an important number, our experience tells us the research *behind* that number is more valuable. Dunbar's theory is that we need to spend time and energy to successfully communicate in groups and that group size affects the amount of effort needed to maintain successful connections. In fact, his early research determined that teams of 150 "would require as much as 42% of the total time budget to be devoted to social grooming." In other words, as teams grow larger, more time needs to be devoted (by everyone) to maintaining group cohesion. In the modern office setting, "social grooming" takes the form of meetings, emails, phone calls, instant messaging, daily stand-ups, shift meetings, and so forth. Large teams are costly when it comes to coordination.

The good news is, Dunbar has more than just one number. He actually identifies a series of numbers starting with 5, 15, 50, 150, and on up into the 1,000s. At the lower end of the scale (e.g., 5 and 15), the coordination cost—social grooming—is very small. In a team of five, everyone knows one another well, everyone knows their job, and—most likely—everyone knows who, if anyone, is *not* pulling their weight in the group. The social grooming time is quite minimal. Even at group sizes up to 15, the communication cost is relatively low. You may notice that the team sizes we recommended earlier in this book hover around the five-person mark (give or take two or three).

This small (five- to seven-person) team is what we call a Dunbar Level One team. It is the size most common for early startups. Dunbar Level Two teams of up to 15 people are often found in young companies that have gotten past their first angel funding rounds and are actively building the business. Many of the IT organizations we talk to work to keep their team sizes at Dunbar Level One and Two in order to minimize communication costs and maximize the effectiveness of the teams in general. Spotify, for example, aims for "squads" of about five to seven people each (see "Teams and Roles at Spotify" on page 209).

Dunbar shows us that team size matters and that communications within smaller teams can be more efficient. Conway reminds us that the interconnection *between* teams determines the ultimate output. The challenge, then, in crafting a successful API management culture is shepherding *lots* of teams inside a large organization. Just as working with a landscape of APIs presents different challenges to working with a single or a small set of APIs, there are unique aspects to confront when you are working with a landscape of teams. Some of the work of physical architect Christopher Alexander can help with this "team of teams" challenge.

---

8 Kevin J. Delaney, "Something Weird Happens to Companies when They Hit 150 People," *Quartz*, November 29, 2016, *https://oreil.ly/Djiz9*.

Enabling Alexander's Cultural Mosaic

Leading and/or supporting a single team is not an easy task. Getting a group up and running, as well as helping them find their footing and style and learn to be positive contributors to the company mission, is hard (but rewarding) work. Those who do this kind of work often also know that every team is unique. Each team has to travel through the same general landscape in its own way. The variations from team to team are key to building diversity and strength into your company. Even though it might seem that you'd want all teams to look and act the same way, that is not a sign of a healthy ecosystem.

This "landscape of teams" presents the same kinds of challenges and opportunities as a landscape of APIs (see Chapter 9), and many of the same landscape aspects we outline in that chapter apply to the landscape of teams too. As you grow your API enterprise, you'll be dealing with more variety, volume, volatility, and other elements of a healthy ecosystem. In fact, human systems (e.g., teams) typically become *better* as variety is introduced. Most of us have experienced cases where adding a new "outsider" to our teams has resulted in a stronger team. There are all sorts of aphorisms along these lines, including "What doesn't kill you makes you stronger"—the notion that unexpected challenges can help us get better. Nassim Taleb's 2012 book *Antifragile* (Random House) is based on this very premise.

Another point of view on the power of "teams of teams" can be found in the writings of the physical architect and thinker Christopher Alexander. His 1977 book *A Pattern Language* (Oxford University Press)—the book credited with launching the patterns movement in software—includes the concept of a "mosaic of subcultures" as a way to organize communities in a healthy, sustainable way.

Alexander's Influence on Software

Although Christopher Alexander is a physical architect, his writing and thinking have greatly influenced software architecture, too. His book *A Pattern Language* introduced the notion of thinking in patterns when constructing large systems and is cited often as the catalyst for the software patterns movement. The patterns book is a heavy read, and only one of our team can claim to have gotten through the entire work. A smaller and more accessible book by Alexander is *The Timeless Way of Building* (Oxford University Press). We often recommend Alexander's writing to software architects dealing with very large ecosystems.

Alexander's "mosaic of subcultures" pattern (*https://oreil.ly/SQ7lt*) describes three essential ways to deal with large collections of people and the smaller groups that emerge within the whole. Alexander's writing is applied to city-sized collections, but in our experience it has important parallels for IT leadership dealing with global and enterprise-level organizations.

Alexander outlines three approaches to how subgroups appear within large communities (his point of view being the city itself):[9]

Heterogenous
People are mixed together irrespective of their lifestyle or culture, reducing all lifestyles to a common denominator that turns out to be homogeneous and dull.

Ghetto
People cluster along their most basic and banal forms of differentiation, race and/or economic status, creating isolated groups that are still homogeneous within each ghetto.

Mosaic
A number of small areas with clear boundaries of separation form, between which people can freely move to experience the lifestyles and cultures that interest and inspire them.

It may take a bit of effort to get past Alexander's city-planning domain, but our experience is that these notions of widespread homogeneity ("We all use the same tools and processes throughout the company") versus ghettos ("We're all data engineers here; the QA people are in the other building") versus mosaics ("I joined this group because I wanted to work on our mobile app") are prevalent in IT organizations, too. Every company has its own shared cultural elements and subcultures that grow up within that organization. Being aware of these subelements of culture is the first step toward dealing with them and, in most cases, leveraging them in the mission of growing a healthy and resilient API management culture.

We've made the case here that it is not enough to just understand the dynamics of communication within a single team (e.g., Dunbar). We've also highlighted the power of interteam connections, as described by Mel Conway. Finally, we introduced the notion of a "landscape of teams" and the importance of paying close attention to the way in which teams are formed (e.g., Alexander) and the ecosystem in which they operate. But what is the payoff here? Why spend time on these elements of culture, especially with regard to managing APIs?

It is your company culture that determines the level of innovation, experimentation, and creativity that teams and individuals can exercise. Your culture is the key to success when growing your company.

We'll touch on this last aspect of culture next.

---

9 Christopher Alexander et al., "Mosaic of Subcultures," in *A Pattern Language* (Oxford: Oxford University Press, 1977), 42–50.

Supporting Experimentation

One important reason for spending time grooming a company's culture is to help foster innovation and transformation of the organization's day-to-day operations. A big reason for this is expressed in a quote attributed to business management guru Peter Drucker: "Culture eats strategy for breakfast."

Essentially, no matter your strategy, it is the prevailing *culture* that drives the company. Therefore, if you want to change the direction of your team, your product group, or even the entire organization, it is culture on which you need to focus. This is the message that Conway teaches us, as well: it is the organization and its boundaries that establish the output of the group.

A key to fostering innovation—the creation of new products, methods, and ideas—is the ability to experiment safely. Experimenting doesn't mean launching some half-thought-through idea into production. Like so many other things we've talked about in this book, experimenting starts small (e.g., within a team) and goes through repeated rounds of iteration to learn from, winnow down, and identify related ideas in order to find something valuable, useful, and desirable—something that might be worth spending precious time and resources on in order to bring to life.

In his 2006 book, *Direct from Dell* (HarperCollins), businessman and philanthropist Michael Dell puts it like this: "To encourage people to innovate more, you have to make it safe for them to fail." The key point here is that failure should be not just easy or common, but *safe*. Teams should be placed in an atmosphere that allows them ample room to experiment but constrains them from making costly mistakes that disrupt important company operations. One way to create this kind of ecosystem is to use the decision elements we outlined earlier in this book (see "The Elements of a Decision" on page 28). When teams know their boundaries, they have a clearer sense of what kinds of experiments they can use in order to learn how to improve.

Another big part of supporting experimentation is understanding that *lots* of teams running experiments is better than a few teams (or just one team). In "The Center for Enablement" on page 254, we discuss the power of having a dedicated team, one that can help establish guidance and guardrails for the enterprise. This is not, however, the place where all the experiments *happen*. Just as in other aspects of IT, heavy centralization and concentration can lead to increased vulnerability and volatility. On the other hand, distributing activities across a wide range of teams and product groups *improves* the chances of successfully generating valuable ideas and *reduces* the likelihood of those experiments causing the company real damage along the way.

This last point might be counterintuitive for some IT leaders. It might follow that *more* experiments adds to volatility, but this is true only if all the experiments are happening in a single place—for example, in a *Center for Enablement* (C4E) or some other experimentation hub. This concentration of risk is discussed by Nassim Taleb in his book *Skin in the Game* (Random House). Author of *Black Swan*, *Antifragile*, and other best-selling books, Taleb reminds his readers, "The probabilities of success from the collection of people does not apply to [one person]." Put directly, an *ensemble* of 100 teams making experiments with new APIs is not the same as *one* team making 100 experiments in a row. You can use your knowledge of the decision elements to reduce risk while you increase experimentation.

And increasing experimentation means more attempts at innovation, which leads to a continuous API management model (see "The API Product Lifecycle" on page 167) that can more easily be sustained over time.

To make this all work at a level that is both sustainable and economical (but not necessarily *efficient*), you need a diverse community of teams working on projects that drive their passions. And that is where Alexander's mosaic comes into play.

Summary

We've covered quite a bit in this chapter. First, we defined a set of roles that capture the decision-making scope and responsibilities needed to design, build, and maintain an API. We also talked about how these roles can be used to put together a physical team of people to do the actual work on the API. And we saw that one person might fulfill multiple roles in the same team, or across several teams.

We also reviewed how the various API lifecycle stages can affect the makeup and need for different roles in an API product team. It turns out teams are dynamic, and the roles reflect the number of people involved and the maturity of the API in question. In addition, we explored the way Spotify has designed a team model that takes into account the way teams interact with one another at various levels within the company. We also pointed out that you can take a centralized or decentralized approach to ensuring efficient knowledge sharing and collaboration across teams within the company.

Finally, we spent some time exploring the power of company culture when it comes to enabling teams. Factors such as team size can affect the quality of communications and the accuracy of the resulting work—and failing to enable cross-team communication can result in "technical ghettos" within your organization that can stifle innovation and creativity.

This last point about the power of culture and enabling cross-team communication leads us to an important milestone in the book. Up until this point, we've been focusing on the management of a *single* API and all the things that go into making sure it meets customers' needs: understanding the typical skills needed to create and maintain an API, how to ensure healthy change management throughout its lifecycle, and the kinds of roles and teams you need to make it all work.

However, as we've mentioned in this chapter, there is another aspect to all of this—cross-team and cross-product work. In all companies we visit, there is more than a single API, more than a single team, and more than a single way of working together. We refer to this world of multiple APIs and multiple teams as your company's "API landscape." And managing a landscape is quite different from managing a single plant or a single API.

When your scope of responsibility grows beyond a single API or product, you need to change the way you look at the challenges and the way you come up with solutions to those challenges. To quote Stanley McChrystal (again):[10]

> The temptation to lead as a chess master, controlling each move of the organization, must give way to an approach as a gardener, enabling rather than directing. A gardening approach to leadership is anything but passive. The leader acts as an "Eyes-On, Hands-Off" enabler who creates and maintains an ecosystem in which the organization operates.

Learning what it takes to enable the gardening of your company's API landscape is what we'll cover in the next several chapters.

---

10 McChrystal et al., *Team of Teams.*

CHAPTER 9

API Landscapes

The theory of evolution by cumulative natural selection is the only theory we know of that is in principle capable of explaining the existence of organized complexity.
  —Richard Dawkins

As the number of APIs grows, it becomes important to manage this evolving set of APIs in a way that maximizes the utility and value of *the overall set of an organization's APIs.* This is an important balancing act to keep in mind, because what may be the best (or a sufficiently good) way to expose an individual service through an API may not be as useful when looking at it through the lens of how easy it is to use that service as part of the overall landscape.

API Landscape Definition

An API landscape is the complete set of APIs published by an organization (see Figure 9-1). The APIs in an API landscape can be in different maturity stages (create/publish/realize/maintain/retire) and can be intended for different audiences (private/partner/public). The APIs may also differ in other aspects, such as style or implementation method.

Other terms you might see being used when people talk about API landscapes are *API portfolio*, *API catalog*, or *API surface area.*

The goal of an API landscape is to provide an environment that helps improve the effectiveness of designing, implementing, operating, and consuming APIs. The API landscape should help the organization to meet business goals such as faster product cycles, easier ways to test and change products, and providing an environment where business ideas and initiatives get reflected in APIs as quickly as possible.

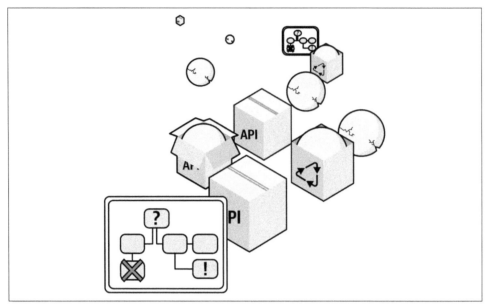

Figure 9-1. The landscape of API products

Modern API landscapes are constantly growing, in terms of API count and the numbers of APIs that are used by new services. With this increasing number of dependencies, it is clear that for the developer of a new service, it is useful to not have to understand and use various completely different API designs. These differences can be fundamental—for example, whether the APIs are using the resource style or an event-based style (see Chapter 6)—but even when the style is coherent, there may be technical differences such as APIs that use JSON representations versus those that use XML representations.

It also would be useful from the API consumer's point of view if vocabularies were aligned. For example, when using multiple APIs that expose customer data in some shape or form, it makes it easier for a consumer if all these APIs share the same fundamental customer model (even if it may be represented slightly differently, it would be useful to have some shared conceptual model across services).

This observation of the usefulness of standardization seems to clearly point us in the direction that more standardization is better. That is true to some extent, but on the other hand, it is well known that standardization takes time and effort, typically does not deliver "the one true and best model" (it simply produces a model everybody can sort of live with), and thus fundamentally has to be looked at as an investment that produces gains and risks.

For example, it probably would not be a good decision for each API to invent its own representation format, meaning that it is better to use existing ones such as JSON or XML. In this case, it seems that what's gained by reusing existing standards outweighs the possible benefits of customized representations. On the other hand, it could potentially be an expensive process to standardize on certain entities that appear across various services, such as the customer model mentioned earlier; in that case it may make sense to avoid the overhead of trying to define the one true model of the customer and simply settle for domain models.

Generally speaking, what we ideally want is for each service to not reinvent the wheel when it is not necessary and instead to reuse those design elements that reduce the effort of creating the design, the effort of understanding the design, and the effort of implementing the design. If we can hit or at least approach that ideal rate of reuse, we allow service creators to focus on those aspects of their designs they *need* to focus on, without being distracted by solving problems for which solutions already exist.

What we see is that an increasing number of organizations are doing exactly this. The most important aspect of getting this right is to understand and make sure that the guidelines informing service designers are continuously evolving themselves: new practices get evaluated and established, established practices get deprecated, and the main force behind these changes is the always-evolving nature of practices in an organization.

Because of this inherent dynamic, it is essential to see the API landscape as a fluid and continuously changing environment. For this to work over time, architecture needs to follow the same continuous evolution path. This landscape then becomes similar to a really large-scale system like the web, which on the one hand is always up and running but on the other hand continuously changes, with new standards and technologies entering the picture all the time.

API Archaeology

While we do see a fair amount of organizations that are just getting started with their API programs, it is important to keep in mind that in any organization with some IT history, it is almost impossible that there aren't already APIs in place that have been in use for a long time.

Looking at its definition, an API is any kind of interface that allows two programmatic components to interact. When we restrict the definition to today's focus on "network/web APIs," then it is any kind of interface that allows two programmatic components to interact across a network.

A Definition of API Archaeology

Archaeology is the practice of unearthing artifacts and understanding them in the context of their origins in time and location. That exact concept can be applied to APIs as well. API archaeology thus is the practice of finding integrations, understanding why and how they were created, and documenting them as a way to better understand the history and structure of complex IT systems. Practicing API archaeology in organizations can be extremely valuable in terms of finding out about existing ways in which IT components interact.

Another term people are sometimes using is that of an *API inventory*. But in that case, the coverage is often limited to listing existing APIs, instead of also looking at non-API ways of how to interconnect components.

In many organizations, these interfaces may not have been called "APIs," and they may not have been designed for reuse (remember the story about Jeff Bezos's famous "API mandate" that we told in "The Bezos Mandate" on page 52?). But in most cases, these interfaces are there, even though they have been created and used for one-to-one integrations (thereby undermining one of the main value propositions of APIs, which is to be reusable). These interfaces are first indications of a need to interconnect components, and we're therefore calling them *proto-APIs,* using the Greek word *protos* (meaning "first") as a prefix, which, for example, is used in the word *prototype*.

Finding and understanding these proto-APIs can be a useful activity because it shows where integration needs appeared (even if they were addressed in non-API ways). Not all of these existing proto-APIs may be worth replacing with actual APIs, but by simply understanding the integration history, one can already gain some insight into how integration needs were observed and met and where it therefore may not be unlikely that additional integration needs will materialize.

Proto-APIs

The need for components to interact exists in all complex systems that are made up of individual components. APIs are one specific way of doing it, but there are many other ways. From the API perspective, any mechanism that is used to allow components to interact, and that is not an API, can be considered a proto-API. In an ideal landscape, all component interactions happen through APIs, with no exception. With this ideal image in mind, any non-API interaction becomes a candidate for modernization, to be replaced by an API. This is the reason why any non-API interaction mechanism between components can be considered a proto-API.

Some organizations, typically those with sizable legacy systems, have dedicated *API librarians*, who are people in the organization who own the history of the legacy architecture, know where services and their APIs are, and know how they work and how to access them. In short, API librarians practice API archaeology and share the results because the organization understands that there is value in doing so.

In summary, practicing API archaeology can help you to better understand the IT landscape, even if there are mostly proto-APIs in it at present. It provides a starting point for understanding the integration needs of the past and also provides a foundation to better understand which API investments may be the best candidates to disentangle a potentially problematic network of many custom integrations. With practice, over time it becomes easier to replace the pre-API integrations with more modern API-based models.

API Management at Scale

API management at scale is a balancing act between imposing some sort of landscape-level design rules and maximizing the freedom of individual API-level designs. It is the classic complex-system struggle between centralized integration for coherence and optimization potential and decentralization for agility and evolvability.

Centralized integration is what brought us the typical enterprise IT architectures of the past. The main driver was to standardize on the *delivery* of capabilities so that they could be provided in an optimized and cost-effective way. High levels of integration do facilitate more potential for optimization, but they also impact the changeability and evolvability of the resulting system.

Decentralization is the opposite approach, with the web being the most widely deployed example available. The main driver is to standardize on the *accessibility* of capabilities so that capabilities can be delivered in a large and evolving variety of ways, but they remain accessible because access is based on a shared set of agreements about how capability interaction works. The main goal of decentralization is to improve *loose coupling* (*https://oreil.ly/GhN2X*), meaning to make it easier to change individual parts of the overall landscape without needing to change any other parts.

The promise and challenges of API landscape management are to take this issue into account and to avoid the trap of SOAP. SOAP said that the only thing that matters is the accessibility of services. That was an important first step, but it failed to address the aspect of *loosely coupling capabilities*. APIs and, with a specific focus on implementation and deployment techniques, microservices[1] allow us to reconsider

---

1 For an in-depth treatment of the microservice architectural style, see Irakli Nadareishvili, Ronnie Mitra, Matt McLarty, and Mike Amundsen's book *Microservice Architecture: Aligning Principles, Practices, and Culture* (O'Reilly).

what matters in large-scale service ecosystems and how to create landscapes that avoid the SOAP trap.

Decentralization and Delivery

If we can learn anything from the not-quite-realized promises of the days of SOAP-based service-oriented architecture (SOA), it is that *carefully managing delivery* is a key aspect of realizing the prospects of service orientation. SOAP addressed the promise of making capabilities accessible, but it failed to address the equally important issue of *how capability delivery is managed*. This meant that while SOAP did provide some value (previously inaccessible capabilities were exposed as services), it did not address the need for increased agility and evolvability of the overall landscape.

The Platform Principle

Many people talk about "platforms" when discussing both APIs and general business goals. However, they may be referring to rather different things. It is important to keep in mind that what may be a good idea to design as a platform on the business level is not always a good indication of how to build it on the technical level.

On the business level, a platform provides a foundation that brings parties together so that they can exchange value, and it really doesn't go any deeper than this relatively abstract way of framing the principle. Often, the attractiveness of the platform is influenced by two major factors:

What is the reach of the platform?
> That is, how many users can I reach when participating on that platform? This is usually determined by the number of people using or subscribing to the platform. Often this is the most important metric, either by sheer quantity or through qualitative factors that identify desirable users that can be reached through the platform.

What are the capabilities of the platform?
> If I am building something on top of the platform, how does it support and/or constrain me in generating value? Also, how easily can I *change* the platform to add new capabilities, ideally without disrupting existing platform users?

While these business metrics are essential, there is a factor that is often overlooked when it comes to platforms: platforms always force people using them to adhere to specific constraints, but they can do it in strikingly different ways.

Web applications can be used by anyone and anything that supports basic web standards. In the simplest case, that may be a modern browser with scripting support.

Anybody can build web applications and make them available, and anybody can use them; there is no central entity involved that controls making the *web platform* work.

Native app store applications can be similar in look and feel to web applications but are provided and used in different ways. They often can only be downloaded from centralized app stores, meaning that the store owner has the exclusive rights to decide what can be installed by users. They also can be used only on specific devices. App store applications are specifically built for the device, meaning that the investment in building one is constrained exclusively to that platform. For the application to be used on any other platform (including the web), it needs to be re-created in a different development environment, and even with a different programming language, meaning that the client side of the application needs to be rebuilt almost from scratch.

Following this pattern for API landscapes and the idea of "providing an API platform for applications," the same thinking can be applied.

Sometimes, an "API platform" is perceived to be a concrete environment in which APIs are made available. Quickly, this can start looking quite a bit like the traditional enterprise service bus (ESB), where the "ESB platform" is supposed to provide the infrastructure, and the APIs made available through it can use this infrastructure.

In other cases, an "API platform" is perceived to be a shared set of principles that services use and provide, and becoming part of the platform has nothing to do with *where* or *how* the individual services are made available. As long as they follow the same principles, protocols, and patterns, they are providing their API on the platform and thus become part of the API landscape.

The second type of "platform" is a more abstract but also a more powerful one. By decoupling the "what" from the "how" of capabilities, it makes it easier for people to contribute to the platform. It also allows more avenues of innovation, enabling applications to experiment with implementation practices without compromising their ability to contribute to the API landscape.

Once again, we can look to the web for an example. By focusing on APIs only, the web allows many different things to change over time. For example, the idea of a content delivery network (CDN) is not something that is built into the web itself. Instead, the sophistication of web content and the flexibility of a web browser to render a web page based on many resources retrieved from potentially different sources made CDNs possible. One could argue that the *potential* for a CDN was already present in the principles and protocols of the very first web pages but that the *pattern* of the CDN emerged only when it became necessary for them to exist.

This is the exact quality of adapting to new challenges that we want in our API landscapes as well. We are architecting the landscape to be based on open and extensible principles and protocols, but we are able and willing to change things when the need arises. We also help applications with supporting patterns that help them to solve their problems more effectively, and we are willing to evolve those patterns over time as well.

Principles, Protocols, and Patterns

The main takeaway of the previous section is that a platform should not require one specific way (*how*) to do things or one specific place (*where*) to do them. Instead, a well-designed platform is designed around principles, protocols, and patterns. We can illustrate these ideas with the web platform, which has proven to be both amazingly robust and flexible at the same time. Over the past almost 30 years,[2] the fundamental architecture of the web has not changed, but of course it has evolved considerably. How is that seeming contradiction possible, while most other systems seem to face challenges much sooner, and after following less radical trajectories?

One of the major reasons is that nothing in the web platform talks about *how* a service is implemented or used. Services can be implemented in any language, and of course preferences have changed over the years as programming languages and environments have changed. Services can be provided from any runtime environment, which have evolved from servers in basements to hosted servers and now cloud-based solutions. Services can be consumed by any client, and those too have radically changed, from simple command-line-based browsers to the sophisticated graphical browsers on today's mobile phones. By focusing exclusively on the *interface* that determines how information is identified, exchanged, and represented, web architecture has proved to be superior in terms of handling organic growth to any other complex IT system architecture we have seen so far. The foundation of this is surprisingly simple.

Principles are fundamental concepts that are built into the very backbone of the platform. In the web platform, one of these principles is that resources are identified by uniform resource identifiers (URIs) and that the URI-identified protocol then allows interaction with these resources. This means that while we could (at least theoretically) transition to a post-HTTP web (and in a sense we are, because the web is shifting toward HTTPS everywhere), it is really hard to think how that would be possible for a post-resource web. Principles are reflected in API styles because these have different foundational concepts that they rely on.

Protocols define concrete interaction mechanisms that are based on the fundamental principles. While the vast majority of interactions on the web these days are via HTTP, there still is some share of File Transfer Protocol (FTP) traffic, as well as more specialized protocols such as WebSockets and WebRTC. Agreeing on protocols

---

2 The initial proposal for the World Wide Web (WWW) project was submitted by Tim Berners-Lee in 1989.

makes interactions possible, and carefully designing the platform allows the protocol landscape to evolve as well, as we are seeing now with HTTP/2 and HTTP/3.[3]

Patterns are higher-level constructs; they are how interactions in (possibly multiple) protocols are combined to achieve application goals. One example for this is the popular OAuth mechanism, which is an HTTP-based choreography to achieve the specific goal of three-legged authentication. Patterns are ways common problems get solved. They may be protocols in their own right (such as OAuth), or they may be practices (such as the CDN example discussed earlier). But as with protocols, patterns will evolve over time; new ones will be added, and existing ones may get deprecated and become historical. Patterns are the shared practice of how to solve problems in the solution space established by principles and protocols.

Often, patterns evolve over time as a response to changing requirements. For example, browser-based authentication was relatively popular in the early days of the web because it could be easily controlled through web server configuration and worked well enough for the relatively simple scenarios of the early web. As the web grew, however, the limitations of this approach became obvious;[4] authentication support became a standard function in all popular web programming frameworks, and the greater flexibility of this approach replaced the earlier browser-based practice.

It is important to realize that this feedback loop was instrumental in the success of the web. Platform architecture starts simple. Applications start to get built, and some push the boundaries of what the platform supports. With enough demand, new features and capabilities get added to the platform, allowing more applications using these new features to be built more easily. The platform architects' role is to observe where applications are pushing the boundaries, help application developers to push and overcome the boundaries more easily, and evolve the platform so that it better suits these observed needs of application developers.

In API landscapes, the same evolution of practices will happen. Instead of seeing this as a *problem*, it should be seen as a *feature*, because practices can be adjusted and improved as teams learn and as new patterns and sometimes even protocols emerge. The secret to a successful API program is to see it as ever-evolving and to design and manage it so that evolution can run its course.

---

3 HTTP/2 and HTTP/3 are good examples of how the web platform can transition across technologies, but they were specifically designed to have few semantic differences to HTTP/1.1; most of the changes and improvements target more efficient interactions.

4 Browser support for authentication was not very user-friendly, for example, making it hard to log out of services.

API Landscapes as Language Landscapes

Every API is a language. It is how service providers and consumers interact when it comes to exposing and consuming a certain capability. For the purpose of this section, it is important to keep in mind that the term *language* refers to the interactions with the API (i.e., to the design of the API) and not the way the API works internally (i.e., the implementation of the API in a programming language).

Certain aspects of an individual API language are decided on fundamental levels:

- The *API style* determines basic conversation patterns (for example, synchronous request/response or asynchronous event-based) as well as primary conversation conventions. For example, in tunnel-style APIs, conversations use function calls as their core abstraction, whereas in resource-style APIs they are based on the concept of resources.

- The *API protocol* then decides the basic language mechanisms. For example, in HTTP-based APIs, it is clear that HTTP header fields are going to be important when it comes to managing the conversation basics.

- Within the API protocol, there often are many more technology "sublanguages" in the form of extensions of the core technology. For example, there currently are around 200 HTTP header fields (*https://oreil.ly/B1PG0*), even though the core standard defines only a small subset of these. APIs can choose which of these "sublanguages" they support based on their conversation needs.

- Certain aspects of the API may be cross-domain and can be easily reused across various APIs (as discussed in more detail in "Vocabulary" on page 238). As one example, these reusable parts of APIs may be defined as media types and then can be easily referenced and reused across APIs to avoid reinventing the wheel.

The main takeaway from this is that *language management* is an important part of *landscape management*. Managing languages is a delicate task. Try to unify things too much, and people living in the landscape feel stifled and cannot express themselves as they want to. Make no attempts at encouraging some language sharing, and landscapes becomes overly varied with the same problem solved in many different ways, and as a result become overly complicated.[5]

One pattern that has become increasingly popular for managing API landscapes is to promote language reuse by carrot rather than by stick.

---

5 This is a good example of complexity versus complication. The *complexity* of an API landscape is determined by the features of various APIs and their reflection in the API. *Complication* is introduced when the same problem gets solved in different ways in different APIs, introducing language variety that is not necessary from the functionality point of view.

The *stick method* was characterized by a small team of leaders deciding on the languages that should be used and then declaring that only those and no others would be allowed. This usually was a top-down decision and often made it hard to experiment with new solutions and establish new practices.

The *carrot method* allows any language to be suggested for reuse, provided it has associated tools and libraries to make life easier for people using it. This means that a language has to prove its utility to be among the promoted ones. It also means that adding to the language repertoire can be done by demonstrating a language's utility.

With the carrot method, the set of promoted languages will and should evolve over time. If new languages emerge, so should new ways to show their utility, and if that's the case, then those should become new promoted languages.

As a result, languages can fall out of favor, either by being eclipsed by competing, more successful languages or by people simply moving on to a different way of doing things. That is what has been happening in the XML/JSON space for a while now. While there still are many XML services around, the default choice for APIs nowadays is JSON (and a few years from now, we might see another technology gradually replacing JSON).

API the APIs

Scaling the practice of APIs means that when the time comes to scale, there is a plan for how to automate an increasing number of tasks both for individual APIs and in the API landscape. Automation requires that how information is made available and can be used and collected is well defined. Come to think of it, this task of making information available is exactly what APIs are for! This leads to the core mantra of "API the APIs":

> Everything that you want to say *about an API*, say it *through the API*.

What this leads to is the idea that an essential part of managing API landscapes in a scalable way revolves around the idea of using "infrastructure APIs" (or rather, an *infrastructure part* in existing APIs). A simple example of such an infrastructure API could be a way to expose status information about an API's health. If each API follows a *standardized pattern* (more on that in "Vocabulary" on page 238), it becomes trivial to automate the task of collecting status information across all APIs. Simply put, it could look like this:

- Starting from the inventory of currently active service instances, visit each of these services every 10 minutes.

- Starting from the services' home pages, follow the link with the `status` link relation to find their status resources.

- Retrieve the status resource for each service and process/visualize/archive it.

In this scenario, it becomes simple to write machinery that collects this information on a regular basis and to build tooling and insights on top of that information. This has become possible because *as part of the API, there is a standardized way that certain aspects of the API are made accessible.*

Following this line of thinking, it becomes clear that managing and evolving an API landscape now in part becomes a matter of evolving the ways in which APIs can be used for these kinds of automation. By designing for change, this information can be added over time, and existing services can be retrofitted as needed.

In this example, exposing status information has become a new pattern, and there is an established practice for what is exposed. This new practice might move from "experimental" to "implementation," if the API landscape is using these kinds of categories for its API design guidance. It might very well also move to "sunset" and then to "historical," with some older services still using it, if at some point in time the landscape moves on to another way of representing API health.

In the last paragraph, we used "experimental," "implementation," "sunset," and "historical" as possible status values for guidance. We are not proposing that you use this specific set, but it is important to realize that all guidance evolves over time. What was once a good way to solve a problem may be replaced by a faster and more robust way of doing it. Guidance should help teams to make decisions about how to solve a problem. By tracking guidance status, it becomes easier for teams to understand how practices evolve, and therefore it is a good idea to keep track of what currently are good solutions, to start noting what might be upcoming good solutions, and to also keep a record of what you once thought was a good solution. "Structuring Guidance in the API Landscape" on page 250 and "The Lifecycle of Guidance" on page 253 discuss the specific ways in which guidance can be structured and evolved in more detail.

Solving this problem in a way that becomes a *design element* of an API makes it easier to manage large API landscapes, because certain design elements are repeated across APIs, and these elements can be used for automation purposes.

Understanding the Landscape

API landscapes are no different from other landscapes of products or capabilities, where the goal is to allow these landscapes to evolve easily and with little friction, and to serve as a solid foundation for building new capabilities, either internally or externally. In all of these cases, there are trade-offs between optimizing for a single well-known goal and optimizing for changeability. Optimization for changeability always requires some trade-offs over fixed goals; the key factors for changeability are to keep the landscape open for evolution and to instrument it in ways that allow insights into its current state and into its trajectory over time.

The idea discussed in the previous section, that everything that should be said about an API should be said through the API, plays a key role in this picture. This can be as simple as providing status information, as mentioned previously, or it could be much more comprehensive, going as far as requiring that any API documentation must be part of the API itself, or managing API security aspects through the API itself. In such an approach, APIs become self-serve products, with as much information made available through them as is needed for understanding and using them.

This approach in some cases can be costly. When taken to its extreme, where the idea is to have APIs that potentially millions of developers can use and access, then it makes economic sense to design these API to be as sophisticated as possible so that it is as easy as possible for developers to understand and use them. In this case, there is one product that is designed for the mass market, and thus it is highly optimized for this use case.

In most API landscapes there will be hundreds or thousands of APIs, and it is neither possible nor necessary to invest in polishing each of these into perfect mass-market products. But a little bit of standardization can go a long way, such as making sure that it is easy to find contact information for the API team, some minimal documentation, a machine-readable description, and examples to get started with.

And when it seems that APIs need a bit more "polish," the evolutionary model of the landscape will help: API teams will start establishing practices for improving the developer experience, and these can become established and supported practices. Once again, the key is to observe changing needs, to observe solutions that are practiced by APIs, and to support whatever is desirable as a landscape-level practice.

The Eight Vs of API Landscapes

Managing API landscapes can be a daunting task. It requires balancing issues of product velocity and independence with the conflicting issues of coherence and robustness over time. But before we discuss how API landscapes mature in more detail, which we will do in Chapter 10, we first provide a qualitative framework for the issues that matter for the long-term development of API landscapes.

In the following model of the "eight Vs" of API landscapes, we make the assumption that APIs are getting designed and developed in a variety of ways (and following a variety of paths through their individual API lifecycles, as discussed in Chapter 7). These eight Vs are like the controls or dials for your API management system. You'll need to observe and tune them to get the best results.

Specifically, the assumption is that the design and execution of the landscape strategy follows a platform model (as discussed in "The Platform Principle" on page 228) where adding APIs to a platform means adhering to the principles, protocols, and patterns of that platform.

With such an open API landscape model in mind, it becomes important to consider the following eight aspects, which in some shape or form all interact with how individual APIs get *designed* and *implemented* and how the whole API landscape is *organized*. Keeping these aspects in mind will also help guide *observation* of the landscape, meaning that insight into them will help you to better understand the continuous evolution of the landscape.

In the following sections, we introduce and describe the eight important aspects to keep in mind for API landscape management. We will use the same aspects in Chapter 10 for our landscape maturity model, which uses risks, opportunities, and potential investments in all these areas as a way to assess and guide the maturity of an API landscape. We will also use them in Chapter 11 to explain how lifecycle management at the landscape level can be guided by and help with the lifecycle of individual APIs.

We have identified these eight Vs—variety, vocabulary, volume, velocity, vulnerability, visibility, versioning, and volatility—as a way to guide and focus the management of API landscapes. We discuss each of them in more detail in the following sections.

Variety

Variety refers to the fact that API landscapes often contain APIs designed and developed by different teams and on different technology platforms, as well as APIs designed and developed for different users. The goal of APIs is to allow this variability and to provide more autonomy for teams.

For example, it may make sense to have one design guideline that promotes resource-style APIs as the default choice for core platform services, because for these, consumption should be as easy as possible for the largest possible number of consumers. However, for APIs that are specifically provided to be backends for mobile applications, it may make sense to support query-style APIs using a technology such as GraphQL, because then mobile applications can very specifically get just the data that they need, in just one interaction.

API landscapes have to balance variety. One goal of API landscape management is to manage and possibly constrain the variety so that API consumers don't have to learn how to interact with too many different API styles. On the other hand, restricting variety to just one design choice may not be a useful thing to do if there are clusters of design preferences where different design choices match those scenarios very well, allowing better products to be delivered to more consumers.

Managing variety in API landscapes thus is a balancing act of constraining choices enough to avoid an unproductive multitude of API flavors, while at the same time being open to identifying choices that allow the API landscape to deliver higher value.

The most fundamental aspect is to treat "managing variety" as an act of governance over time: do not build anything into your landscape that makes it fundamentally hard to evolve your understanding of the variety that you want to support over time. If one thing is certain, it is that API landscapes in a few years will not look the same as they do today—so keeping paths open to deal with evolutionary variety is essential to avoid painting yourself into a corner.

API Preferences over Time

You might have certain preferences for how APIs should be designed, and use those preferences to inform your governance. You might encourage developers to follow those preferences, because from the landscape perspective they seem to provide the best cost/benefit combination.

But you should not place all your bets on that one set of preferences. Something better might come along that makes you change your mind, or you simply might have API consumers asking for certain APIs and want to make those consumers happy.

One example of this is GraphQL: regardless of what you think about that specific technology, if you work on APIs, you may hear strong preferences for GraphQL from some consumers. Being able to support these "preference clusters" over time is essential, as they will evolve and will drive the way in which your landscape is evolving.

Never assume you have found the one best way to do APIs: whatever you do is contextual with regard to technologies and consumer preferences, and it will change over time.

Allowing and controlling variety is a long-term activity. Allowing it should be built into the landscape from the very beginning. Constraining it by encouraging principles, protocols, and patterns is a balance of understanding how APIs are being used and how much value they deliver and making choices to maximize that value. With increasing maturity of the API landscape (see Chapter 10), it should be possible to gain better insights into the status, evolutionary path, and usage of the landscape. Variety can then be controlled by balancing the cost of increased variety (which reduces coherence across the full landscape) and more specifically designed APIs (which improves API value for a subset of the APIs in the landscape).

Vocabulary

Every API is a language, as discussed in "API Landscapes as Language Landscapes" on page 232. It defines how developers can interact with a service, and it defines these interactions through interaction patterns, underlying protocols, and exchanged representations. Standardizing on API building blocks through shared vocabularies is a powerful way to increase coherence across the API landscape.

For some aspects of that language, it might not be necessary to reinvent the wheel every single time. A simple example is the issue of error messages. Many HTTP-based REST APIs define their own error messages because they want to expose error messages beyond just using the standardized HTTP status codes. It is possible to define such a format individually, but the "problem details" format of RFC 7807 (*https://oreil.ly/xhg98*) defines a standard representation for this (as long as the API is using JSON or XML). Reusing this "problem report vocabulary" has two advantages.

Teams *developing* APIs do not need to invent, define, and document a new vocabulary for error messages. They can simply adapt the existing vocabulary and possibly extend it to expose specific aspects of their error messages.

Teams *consuming* APIs do not need to learn a proprietary format and instead will understand that part of the "API language" after they have encountered that particular vocabulary for the first time. This makes it easier for developers to understand aspects of an API that are used in other APIs as well.

The following example is taken from RFC 7807 and shows how such a format can combine standardized and proprietary vocabularies. In this example, the type, title, detail, and instance members are defined by RFC 7807, while the balance and accounts properties are proprietary members defined by a specific API. It is perfectly possible that in an API landscape you might always use RFC 7807 problem reports, but the set of properties is actually evolving over time, as APIs are exposing specific problem details:

```
{
    "type": "https://example.com/probs/out-of-credit",
    "title": "You do not have enough credit.",
    "detail": "Your current balance is 30, but that costs 50.",
    "instance": "/account/12345/msgs/abc",
    "balance": 30,
    "accounts": ["/account/12345",
                 "/account/67890"]
}
```

In many cases, this kind of vocabulary reuse can be achieved by using standards. Whether these standards are formal standards on the internet/web level or informal/internal standards of an API landscape does not matter all that much. The important thing is to avoid reinventing the wheel as much as possible.

In fact, having the ability to treat formal standards and informal standards in the same way is essential to being able to decide when, for some aspect of the API language, switching to a standard makes sense.

EIMs and APIs: Perfection Versus Pragmatism

While using official standards is a rather straightforward way of avoiding reinventing vocabularies, in some cases organizations go beyond this. The most extreme case is the idea of an *enterprise information model* (EIM), where the goal is to have a complete and coherent model of *everything* that has to be represented in an organization. In many cases (and often in larger organizations), the ideal of the EIM has proven to be elusive: the effort of documenting the complete vocabulary of a complex organization is substantial, and by the time the exercise is completed, reality and systems have already changed, turning the EIM into a snapshot of the past.

As the organization evolves, so should the EIM, but it is hard to keep both in sync. For example, an organization might have a certain model of a customer and information related to them. That information very likely evolves all the time, and different products will extend/enhance the customer model in ways that work for them. Trying to make sure that these extensions and enhancements are always done in a coherent and coordinated way is likely to slow down service design and delivery. In practice, this means that the choice often is between having an EIM that reflects a static model of the organization, or increasing the organization's ability to change when needed but giving up on the ideal of a perfectly designed and harmonized model of everything.

A more realistic approach is to assume that the EIM effectively *is* the union of all capabilities that are accessible through APIs. With this way of thinking, it is still up to the API landscape management to decide how much vocabulary standardization makes sense. For some clear cross-domain concerns (such as the error messages mentioned previously), deciding on a standard vocabulary might be an easy decision to make.

For more domain-specific concepts, the API will expose those concepts in its design, and this design then is the EIM of that domain. The downside of this approach is that this does not produce the one highly aligned and uniform model of everything that EIMs often strive to be. The upside of this approach is that the "domain model" now is directly actionable (through the API), and by the very definition of this approach, what is not exposed and/or actionable in the API is not part of the EIM.

Vocabulary management at scale succeeds best if the main focus is on making vocabularies findable and reusable, instead of creating the one true model of a concept. If vocabularies can be easily found and reused, developers are interested in reusing them as long as they fit their purpose, because then they do not have to design their own.

How to *define* vocabularies is a tricky subject. Without getting into the weeds of UML and XML and how to define and document and compose vocabularies, it is important to keep in mind that one important goal of APIs is to *not* expose implementation models but instead create an *interface* for them, which often will be different from the internal model of a service or a domain (as described in Chapter 3, one strategy is to *start* with that interface model without even considering its implementation initially).

Vocabularies can be managed in a variety of ways, each of them having different advantages and limitations:

- When used for *complete representations of API interactions*, vocabularies become complete models of the meaning and the serialization of domain concepts. Typical examples for this might be XML or JSON schemas. How these vocabularies are *identified* also differs: in some cases, and for web-based APIs, people use media types, but in other cases people might use identifiers for schemas and then associate those identifiers either implicitly or explicitly with an API representation.

- Vocabularies sometimes also are used as *building blocks within representations*, allowing an API to support representations where certain parts of it follow that specific vocabulary. XML has a rather sophisticated mechanism for this with XML namespaces, whereas JSON has no formal way of identifying that a part of a JSON representation uses a standardized vocabulary. We looked at the example of RFC 7807, which has a vocabulary of built-in properties but also allows APIs to add their own properties to the problem detail format.

- Vocabularies may also be essentially *shared data types*, in which case there often is a pattern of defining and supporting an evolving set of values for the data type through a *registry*. Registries allow a community to share an evolving set of well-known values for certain data types, and they are a widely used pattern for fundamental technologies of the internet and the web. One example is hypermedia link relations: there is a registry for link relations that makes it possible for developers to find out about existing relations, or to add new ones if necessary.

Picking the right way to establish and manage vocabularies is important and is a key determinant of how easy it is for API teams to (partly) assemble their APIs from existing building blocks, instead of always starting from scratch. But establishing vocabularies makes sense only if there is a clear model for how they can be easily found and reused. Tooling is an excellent way to use vocabularies so that designers have a well-defined set of choices. When designing resource-oriented APIs, for example, HTTP has a set of concepts that are open and evolving vocabularies.

As shown in Figure 9-2, HTTP has quite a few vocabularies associated with it (the figure is a screenshot of *Web Concepts*, an open repository that makes standardized and popular values for these vocabularies available). An API landscape would probably not encourage HTTP API designers to use all of the approximately 200 existing HTTP header fields, but API design and implementation tooling could be based on a *subset* of these values, thereby establishing the shared practice of which HTTP header fields to consider within the organization.

Figure 9-2. Web Concepts: HTTP vocabularies

The HTTP vocabularies are an example of a rather technical focus, where it is important to share a set of practices for how to use a certain technology. On a more domain-specific note, the very same principles can apply to domain concepts such as customer types. For example, a company may have an existing vocabulary of five different customer types, which might grow over time to cover additional customer types. Managing this domain vocabulary in a registry is a good way to ensure that the set of shared values is accessible to developers and tooling and can evolve over time.

Another possible way to effectively manage vocabularies is to use industry standards. While industry standards may not always be a perfect or complete fit for an API, they may still be useful as a building block. As a simple example, think of something like how to represent country or language information (there are ISO standards for this). There also are more complex (and often more verticalized) standards such as Fast Healthcare Interoperability Resources (FHIR) for the interoperability for electronic health records.

Volume

Once an organization gets serious about its digital transformation strategy, the *volume* of services that exist (or get exposed through APIs) can grow quickly. One reason for this is that as more and more of the organization gets reflected through digital shadows, its "digital footprint," and thus naturally the number of its APIs, increases. It can easily reach into the hundreds or even thousands, for organizations beyond a certain size and with some history of developing APIs. API landscapes must be able to deal with this scale easily so that it becomes primarily a business decision of how big the API landscape is going to be.

A second reason is that with the API-as-a-product strategy (Chapter 3), anything and everything that is done in the organization is conceived with an API-first mindset, because only then can it become part of the network effect of the increasing API-enablement of the organization. This might very well mean that quite a number of these API-as-a-product initiatives don't make it very far, because not only should APIs enable the organization to combine services more easily and more quickly, but they also should help the organization to do this more economically so that products can be built and evaluated (and possibly discontinued) quickly.

When it comes to the volume of APIs in an API landscape, there often is a difference in preference. Sometimes the approach is to keep the volume down as much as possible (which can be a very relative term in complex organizations) and to attempt to have a carefully curated landscape of APIs. In other cases, the focus is more on making it easy to handle volume, and to gain and provide insights into an API landscape, so that volume is mostly a management problem and can be handled by improvements over time, if required.

Either way, it often is natural that volume goes up over time, as the API landscape matures and new services enter the landscape. This means that it is equally natural that with growing maturity, handling volume becomes something that is based on policy and not on fundamental problems of having to deal with a growing volume of APIs.

Velocity

One important value proposition of digital transformation is that it becomes faster to design, release, test, and change products, and that is because the organization's increasing maturity in managing individual APIs and the API landscape allows it to move faster than it could without those skills. This also means that the organization becomes a network of individual but interdependent services: instead of many building blocks being stable for a long time and new ones being added relatively slowly, things can change more quickly and be added faster.

While this added *speed* is one of the key differentiating aspects that organizations are able to benefit from, at the same time it becomes important that this can be done *safely*. If not, the increased speed comes at the unacceptable cost of threatening the robustness of operations.

For many organizations, velocity is one of the key motivations to start digital transformation initiatives: with markets changing faster and the competition becoming faster, it is essential for organizations to be able to act or at least react quickly. Any factors that slow down time it takes for ideas to be turned into products, or hinder the management of the constantly growing and evolving product portfolio, also harm the organization's competitiveness.

In API landscapes, velocity is accomplished to a large degree by giving teams more freedom to design and develop according to their preferences and choices and schedules. The goal is to minimize all parts of the process that potentially slow down API delivery. As mentioned earlier, one key lesson from earlier IT approaches is that *decoupling delivery* (i.e., the ability to change and deploy individual components independently of others) is essential to decreasing delivery time.[6] But allowing individual capabilities to be added and changed and delivered independently also means that traditional practices of testing and operations have to be changed.

As discussed in "The Platform Principle" on page 228, one of the common approaches to avoid coupling and the resulting loss in velocity is to move away from integration. Using a platform as described means giving up on the idea of integration and embracing the idea of decentralization. The benefit of this is that the loose coupling allows higher velocity of individual parts because there is less coordination effort for making changes. The cost of this approach is that delivery and operations need to adjust to this new landscape and make sure that the overall ecosystem meets the standard of robustness that the organization needs.

Taken to the extreme, looking at the web once again is an interesting exercise. The web changes fast because new services can be deployed, existing ones can be changed, and users might or might not be affected by these changes. At some level, one could argue that the web never "works": something is always broken, with a service not being available or a user being affected by a service change. But the resulting velocity of the overall system more than makes up for this inherent brittleness, and by managing change well and using appropriate methods for deployment and testing, it is possible to find a good balance of velocity and value in such a system.

---

6 Earlier, we contrasted this with SOAP, which focused on APIs only, without providing any guidance on how to manage the growing and changing landscape of SOAP services.

Vulnerability

Only organizations that have no IT are not (directly) vulnerable to IT-based attacks. But with the trend toward more IT, more alignment between business and IT, and the opening up of IT capabilities through APIs, many vulnerabilities are created, and these have to be managed. API landscapes must make sure that the risks of a bigger attack surface are more than compensated by the rewards of increased agility and speed.

One of the value propositions of the *API economy* is that businesses can react and restructure quicker when they use APIs internally, and when they also can outsource capabilities via APIs. But of course there is a flip side to this, because it creates dependencies. For example, in June 2018, Twitter acquired anti-abuse technology provider Smyte. Many companies used Smyte's services via its APIs, which offered tools to stop online abuse, harassment, and spam. These companies even had contracts with Smyte. Directly after the acquisition, and without warning, Twitter closed down Smyte's APIs, creating problems for companies relying on these APIs.

The lesson of this and similar cases is to always treat *external dependencies* as brittle, to always build resilience into services to handle potential service interruptions responsibly, and to make this a fundamental development practice. One can even go one step further and make this a rule for *any* dependency, not just the external ones—because as velocity increases, the likelihood increases that there may be problems with runtime dependencies, and any nonresilient use of a service is a predictable potential problem.

Implementing resilience often is not trivial; in some situations dependencies may be critical, and not much can be done to compensate for them not being available. But even then it is important to handle the situation responsibly: instead of crashing or hanging or going into undefined operational states, services should clearly report the situation so that it can be analyzed and fixed.

Another aspect apart from the technical vulnerability is the fact that more and more services are made available and thus have APIs as attack surfaces. This can be a problem when it comes to malicious attempts to gain access to systems or simply disrupt operations. It can also be a problem when APIs expose information or capabilities that for legal, regulatory, or competitive reasons should not have been made available. This can have a major impact on how organizations are perceived and thus needs as much attention as the more directly malicious threats.

In summary, vulnerability needs to be addressed by handling APIs safely and securely. Safety means to treat all dependencies as brittle and to never depend on the availability or specific behavior of an API. Security means to always make sure that malicious players cannot gain access to or disrupt the operations of APIs in the landscape.

Visibility

Visibility and scale are almost natural enemies. If there are few things and everybody designing and developing and using and managing them is in a relatively small team, then most things are visible, or at least can be discovered using the simple discovery process of asking the people around you. They will quickly guide you to find what you are looking for. They also can explain how that thing works. If you need an overview across all of the things, you can manually inspect them to gain insights. None of these assumptions is true anymore for larger API landscapes.

In large and decentralized settings, visibility is a much harder goal to accomplish. However, direct "line of sight" is not a natural requirement for establishing visibility. Typical patterns for large-scale visibility in real life as well as in IT systems often combine two aspects (and we'll look again at the web to explain that in terms of the biggest visibility scenario there currently is).

Publishing things needs to be done in such a way that they are *discoverable*. In terms of the web, being discoverable means having a working web server and publishing HTML that can be used to crawl and index content. There are mechanisms such as *Sitemaps* and *Schema.org* to improve discoverability, but all these improvements were invented quite a while after the search engines started operating.

Searching things often is a much more contextual task than just discovering them. Search often revolves around the context of the search and how "useful" and "less useful" search results are delivered. Google revolutionized the web with its PageRank algorithm (*https://oreil.ly/xnt6Z*), by calculating relevance according to popularity. In many cases, search is treated as an extra service after the initial task of discovering and collecting information (an activity that is called *crawling* on the web).

As discussed in "API the APIs" on page 233, the prerequisite for API visibility and use in the landscape is to expose information *about* APIs *through* the APIs. That was the core of what made the web work: Everything *about* a web page is *in* the web page, and there is a uniform way to access all web pages. The visibility aspect therefore means keeping track of "how" users could be aided by making APIs more visible; thinking about whether that is a problem of discoverability (can the APIs even be located?), representation (is the necessary information accessible through the API?), or search (are there search services using the exposed information?); and tweaking those factors of the landscape that are needed to improve visibility.

While visibility of APIs is important, it is equally important to make things visible in APIs. For example, aspects such as the standard "problem details" format discussed in "Vocabulary" on page 238 help visibility inside APIs, because now it is possible to use tooling that understands problem details across APIs. Actually, there is a tight relationship between vocabularies and visibility: the more vocabularies are shared across APIs, the easier it becomes to leverage this shared aspect of these APIs. The

"API the APIs" model discussed earlier therefore is one that benefits a lot from visibility through shared vocabularies: if you want to say something about your API, say it through your API, and ideally say it in ways that are shared across APIs.

Versioning

One of the challenges when moving from integration to decentralization is that changes also happen in a more decentralized way. That is good because it allows the velocity that often is one of the important benefits that API landscapes provide. But in order to handle changes in the API landscape in a reasonable way, *versioning* cannot be handled in the same way as in integrated systems anymore.

One important consideration is to *avoid versioning* as long as possible, or at least to avoid it in the sense in which the term is often used: to describe how different versions are released and then must be used differently by consumers. We can once again look to the web for examples: few sites release "new versions" where users have to relearn the way the site works. Instead, the goal is to improve sites in ways that can be picked up by existing users if they want to use new features, without disrupting established workflows that users rely on to use the site.

The general goal for versioning in API landscapes should be similar to that of websites: avoid breaking existing consumers, and design all APIs for extensibility from the very start so that there is loose coupling between the "version" that users expect and the "version" that the service provides.[7]

In such a model, "hard versioning" of the API does not really happen: changes are treated as *an improved/extended version of the API* that consumers do not need to learn about unless they want to use the new capabilities. Incompatible changes break the API; a new one has to be released, and consumers must migrate from the old to the new one. In that case, it is a *new API*, and not a new version of the old API.

So, one might say that versions of the API are not relevant. But the API does evolve over time, and it is useful to be able to talk about the "snapshot" of an API's capabilities at some point in time and possibly also to learn what has changed since then. Because of this, version numbers still are a useful concept because they help to identify the evolving capabilities of an API and navigate its history.

---

7 One way to follow patterns for robust extensibility (*https://oreil.ly/HTk61*) is to use meaningful core semantics, have a well-defined extensibility model, and have a well-defined processing model of interactions with APIs and possible extensions work.

Semantic versioning

Semantic versioning (*https://semver.org*) is a simple versioning scheme that is based on using version numbers in a structured and meaningful way. Semantic version numbers are structured according to a `MAJOR.MINOR.PATCH` pattern. These parts are numeric and have the following meaning:

- `PATCH` versions are bug fixes, not affecting any specified interfaces and instead correcting incorrect behavior or making any other changes that affect only the implementation.

- `MINOR` versions are compatible changes to the interface, meaning that clients can continue using it as is without the need to adjust to changes in the interface. This minimizes the efforts clients have to spend adjusting to new versions: They only have to change when a new minor version is released when they want to take advantage of new functionality that has been released with that version.

- `MAJOR` versions are breaking changes that require clients to update their use of the API; they cannot expect to smoothly transition across major version changes.

When using semantic versioning for API products, version numbers effectively become part of the documentation, because they imply information on what has changed between versions. Usually, it is good practice to also document what exactly has changed, but semantic versioning provides a good starting point for clients to decide whether they want to investigate API updates, or not necessarily.

Volatility

As already discussed for the *velocity* and *versioning* aspects, the dynamics of API landscapes are different from integration approaches, and thus services must keep those dynamics in mind. *Volatility* is a fact of life in large decentralized systems: services can change (avoiding breaking changes can help a lot), services can stop working (decentralized deployment and operations mean a less centralized model of availability), and services can disappear (services do not live forever). Responsible development practices in an API landscape keep those considerations in mind for all dependencies.

Volatility can be seen as the result of decentralizing implementation and operations, and accepting that such a move results in a more complex set of failure scenarios than the binary does versus doesn't work of integrated monolithic systems. This is the unavoidable side effect of radically separating components, and there definitely is a cost to dealing with this added complexity (this is one of the aspects of Jeff Bezos's famous "API mandate" and its consequences, as told in "The Bezos Mandate" on page 52).

For developers, the move from "programming as part of a system" to "developing as part of an ecosystem" can be challenging. Traditional assumptions about robustness and availability are not true anymore, and moving to a model where an application is handling every external dependency as a potential failure point takes development discipline.

On the other hand, techniques for graceful degradation are well-known. Once again we can look at the web, where well-designed web apps often do implement graceful degradation in robust ways. This principle applies to runtime dependencies to other services, as well as to runtime dependencies for the execution environment (the browser). Web apps operate in environments that are much harder to control than traditional runtime environments. Because of this, they need to have robustness built in or they will fail to work for too many browsers or too many environments.

Similar development thinking is necessary for applications in API landscapes. The more defensively an application is programmed, the more likely it is to be resilient against variations in the runtime environment. This is the ultimate goal of applications in API landscapes: operating as robustly as possible and not making any assumptions that depend on the availability of other components.

Summary

In this chapter, we have delved deeper into the idea of *API landscapes*. We have looked at how existing integration solutions can be regarded as "proto-APIs," how scaling up the API practice introduces more challenges, and what an API platform should ideally look like.

The most important thing to keep in mind is that for API landscapes to deliver their main value, it is vital to treat them as continuously changing environments, where change is triggered by observations of the practices of individual APIs. The landscape's role is to distill changing practices into principles, protocols, and patterns that help API teams to be more productive.

This chapter also introduced the eight Vs of API landscapes, a set of aspects that are helpful to keep in mind when it comes to considering the specific challenges of an API landscape. Because managing and fostering an API landscape is always an evolutionary and gradual process, we will use these landscape aspects in the following chapter, where we discuss how they can help inform investments in the API landscape and how that translates into increased maturity for all these aspects.

CHAPTER 10

API Landscape Journey

The real problem is that programmers have spent far too much time worrying about effi-ciency in the wrong places and at the wrong times; premature optimization is the root of all evil (or at least most of it) in programming.
　—Donald Knuth

In Chapter 9, we looked at API landscapes in depth, focusing on foundations and key aspects. We will now move on to discuss what it means for API landscapes to become more mature. As we have done so far, we will consider this a journey rather than a destination: an API landscape is never "done," as it will always continue to evolve, following the evolution of business and technology (as discussed in Chapter 7).

Evoking an analogy that we have used previously, this view of API landscapes is similar to the ongoing evolution of the web. The web is never "done" either: new technology developments, new scenarios, and new usage patterns continuously feed its evolution. While this may seem daunting, it is exactly this continuous evolution that is the reason for the web's success over time. Without it, the web would have become irrelevant at some point, and a different approach would have taken over.

In the same way as the web is continuously evolving, API landscapes must contin-uously evolve as well. Landscape architecture itself has to evolve in response to changing needs and evolving principles, protocols, and patterns.

But even the best architect has to deal with limited resources that can be dedicated to changing architecture. Furthermore, API teams can deal only with a maximum rate of change: in the end, as long as the current landscape works well enough as a platform for API products, it may be more economical to reuse the established principles, protocols, and patterns, rather than trying to have the perfect platform for each individual problem.

For this reason, understanding maturity at the landscape level means knowing what to observe in the landscape, and where and how to invest to improve the landscape. We will again use the "eight Vs" that we introduced in "The Eight Vs of API Landscapes" on page 235. This time, however, we will use these areas to consider the risks of not improving them and will point out ways to make improvements. To this end, a number of checkpoints are defined that help you better understand the maturity level in different areas and where to direct investments to get to a more consistent maturity level across various areas.

Before we get to discussing these maturity measures and methods, however, we will first discuss some of the organizational aspects that go along with increasing the awareness and the proactive management of your API landscape.

Structuring Guidance in the API Landscape

Creating and managing guidance is an important part of API landscape management. It communicates to everybody *why* certain things are important, *what* is done to address these issues, and *how* implementations can follow the guidance. The guidance should be managed as a living document that everybody can read, comment on, and contribute to. This way, every developer is part of the community establishing and evolving the document.

A common theme for improving the effectiveness of an API landscape is to strictly separate the "what" from the "how" when it comes to requirements for APIs, to always provide a "why" story explaining the rationale, and to provide tools and support for specific ways that requirements can be satisfied:

"Why" (guidance motivation)
> Describes the rationale behind a requirement or a recommendation, making sure that it is not an opaque rule that has been created with no explanation. Documenting the rationale also makes it easier to determine, when alternative ways are being proposed, whether they are targeting the same rationale.

"What" (design guidance)
> Explains the approach that is taken to address the "why" so that it becomes clear what APIs need to do to address these concerns. This should be done by defining clear requirements for the API itself and not by defining requirements for the implementation. The most important aspect of describing the "what" is to make sure that it does not get mixed with "how" to do something, which is explicitly addressed separately.

"How" (implementation guidance)
> Provides specific ways "how" to address the issue so that the guideline can be implemented. These might use specific tools or technologies, and there can be various "how" approaches associated with a single "what" that they address. Over

time, as teams developing APIs discover or invent new ways to solve problems, new "how" methods may get added to existing "what" approaches, allowing new solutions to get established over time.

Guidelines should help everybody to be an effective team player in the overall API landscape. They are established to help the productivity of API teams and to enable the changing culture and practice of designing and developing APIs to be tracked and managed.

The following is a concrete example of how this works. It uses the common challenge of decommissioning APIs, and specifically how upcoming decommissionings can be communicated to API consumers. The example we are showing has one "why," two "whats," and three "hows":

"Why" (guidance motivation)
Service users can benefit from learning about the upcoming decommissioning of an API. APIs should therefore have a mechanism to announce that they are going out of service.

"What" (design guidance #1)
APIs can use the HTTP Sunset header field to announce their upcoming decommissioning. They should specify which resources will use the header field (a popular choice is the home resource) and when it will appear (a popular choice is that it will appear as soon as there is a planned time for decommissioning). APIs might also specify that the header field will appear at least a certain amount of time before an upcoming decommissioning (giving API users a guaranteed grace period to manage mitigation and/or migration).

"How" (implementation guidance #1 for design guidance #1)
One implementation method is to control the HTTP Sunset header field through configuration. As long as there is no configuration, the header field will not appear in responses. When the upcoming decommissioning is known, the configuration is added, and the header field appears for those resources where the API defines it to be used.

"How" (implementation guidance #2 for design guidance #1)
One implementation method is to add the HTTP Sunset header field through an API gateway. Instead of the API implementation itself adding the header field, it is added by the API gateway as soon as such a policy is configured and enabled. After the policy is configured in the API gateway, the header field appears for those resources where the API defines it to be used.

"What" (design guidance #2)
APIs that have registered consumers may use a channel outside of the API to communicate with them and to announce the upcoming decommissioning. This

guidance applies only when such a consumer list exists and when the associated communications channel is deemed to be sufficiently reliable.

"How" (implementation guidance #1 for design guidance #2)
One implementation method is to use email messages to communicate with all registered users of an API. The email ideally references an available resource (the API change log or part of the API documentation) that contains information about the upcoming decommissioning. That resource should have a stable URI so that it can be referenced throughout conversations with users.

Many organizations where APIs play a role in their strategy have some form of API guidance. Some are even published openly, which allows you to freely browse them; for example, you can see what organizations like Google, Microsoft, Cisco, Red Hat, PayPal, Adidas, or the White House are using as their API guidance.

The API Stylebook

The well-known "API Handyman" Arnaud Lauret has compiled a number of published guidelines in his API Stylebook (*https:// oreil.ly/x4NwM*), sourced from (typically large) organizations as different as Microsoft and the White House. It is an interesting resource to explore in terms of what large organizations have created as their API guidelines.

For these openly available API guidelines, without even looking at the content, the publication channel chosen already tells an interesting story of document creation and management (and the general philosophy behind the guidelines and their management):

- PDF documents have the clear "smell" of a read-only document. The PDF is published from some inaccessible source; it's a way of compiling, formatting, and distributing existing content. There is little feeling of "being involved in the management and evolution of the guidance" in this case.

- HTML often is a bit better because in most cases the published HTML *is* the source, so readers actually look at the source of the document itself, and not at a formatted and detached product, as in the case of a PDF. But still, the management of the HTML source is not necessarily obvious, so there still is the feeling of detachment from the creation and editing stages.

- Many version control systems have some form of publishing feature and thus can be used to host and publish guidance content. For example, GitHub has simple built-in ways of formatting and publishing content (as Markdown files, in the simplest case), though it's likely you'll find that some essential formatting capability is missing.[1] GitHub has easily usable features for commenting, raising issues, and suggesting changes. In addition, these functions are not something most developers have to learn, because many are already used to GitHub and feel comfortable using it. Guidance published in the same way as code makes it easy for others to contribute to it.

There is an additional rule that guidance can follow: there can only be guidance that is testable (i.e., where there is tooling in place that helps developers to determine whether they have successfully addressed some guidance). This not only makes guidance more explicit and following it more objective, but also means that guidance can be tested for in an automated way. While it may not be worth the investment (or even be possible) to test all guidance in a fully automated way, this should be at least seen as an ideal, and therefore we suggest that the more typical "why/what/how" pattern described previously be extended with a fourth element:

"When" (guidance testing)
> "When" describes for everything that needs to be done *when* it can be said that it has been done. This means that there is a way to test for it being done properly, and there potentially is an automated test in the deployment pipeline that will run this test and make sure that guidance is being followed as intended.

As with everything in a well-managed API landscape, tests can be improved over time. They may start with simple plausibility tests to give a minimum assurance and positive feedback that guidance has been addressed. If over time it is seen that this feedback is not as helpful as it should be, then the tests might get improved to provide teams with better feedback and thus make it easier for them to validate their compliance with certain guidance.

The Lifecycle of Guidance

Since guidance is an evolving set of recommendations, it too has a lifecycle: things get proposed and maybe explored for a while, and they might become recommendations for what to do or how to do it. But like everything in a landscape, they will eventually get replaced with newer and different ways of doing things, so these recommendations will go through a sunset phase and eventually become historical. The lifecycle stages of guidance can therefore be defined as follows:

Experimental
> This is the phase where guidance is being explored, meaning that it is used in at least one API product. This is used to better understand whether it makes sense

---

1 Markdown content will render directly in the web view of the repository. More ambitious writers/publishers can use GitHub's *Pages*, which is a way to generate a website directly from a repository.

as landscape-level guidance. At this point, the guidance is documented, but there is no investment to make it easier for teams to follow the guidance.

Implementation

When guidance is established at the landscape level, it should be supported (there is at least one "how"), and it might become something teams have to at least consider before opting out. For some guidance, there may be no opting out, and therefore teams have to follow it.

Deprecation

Once newer/better ways of doing something are known, guidance may enter the deprecation period, where it is still possible to follow it, but where teams ideally should consider following guidance that is in the implementation stage.

Historical

Eventually, guidance is retired, and it should not be used in new products anymore. Refactoring existing products to migrate to a more modern way of doing things may even be considered. Historical guidance is still useful to keep around for historical reasons and to document the way in which older APIs were designed and implemented.

These stages are just one way of managing how guidance may evolve, and you should feel free to define your own. In addition, there might be ways of marking guidance with different compliance levels, such as marking it as "optional" or "required." Complementing such compliance levels, there also might be a process for granting exceptions so that, for example, required guidance can be skipped when there is sufficient evidence that following it would create problems.

The important takeaway for the guidance lifecycle is to accept that guidance will be continuously evolving, so you need to have a way to track this evolution, and a way of managing it in your organization. This is what we discuss in the next section, which introduces a popular way that large organizations tackle the challenge of guidance management.

The Center for Enablement

There are various names that organizations use for teams that manage API guidance and usually also have the role of driving the API program. One popular name is *Center of Excellence* (CoE), but to many, this has negative connotations in the sense that anybody outside seems to lack excellence. For this reason, a name we like better is *Center for Enablement* (C4E), which nicely reflects the changing role of today's IT teams.

Managing guidance may seem like a technical detail, but in practice it can make a significant difference. The role of the C4E mostly should be that of a collector and editor, with the individual API teams being the main contributors, or at least drivers, of the content that goes into the guidance. The C4E is also responsible for identifying aspects of the guidance that warrant an investment in terms of supporting infrastructure so that something that was initially a problem that had to be solved by individual teams can now be solved by available tooling.

Another part of the C4E's role is to ensure that following API guidance does not create any bottlenecks. The ideal picture is that teams know the guidance, know how to follow updates, and have enough internal skills and support from the C4E through tooling that complying with the API guidance does not slow them down. Any bottlenecks should be identified and resolved so that the "API" part of developing "API products" can be implemented with as little friction as possible.

Of course, this all depends on the constraints of the organization. For example, in some areas, there are regulations or legislation in place requiring organizations to review and sign off on releases. In this case, these processes have to be followed and cannot be fully automated through tooling. But these cases are typically the exception rather than the rule, so most guidance really should be seen as something that *should* be followed, and the C4E's main role is to enable the API teams to effectively and successfully follow it.

Engineering the Engineers: Chaos Monkey

Another interesting role of the C4E is to determine ways in which nonfunctional requirements can be transferred into the general design and development culture of the organization. An example is that of Netflix's popular Chaos Monkey tool. The story behind it is that as a general developer practice, in an environment like Netflix's complex and interdependent API landscape, services should be maximally resilient so that problems with individual services affect as few dependent services as possible.

One problem with "resilient code" as a requirement is that it is hard to test. Netflix's solution is the ingenious Chaos Monkey, a tool that simulates isolated and controlled failures in the infrastructure and observes the behavior of services in the light of these outages. This allows engineers to observe the resilience of services in a controlled way. This is an example of an approach that we call *engineering the engineers*: by building tooling that will identify nonresilient code, the landscape managers ensure that engineers are more disciplined when it comes to making their code more resilient. If they fail, there is testing in place that will reveal problems before they become critical, meaning that developers have this additional "testing in production" safeguard that makes sure that code behaves in a resilient way.

This approach makes it easier for the C4E to scale the API landscape to more APIs being designed and deployed. It also makes it easier for individual teams to understand what the requirements are and gives them (at least partially) automated ways to test for them. Some review and discussion might still be required for some of the guidance, but the easier it becomes to focus on those aspects that cannot be automatically tested, the better the C4E can scale.

In summary, the role of the C4E is to be the steward of guidance at the landscape level. The goal is twofold: to make it as easy as possible for API teams to *create new products* and to make it as easy as possible for API consumers to *use APIs across the landscape*. Because the C4E has this role of managing the balance between ease of production and ease of consumption, its most important tasks are to constantly gather feedback from producers and consumers and to figure out a way to continuously evolve the API landscape to best serve both groups.

This constant evolution of the API landscape means that it has to be aware of the landscape aspects introduced in "The Eight Vs of API Landscapes" on page 235. It also means the C4E has to decide when to invest in which aspects, by observing for which of the Vs it is acceptable to not provide sophisticated support and where an investment makes sense. For example, for the *volume* aspect, it might be acceptable that for a little while, not much effort is invested in scaling to hundreds or thousands of APIs, but once more and more teams are building and using APIs, handling the volume in a scalable way becomes critical and requires investment.

The main idea of the C4E is that it helps API product teams to be more effective contributors to the API landscape. We discussed API product teams in Chapter 8. Complementing this discussion, in the next section, we talk about C4E teams and how managing APIs and the API landscape translates into putting together a team that supports individual API product teams in the best way.

C4E Team and Context

One role of the C4E is to be the steward of landscape guidance, and to support teams to follow that guidance. By interacting with API product teams, the C4E gathers feedback on which new patterns may be emerging and can learn about how principles, protocols, and patterns may have to evolve to improve the API landscape.

To do this, the C4E needs to evolve along with the landscape. Initially, it is likely that it will not even be a physical team with dedicated members but instead that different API product team members (as discussed in Chapter 8) will take on the roles described here. Over time, however, it is likely that in large organizations, the C4E will develop into an actual team with its own staff. Even then, it is important to always keep in mind that its primary responsibility is to support product teams in their delivery. As Kevin Hickey puts it:[2]

> Instead of a centralized [Enterprise Architecture] group making decisions for the development teams, you are now an influencer and aggregator of information. Your role is no longer to make choices, but to help others make the right choice and then radiate that information.

The team roles we identified in "API Roles" on page 196 are also relevant for the C4E in many cases, or at least provide relevant input to the activities happening on the landscape level. But some roles are added at the landscape level that typically do not exist at the team level.

One example are roles related to compliance. In many organizations, there are dedicated roles for making sure that the organization complies with regulations and legislation, tracking changing compliance needs, and ensuring that the organization adjusts accordingly. For the API landscape, this often translates to existing guidance that is mandatory to follow (as discussed earlier in this section). To avoid this becoming a bottleneck, compliance ideally should be something API teams can test for so that it can become part of the delivery pipeline. In practice, this often may not be entirely possible and may not even be allowed (somebody may have to sign off after performing a review). Whatever the organization's exact needs are, the important thing is to think about compliance from the API perspective, identify areas where compliance needs to be turned into guidance, and support API teams so that it becomes as easy as possible for them to create products in a compliant way.

Another role that typically is unique to the landscape level is that of providing infrastructure and tooling. As introduced in "Structuring Guidance in the API Landscape" on page 250, typical guidance in an API landscape is structured into "why," "what," and "how." Our recommendation is that every "why" (guidance motivation) should have at least one "what" (design guidance) and one "how" (implementation guidance), as well as possible testing infrastructure and tooling for helping teams to more easily verify their alignment with existing guidance. For each "how/test," the role at the landscape level is to enable teams to address and verify that guidance as effectively as possible. This may mean providing tooling and/or infrastructure to address and verify that guidance. Creating and maintaining this tooling/infrastructure then becomes an important role at the landscape level. The better assistance and tooling work there is at the landscape level, the more teams can focus on addressing their business and product needs, instead of having to focus on fitting into the landscape. Any friction experienced by product teams should be treated as an important signal that something needs to be addressed with better assistance and tooling.

---

2 Kevin Hickey, "The Role of an Enterprise Architect in a Lean Enterprise," November 30, 2015, *https://oreil.ly/OYmKt*.

One example of such tooling is *API linting*, which is the process of checking API descriptions (such as OpenAPI or AsyncAPI) against rules that formalize certain requirements. To make it easier for API designers to follow design guidance, the C4E can provide linting tools or services that allow for automated testing. This tooling can be integrated into CI/CD pipelines, further reducing the effort required by development teams to follow the available guidance.

In the end, the C4E team plays a critical role as supporters and enablers for API product teams. They make those teams aware of the decisions that are necessary by providing guidance about relevant decision-making points, and help them by providing infrastructure and tools that enable common API tasks to be solved effectively so that most of the API product teams' energy can be spent focusing on solving business problems. In other words, the C4E team is responsible for ensuring each API product team can move its API through its maturity journey effectively, making the right decisions along the way, and that this effectiveness can be scaled up to many APIs.

Maturity and the Eight Vs

The eight Vs of API landscapes introduced in Chapter 9 are important areas of consideration when it comes to planning API landscapes and their evolution. They can also serve as guidelines when it comes to determining the maturity level in these areas, reflecting on the motivations and advantages of improving maturity, and deciding on possible investments in these areas.

It is important to understand that investment in these areas should be evolutionary and should be driven by the concrete needs of an API landscape. If architected well, these investments can be done as needed and incrementally and will not require a rearchitecting of the API landscape. This means that the maturity of an evolving API landscape itself is ever-evolving, driving improvements as needed, and the landscape is continuously improved based on feedback from developers and users.

Like any evolution, this continuous improvement is not a process leading to some finite or even predictable goal. A landscape's value is determined by how well it supports the products being developed in it and how well those products serve consumer needs. Both development practices and consumer needs change over time, making it inescapable that continuous improvement is a permanent process.

The main goal of landscape architecture is to make this process as simple as possible, by allowing the landscape to adapt to the changing needs of producers and consumers. Landscape maturity can be measured by how much support the landscape can provide. For the eight Vs that we have identified, it is possible to individually look at how maturity can be framed for them and what a strategy to manage maturity for each of them can look like.

This idea of a "maturing landscape" is a little different from the maturity cycle of API products discussed in Chapter 7. Products come and go, and do so in a journey through their own lifecycle, which has a start and an end. The landscape is there to support products and should do so by continuously evolving. There is no single linear path and no end state. Therefore, there are no stages, and we have addressed this by investigating how the eight Vs we identified can serve as guiding principles for continuously improving the landscape, developing your landscape strategy, and deciding what investments to make at the landscape level at different times.

Variety

As described in "Variety" on page 236, the variety of a landscape depends on how many constraints are put in place when teams want to design and implement APIs, and how much freedom teams have when it comes to designing API products that they consider good solutions.

Variety is a tricky thing to deal with because variety in ecosystems is always a balancing act between promoting some level of coherence and reuse, while at the same time not overly constraining teams and forcing them to use solutions that are a bad fit for their problems. For this reason, variety has two "bad extremes" in its spectrum.

No variety implies that a chosen pattern becomes the proverbial "Maslow's hammer" (*https://oreil.ly/QKFSK*) for everything, being the only way a problem can be solved[3] (which often ends up being a bad fit for at least some of the problems).

Too much variety results in "precious snowflakes," where diversity means that teams invest effort in solving problems for which adequate solutions already exist. As a result, users have an unnecessarily hard time understanding APIs because there is no coherent "look and feel."

This balancing act is not easy, and there is no "one true solution" for how to pick a spot on the spectrum between Maslow's hammer and precious snowflakes. It is therefore not appropriate to define maturity for variety in terms of how much variety an API landscape exhibits. In many cases, it may actually be the case that the variety is accidental, resulting from either inflexibility in allowing diversity (resulting in low variety) or inability to promote and manage coherence (resulting in high variety).

---

3 The famous quote by American psychologist Abraham Maslow is "I suppose it is tempting, if the only tool you have is a hammer, to treat everything as if it were a nail."

Variety Maturity

What does it mean to manage variety with a high degree of maturity?

- *Maturity for variety* means that variety is consciously managed in an API landscape. The currently used choices and the reasoning behind them are clearly documented.

- Those choices should evolve as needed: variety is managed and driven by a balance between promoting reuse and allowing new solutions if existing ones are inadequate.

- Increasing variety can be done without disrupting the landscape. It is possible that some tooling and support in the landscape will need to be adjusted, but all tooling and support infrastructure must be designed so that increasing variety can be done incrementally and is part of the underlying architecture.

Variety exists for many different concepts in an API landscape, depending on how the landscape is organized. For example, for landscapes that are HTTP-based and use resource-style APIs, one variety factor may be the choice of serializations. While most of those API landscapes nowadays will probably use and allow APIs to support XML and JSON, those are simply the most popular choices of today and the recent past.

It may very well happen that new serializations appear or are considered by API designers. The question should be whether the new format is considered to be a potentially valuable addition to the landscape. It should be possible to start with a few APIs and see how they do with the new option. These APIs may not be able to benefit from existing tooling and support, as long as the new format's use is *experimental* (there is no investment at the landscape level at this stage).

Once a new variation is considered *productive*, it may trigger updates in available tooling and support. Mature landscapes can handle these updates as incremental changes that are added as needed, meaning that adding variety is purely a function of assessing the utility of the added variation and the incremental cost of tooling and support updates.

The most important consequence of this view is that *all* tooling and support should be capable of these kinds of updates. Any tooling and support not capable of handling increased variety creates limitations that are not driven by the value that variety can bring to the API landscape. Instead, tooling and support then *prevents value from being added* and therefore is problematic from the API landscape perspective.

One important consequence of a variety strategy is looking at the *API capabilities of tooling and support*. As discussed in "API the APIs" on page 233, when everything is done through APIs, including interactions of tooling and support, then it becomes easier to extend variety. As long as new variations support the same APIs, they still can interact with existing tooling and support infrastructure.

Variety Maturity Strategy

When investing in tooling and support, always consider how these investments translate when variety increases. Try to avoid tooling and support that has no clear evolution path. Tooling and support should be able to adapt to your choice of the most productive level of landscape variety instead of dictating it.

Vocabulary

As discussed in "Vocabulary" on page 238, many APIs use vocabularies that determine certain aspects of the API's model. Vocabularies can come into play in many different ways, and in many cases an API may use a certain vocabulary when it is initially released, but also foresee that this vocabulary may change over time. In that case, the vocabulary becomes part of the API's extension model, and the question then is how this extensibility is designed and managed.

The fact that vocabularies used in an API landscape *do* evolve is a result of the fact that domain models of APIs tend to evolve over time. Vocabulary evolution in the API simply is a reflection of that reality. Vocabularies often evolve by refining the understanding of the problem domain: for example, adding social media handles to a customer model that previously only had basic personal information. The question then is how to deal with data (existing customer records without social media handles) and code (applications without built-in handle support) that came to existence before the customer model evolved. Managing this vocabulary evolution in a disciplined way is what defines the maturity of how vocabularies are handled in an API landscape.

Vocabulary Concepts

"Vocabulary" on page 238 discusses which vocabularies may be used for APIs, such as domain-agnostic concepts (for example, language codes), domain-specific concepts (the domain reflected in the API), and the domain of concepts for API design itself (such as HTTP status codes).

Vocabulary Maturity

The basic starting point from an individual API point of view is for each API to identify potential vocabularies where the API may evolve. This goes hand in hand with identifying extensibility points of the API: if an API team expects a vocabulary to evolve, then it must identify this in the API itself and provide a processing model for API users.

Once vocabulary evolution becomes a natural part of APIs, it becomes important to manage it responsibly. On the one hand, that means responsible versioning on the API side and documenting versions across time. On the other hand, it means helping clients to use APIs in a way that handles evolution correctly. What this means depends largely on how individual APIs decide to implement vocabulary evolution.

It can be left to individual APIs to manage the evolution of their vocabularies. However, an alternative model is that the API landscape supports this approach and allows the vocabularies to evolve independently of the APIs. One typical pattern to do that is through the *use of registries (https://oreil.ly/VhE3a)*, and supporting and managing registries is something that can become part of an API landscape itself.

This last maturity aspect warrants some additional explanation. There are two different ways vocabulary evolution can be "delegated" (i.e., managed outside of the API itself). One is by reference to an external authority that is in charge of managing the vocabulary, and the other is by managing the vocabulary in the API landscape, but in a way that separates APIs from the evolving vocabularies:

External authority
> One typical example for this is the use of language tags (i.e., identifiers for human languages, such as "English" or even possibly "American English"). In most cases, APIs probably should not include a static list of these language tags. Instead, it makes sense to refer to one of the lists managed by the International Organization for Standardization (ISO) in its ISO 639 standard (*https://oreil.ly/a23v2*). Using this pattern, an API can define that a language tag's value space is whatever the ISO decides are possible language tags at any point in time. ISO guarantees that language tags evolve in nonbreaking ways by never removing or redefining existing tags.

API landscape support
> Not all concepts have external entities and managers (such as the ISO for the list of language tags), but it is possible to use the same pattern for other vocabularies as well. API landscapes can support registries, allowing APIs to decouple the API definition from the evolving value space of vocabularies. Operating such a registry is not an extremely complex task but still should not be the responsibility

of individual API teams.[4] Instead, there should be landscape-level *registry support* in the same way as, for example, the Internet Engineering Task Force (IETF) manages its registries for its specifications in the more than 2,000 registries managed by the Internet Assigned Numbers Authority (IANA).[5]

The role of architecture for managing vocabularies is the same as for other aspects of nurturing a productive and supportive environment for APIs: monitor the needs and practices of existing APIs, and step in with good practices and support when vocabulary evolution seems to become a repeating patterns across APIs.

The initial good practice should be to at least identify potentially evolvable vocabularies in APIs and document them, which can be part of a general extensibility good practice. If there are repeating occurrences of APIs evolving simply as an unintended consequence of vocabulary evolution, then this may indicate that API landscape support for vocabulary evolution could help reduce the need for API updates.

Maturity for the vocabulary aspect might be harder to achieve, because it is not trivial to come up with ideas of how vocabulary use in APIs can be made observable. This may be one of the cases where some up-front investment may help to improve observability. For example, by creating tooling to document vocabularies, it may become easier to observe their use and evolution across APIs. But that's assuming that API teams find such documentation support useful enough to use it, which in turn might require better observing how teams typically document their APIs. As can be seen, the maturity journey often is not just a question of landscape-level support and tooling: it may start with understanding what should be observed and then devising methods for observation.

Vocabulary Maturity Strategy

Promote good practices that decouple API design from the evolution of vocabularies, if possible. Start by promoting the reuse of externally defined and managed vocabularies, such as those defined and managed by standards-defining organizations. Monitor how many API changes may be (mostly) driven by the need to update vocabularies, and consider providing support for managing vocabularies in the API landscape independent of specific APIs by setting up the infrastructure for it.

---

4 After all, one of the main motivations of a registry is to *decouple* the management of a list of well-known values from places where they are used.

5 The IETF's IANA registry model is a very good one to illustrate how simple and yet effective such an infrastructure can be. It also is a good demonstration of how, by applying this design pattern systematically across its many specifications and API definitions, it was possible to make these specifications more stable, because for many changes only registries need to be updated.

Volume

"Volume" on page 242 suggests that having more APIs can be better than having fewer APIs. This is not necessarily the case, of course, but it hints at the fact that decisions on whether APIs should be allowed into the landscape or not should not be driven by considerations that the API landscape simply cannot handle the volume. More volume isn't necessarily better, but it also shouldn't be automatically considered to be worse.

Instead, the overall goal should be that APIs are always allowed to be created, changed, and withdrawn. The role of the API landscape is to be able to scale to whatever level that is, and the ability to handle the volume should ideally never factor into strategic decisions about landscape size and rate of change.

Managing volume in an API landscape mostly revolves around considerations for economies of scale. Things that may make sense to not support or automate at a smaller scale may be reasonable targets once the landscape starts growing. This is a simple pattern around return on investment (ROI): investing in support or automation makes sense past a certain threshold, when the expenditure to solve problems individually (and over and over again) is higher than the expenditure for support or automation.

Once volume drives support or automation, some coherence may appear in the landscape, since more APIs will start to use these supported mechanisms. This will make them more similar, thus helping landscape users to more easily understand and consume APIs because they approach certain problems in a certain way.

However, as mentioned in "The Center for Enablement" on page 254, one important thing to keep in mind is that support or automation (the "how") should never be the one and only allowed way to do something. It is something that a C4E should identify and provide as part of the general API platform support, but it should always be something that can be replaced with a better way of solving the same problem once a better solution has been found.

As pointed out earlier, the most important aspect of volume maturity is to not let volume get in the way of making decisions about whether and how an API landscape can grow. The best way to do this is to monitor the ongoing evolution of the API landscape, track *what* teams are implementing and *how* they are implementing it, and invest when it seems that support or automation could step in to help teams be more productive.

Volume Maturity

- Monitor how API teams are solving the problems associated with designing, building, and operating their products, and consider investing in support or automation as needed (i.e., when it becomes useful from the ROI point of view).

- For all potential support or automation, consider the value created both for teams producing the API and for consumers of the API. The overall value created by support or automation is the sum of these two values.[6]

- The most important activity from the API landscape point of view is to identify repeated design or implementation activities that teams are doing and to explore possibilities to improve productivity by investing in support or automation.

This approach implies that the API landscape is actively monitored and thus allows these decisions to be data-driven. One good pattern to enable this in a scalable way is to follow the "API the APIs" principle described in the previous chapter, by making sure that APIs themselves expose information *about* themselves. That way, it becomes possible to build support and automation into the monitoring of APIs as a way to decide when to invest in support and automation for the design and development of APIs.

One good way to evaluate maturity for the volume aspect is to reflect on what information about the API landscape is readily available to those assessing the landscape. Keep in mind that this information can be collected in any way, as long as it is available. It can be made available through the APIs themselves ("API the APIs"), through instrumentation of runtime infrastructure (for example, capturing data from API gateways), or through instrumentation of design-time/development infrastructure (for example, collecting data from shared development/deployment platforms of API products). As long as this information is available, it becomes easier to understand and manage the trajectory of the landscape.

---

6 One could also consider the creation of "technical debt" as something that should be taken into account. We'll skip over this here, but taking a proactive approach of always considering how hard it will be to move away from support or automation is an important landscape management aspect as well.

Volume Maturity Strategy

Handling volume requires a foundation that can be used to observe APIs in a scalable way and thus understand the evolution of the API landscape. Observability should include API information that can be used to make investment decisions based on trends in the API landscape. Managing volume itself can be scaled up to handle larger volumes when the information required to understand the API landscape is part of the APIs themselves. This "API the APIs" approach will evolve over time, changing the set of observable information that is used to understand the ongoing evolution of the API landscape.

Velocity

As discussed in "Velocity" on page 242, *velocity* refers to the fact that API landscapes are likely to change continuously and at a relatively fast pace. On the one hand, this is the result of more and more APIs to be created and used, but on the other hand, it also results from APIs being treated as products, and as a result being observed and changed in response to user feedback and requirements (as described in Chapter 3). Also, in most cases this change happens in uncoordinated ways, since one of the goals of API landscapes is to allow products to evolve individually, instead of having complex coordinated release processes that allow products to evolve only in highly interdependent ways.

Handling velocity in a mature way means that API releases and updates can be done as necessary and that the API landscape is capable of supporting a high rate of change. Maturity along this axis should be able to evolve itself. While initially an API landscape may be small enough so that even relatively high rates of changes still mean a smaller number of API changes, this will change over time. Particularly, the combination of increasing volume (as discussed in "Volume" on page 264) and velocity of API changes means that handling velocity does become increasingly important as an API landscape grows and matures.

Velocity Maturity

- APIs should always be designed for changeability. Depending on the API style, that can mean different things, but asking teams about their extensibility roadmap is a good first step to make it part of the API design culture to see API evolution as a natural part of the API lifecycle.

- Evolving APIs mean a change in practice for API consumers as well: API consumption needs to be resilient enough to handle API evolution so that the evolution of the API and of its consumers are decoupled.

- Increasing the velocity of API changes is possible by making sure that coordination overhead between API implementations is reduced. One way of doing this is by adopting microservices as a pattern of implementing services.

These considerations also make it clear that velocity has an impact on producers and consumers. With growing size and popularity of an API landscape (and hence an increasing number of consumers), handling velocity in a mature way becomes more important. Having to coordinate updates between an API and all consumers becomes increasingly expensive and quickly reaches the point where the coordination cost may cause teams to reconsider product improvements.

As pointed out in "Versioning" on page 246, there can be different strategies for how to deal with changing APIs. They might change transparently, so users are experiencing a changing API and these changes are made clear through the API's semantic versioning number (see "Semantic versioning" on page 247). Another possibility is that the promise of stable versions and velocity then translates to an ongoing stream of new versions being released and made available in parallel. This latter pattern implies that it should be easy for consumers to learn about new versions and find information about them, as discussed in "Visibility" on page 245.

While it is important to enable velocity, it is equally important to manage it. With increased velocity, consumers need to be able to keep up. This can be done in various ways, such as promising stable APIs that will remain operational for a certain period of time,[7] or continuously evolving APIs and thereby removing the need for keeping older versions operational.[8] Whatever pattern the landscape supports, this is an area where individual APIs can benefit from landscape-level support, so establishing practices and supporting them becomes a worthwhile investment.

Velocity Maturity Strategy

Enabling agility (i.e., the ability to change things quickly based on feedback and requirements) is one of the main driving factors of API landscapes. On the one hand, designing for change means designing APIs so that they can be changed quickly and easily by producers. On the other hand, consuming changing APIs means that there must be a consumption model that allows consumers to handle changing services. Anything that makes changing things hard should be carefully identified and

---

7 In this case, convenience is higher on the consumer side, and the producer has to invest in the operational effort of running various API versions concurrently.

8 In this case, convenience is higher on the producer side, and the consumers have to invest in making sure that the ongoing evolution of the API is handled by their applications.

examined. This can be an incremental process where one factor that reduces velocity is identified and improved, and then this process is repeated as needed.

Vulnerability

As discussed in "Vulnerability" on page 244, increasing *vulnerability* is a logical conclusion of a journey toward a bigger API landscape. Having no APIs means having no potential vulnerabilities through APIs, and any API that gets added from there on is a potential vulnerability. Being aware of this simple and inescapable fact is a good first step toward maturity regarding the vulnerability landscape aspect.

Depending on their audience, APIs may just be exposed to internal consumers (private APIs), or they might be exposed to external consumers as well (partner and public APIs). As shown in Figure 10-1, in many cases these two or even three scenarios are secured differently, often even with separate components put in place.

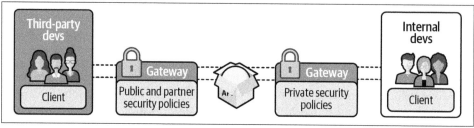

Figure 10-1. Securing APIs with API gateways

From the security point of view, it is understandable that this is implemented in a relatively centralized way, making it possible to observe and manage (and possibly interrupt) traffic to better understand usage and potential problems. On the other hand, this security-driven centralization conflicts with the general decentralization effort, raising the question of how much control individual API products have (and should have) over the control and configuration of the centralized security enforcement point. Balancing speed and safety is a challenge here, but once again it should mostly be driven by organizational and security needs and not by technical constraints of the architecture.

Following the general pattern of how we look at the maturity journey, the same applies to vulnerability: it is important to observe the development of APIs in the API landscape and to distill common themes and areas where landscape support and tooling can help. The only exception to this general rule is that vulnerability is a higher-risk aspect, which means that landscape observation and taking action in a more prescriptive way may be appropriate.

One example of this is the recent developments around personally identifiable information (PII) being exposed through APIs. The growing popularity of APIs means that there is a higher risk of PII being exposed through APIs. Exposing PII is risky for an organization because of potential legal, regulatory, or reputational consequences. These risks may not always be immediately visible to the teams creating API products. In addition, while information being exposed by one API may look sufficiently anonymized to not be considered PII, the increasing availability of complementary information through other APIs means that de-anonymization is becoming a risk that often is better assessed at the landscape level than on the level of individual APIs.

Another issue is the unintended consequences of exposing certain data through APIs. In 2016, the European Union (EU) enacted the general data protection regulation (GDPR). This regulation pertains to processing PII and requires all organizations in the EU to provide information about the PII in their possession and to make it available on request. This means that creating API products that manage PII has far-reaching consequences for an organization. Depending on the size and maturity of the organization, implementing the required processes for GDPR compliance can be complex.

What these examples show is that even though velocity is beneficial in API landscapes and one of the reasons why organizations switch to API strategies in the first place, it still is necessary to manage the risk—and depending on the business sector of the organization and the APIs being developed (and their intended set of consumers), in many cases vulnerability considerations and vulnerability management are necessary for responsible risk management.

Vulnerability Maturity

- APIs by definition expose business capabilities that previously were not (or not as easily) available to consumers. Assessing the risk of every single new API is necessary to avoid scenarios with information leaks or other problems that create organizational risk.

- API products should document all the information they store and the reason for storing it. Information is potentially valuable, but it also can increase risk; managing information should always be treated as something potentially introducing legal, regulatory, or reputational risk.

- Securing APIs is essential to a responsible API strategy and should be treated as an essential component of the organization's overall information security strategy.

When compared to other landscape aspects, vulnerability stands out in the sense that it introduces greater risk than the others, because of the inherent problems of APIs providing access to business capabilities and the potential problems arising from that general perspective.

Apart from the issues of security against malicious attackers or potential legal, regulatory, or reputational risk, there also is the issue of service stability and testing. As the quote goes, with great power comes great responsibility—meaning that when API products have more autonomy in terms of how they are designed, developed, and deployed, this also has the potential of adding new failure scenarios. In his famous "Google Platforms Rant," Steve Yegge says, "Every single one of your peer teams suddenly becomes a potential DOS attacker. Nobody can make any real forward progress until very serious quotas and throttling are put in place in every single service."[9] This quote highlights that robustness and resilience also play a part in the stability of an API landscape and that it does become vulnerable to failure models that are introduced by decentralization and could be handled more easily in centralized scenarios.

One of the biggest challenges for the landscape aspect of vulnerability is to adjust to the new reality of more accessible business capabilities. Since API landscapes have the explicit goal of making these available, this is simply a reality that has to be managed. By assessing and managing the vulnerability of every single API, and making it easy for API products to fit into this architecture, vulnerability management can fit into the new decentralized view of an API-focused IT landscape.

Vulnerability Maturity Strategy

The transition to API landscapes requires a different way of managing vulnerability. The traditional model of inside versus outside has to be replaced by a model that treats all services as individual and potentially externalized components and allows us to apply the same security models to all of them. The landscape must make it easy for services to protect themselves from malicious or problematic behavior. There may be "private/partner/public" services, but switching categories ideally should mean nothing more than applying different security policies.

Visibility

One of the important aspects of *visibility*, as discussed in "Visibility" on page 245, is the *observability* of APIs. It follows the principle described in "API the APIs" on page 233, which states that "everything to be said *about* an API should be said *through* the API." Following this principle, everything necessary becomes visible through the API, making it accessible in the API landscape so that over time, and when needed, additional services can be built on top of this information.

---

9 "Stevey's Google Platforms Rant," GitHub Gist, October 11, 2011, *https://oreil.ly/jxohc*.

As with everything in API landscapes, this is an evolutionary and incremental process. Initially there may not be much information *about* an API that needs to be exposed *through* the API. Over time, however, this view might change as increasing volume and velocity dictate that certain aspects of the API landscape need better support and automation. If this support and automation can be built on top of APIs, it becomes part of the API landscape itself, meaning that it does not need non-API ways to interact with services.

After all, one of the fundamental properties of APIs is to provide encapsulation, meaning that an API should encapsulate *everything* about its implementation, making the API the only interface to interact with. Any path around this, even for "internal" purposes, thus could be considered a violation of the API landscape approach.

If APIs are an organization's chosen approach to make *all* dependencies explicit, well defined, and therefore visible and manageable, then *any* practice creating invisible dependencies undermines this approach. This is the reason why Jeff Bezos's famous "API mandate" (discussed in "The Bezos Mandate" on page 52) has the final message that no practice circumventing the API strategy will be tolerated: "Anyone who doesn't do this will be fired."

One common way dependencies are created without API landscape visibility is through the use of (potentially shared) libraries.[10] While many developers might think that using libraries is different from creating "API-level dependencies," it really is not, in particular when it comes to using libraries that are either shared across API products or that imply runtime dependencies on other components. This means that treating libraries in the same way as other APIs can go a long way toward avoiding scenarios where dependency management problems creep back into the landscape, and not even at the visible and managed level of APIs.

Visibility Maturity

- One important aspect of visibility is to expose everything about an API that is needed to use or manage it in the API landscape. That information will probably evolve over time, so being able to change the API easily in response to the changing information needs of users and managers is important.

---

10 Ironically, this is the original meaning of the term *application programming interface*, where an API was conceived as the interface between two colocated software components (often user code and a library). More recently (and in this book), in most cases people now refer to *network interfaces* when talking about APIs, switching the meaning of the term to something that does not cover the traditional "local API" scenarios any longer.

- Another important aspect of visibility is to expose every dependency through APIs so that APIs become an accurate reflection of dependencies and there are no hidden dependencies that use side channels instead of APIs.

- Once the API landscape grows, API-level visibility needs to be complemented with landscape-level visibility, i.e., with the ability to find APIs based on their visible information.

- Finally, visibility also applies to how easily API information can be used. For example, when APIs standardize on certain capabilities such as how to represent error messages or status information, this information can be more easily used and aggregated at the landscape level, which will increase the visibility of these API aspects.

API-level visibility nicely feeds into landscape-level visibility: whatever is made visible at the API level can be used at the landscape level to improve the discoverability of APIs, making them easier to find (and thus more visible) at the landscape level.

For example, if APIs expose their dependencies clearly and visibly at the API level (taking into account the principle we discussed about *all* dependencies being treated as API dependencies),[11] then this information can be used to create a dependency graph and even create higher-level information, such as computing API popularity.

In a feedback loop, visibility needs at the landscape level might feed into visibility requirements at the API level, and observing the needs of API users and the practices of API providers will allow the landscape to adapt to new visibility needs.

As visibility matures and gets to the point where APIs are maturing to be better landscape citizens (by adapting to visibility requirements that were triggered by visibility issues at the landscape level), it may become a pattern to separate the "landscape-assisting" parts of an API from its functional aspects. This practice may have to be accompanied by robust vulnerability practices, if the "landscape-assisting" part should be restricted to be available to landscape tooling only.

---

[11] Exposing dependencies can be done in many different ways: it could be done by developers explicitly listing dependency information, by using tools that do code inspection of the implementation, or by runtime observation at the API level.

Visibility Maturity Strategy

For APIs to provide value, they must be useful and findable. To be useful to the landscape, they may have to improve the visibility of some of their information. Any problem in the API landscape should trigger the question, "What information would help with solving that problem?" If there are implications for visibility at the API or landscape level, this should trigger updated guidance (adding visibility to APIs) or updated landscape tooling (adding visibility to the landscape).

Versioning

Velocity—the ability for API products to change quickly in response to feedback or evolving requirements—is an important motivation for moving to an API landscape. *Versioning* is an inescapable part of that, because every time an API product changes, it becomes a new version. As discussed in "Semantic versioning" on page 247, this might not necessarily mean that a consumer has to do something about it (minor-level version number increases indicate compatible changes), or even has to know about it (patch-level version number increases indicate that there are no changes to the interface). But managing this versioning process to minimize negative impact on the landscape is essential to make sure that velocity is not compromised more than necessary.

Versioning applies to APIs of all styles. In the tunnel, resource, and hypermedia styles, it is concerned with changing the interface of the resource that is used for interactions (either procedures for tunnel APIs or interactions with resources for resource/hypermedia APIs). In query-style APIs, versioning is not part of the interface itself (which is the generic query language), but the discipline of managing the schema of the data to be queried in such a way that existing queries keep working. In event-based APIs, versioning applies to the message design, making sure that consumers of new messages have the robustness to treat new messages like old ones instead of rejecting them because of changes to the message schema.

Managing versioning for APIs can follow different paths, and these are in part motivated by different goals for the APIs: promising customers stable APIs that will never change (like Salesforce does) has value for customers and thus may be a good investment, but on the other hand, this strategy incurs operational costs in running many different versions in parallel. Another strategy is to follow the path of Google (*https://oreil.ly/YMIVU*) and make no promises of complete API stability but implement a disciplined API change policy. This strategy carries a greater risk of consumers getting it wrong, but on the other hand, it reduces operational complexity.

Versioning Maturity

- Making sure that every API has a versioning strategy is a first step toward versioning maturity. This might include accepting that APIs make a conscious choice of not supporting versioning and that any updates will be breaking changes and essentially new products.

- Versioning models heavily depend on the API style and usage model of APIs and the cost/benefit balance of what producers and consumers must invest in these models.

- Versioning benefits a lot from being treated consistently, if not across the entire API landscape, at least for certain classes of APIs and users.

- Depending on the versioning model, API landscape support may be able to help API producers and/or consumers to make sure that the landscape's versioning model is supported and properly used.

Generic models for versioning are still in their infancy, both in standards and in tooling. For example, the popular OpenAPI description standard has no model of "versions" or "differences," making it hard to use it as a solid foundation for versioning. Instead, the standard encourages code generation from the descriptions, never addressing the question of how to manage this in scenarios where the API evolves and thus has a new description. This in turn raises the question of how to change the consuming code to adapt to the changed API.

It is likely that with increasingly complex and dynamic API landscapes, the importance of versioning will increase, and standards and tools will adapt to this development. For now, versioning maturity still requires attention and good management at the landscape level, and individual APIs will be able to benefit substantially from guidance and/or tooling provided at this level.

As with everything at the landscape level, versioning should not be addressed under the assumption that there is one true way of doing it. Having a strategy and supporting it is good, but being open to other models and being able to transition to them is even more important. Versioning might differ substantially across API styles, certain classes of APIs, or certain groups of API consumers, so being able to evolve those strategies and where they apply over time is important.

> # Versioning Maturity Strategy
>
> For versioning to be as nondisruptive as possible in API landscapes, hard versioning should be minimized as much as possible, and soft versioning should be supported as much as possible. Soft versioning approaches come in a variety of flavors, but the most important consideration is that versioning is disruptive enough in itself that a consistent versioning strategy (and possible tooling and support for it at the landscape level) should be in place as early as possible.

Volatility

Programming models are hard to change, especially in the minds of those doing the programming. As we saw in "Volatility" on page 247, programming in distributed systems is particularly challenging because many failure modes exist that would not exist in a more integrated environment, where failure models are less complex. Handling the inherent *volatility* of services in API landscapes requires a change in the mindset of developers.

When initially moving to an API landscape, it is likely that developers will stick to their programming models and write applications that make overly optimistic assumptions about component availability. Particularly in landscapes where there are many dependencies, this can make it hard to locate the source of problems: when one application exhibits problems, finding the root cause might require a "trace" through various services, a different task from the more traditional approach of being able to instrument and subsequently debug monolithic code.

Ideally, applications will handle *all* API dependencies and have resiliency built into them, including approaches such as *graceful degradation*. To better deal with volatility, it also is possible to develop in a style that is more defensive and that attempts to make the most out of the operational reality of a landscape. Not all dependencies that an application has may be essential, meaning that it is possible to develop an application to have reasonable fallback behavior (and still be operational and provide value) even when some dependencies are not available.

Volatility Maturity

- Locating error conditions is the most fundamental requirement that must be satisfied in an API landscape. The ability to trace traffic and gain insight into the traces often is an essential part of the ability to locate problems.

- Changing development practices to better accommodate decentralized failure modes helps with making sure that individual failures do not necessarily turn into cascades along the dependency chain.

- The more developers can be helped or nudged toward more resilient development practices, the more robust the API landscape will be.

While volatility is an inescapable fact of decentralization, it should be kept in mind that the move from integrated to decentralized models changes the failure model. With individual services now being able to fail, the reliability of the overall system gets impacted by individual service reliability in a more complex way, and the compound effect of these individual failures grows as the API landscape—and the dependency graph between APIs—grows.

Dealing with the potential increase in the overall failure rate means that it's necessary to minimize the propagation of failures. In part, this can be done by making sure that components are resilient against failures, isolating them instead of propagating them.

Volatility is one of those aspects that you may think you can put off dealing with for a while, but problems can quickly spiral out of control, in particular when the dynamics of an API landscape start picking up. And of course, the worst possible moment for landscape-wide reliability problems to manifest is when the growth and change rate of the API landscape are increasing. For this reason it is a good idea to start investing in handling volatility early on and to see it as a necessary first step in the general API-landscape maturity journey.

Volatility Maturity Strategy

Managing volatility in an API landscape requires a change in developer practices to write applications that behave responsibly in a distributed system. It also requires the landscape to provide the tooling that is needed to handle volatility in distributed systems, such as tracing errors. The impact of not handling volatility in a mature way will be felt quickly, in particular when the landscape grows quickly and/or when services in the landscape have different operational stability.

Summary

In this chapter, we have explored the API landscape maturity journey, using the landscape aspects (the eight Vs) introduced in Chapter 9 as a way to frame the journey toward a more mature API landscape. For each of the aspects, we looked at individual factors that influence maturity. We also looked at how investments in maturity improvements will manifest themselves on the landscape level. We have chosen not to show one linear path to "API landscape maturity," but instead have used the landscape aspects to show this journey as a multifaceted path. The most important thing to keep in mind is that *all aspects* have an impact on the overall API landscape maturity and that it is therefore always important to keep all of them in mind when assessing a landscape's current maturity level and possible paths to improving it.

In the next chapter, we will connect the dots, looking at how API landscape maturity interacts with the API product lifecycle as presented in Figure 7-1. After all, the purpose of API landscapes is to provide good conditions for APIs to be developed, used, and improved, and thus we need to understand how the practice of building individual API products is affected by the landscape in which these products get developed and deployed.

CHAPTER 11

Managing the API Lifecycle in an Evolving Landscape

Many drops make a bucket, many buckets make a pond, many ponds make a lake, and many lakes make an ocean.
—Percy Ross

Ideally, if you've been following along in the book up to this point, you've noticed that there are some key differences between managing the lifecycle of a single API and managing the lifecycle of an entire landscape of APIs. In, fact, it is our experience that companies that notice—and act according to—this important distinction between "the one" and "the many" are the companies that have the best chance of long-term success in their digital transformation efforts.

In this chapter, we'll touch briefly on these differences and then dive into the lifecycle pillars we introduced in Chapter 4—this time, we'll focus on the landscape (the many, as introduced in Chapter 9) instead of the API (the one). This should give you some perspective on how the challenges of scope, scale, and standards we discussed in Chapter 1 come into play when you are growing your API ecosystem.

Along the way, we'll return to the eight Vs of the API landscape (introduced in Chapter 9 and refined in Chapter 10) and touch on some of the decision-making elements to employ (described in Chapter 2). Bringing all these elements together will help you gain a point of view on how you can best apply these patterns and practices in your teams, for your products, in a way that fits your company's culture and values.

But, before we revisit the landscape and API product models, let's go over some pragmatic approaches to making API management work at the complex level of the evolving landscape.

Managing an Evolving Landscape in Practice

In any medium- to large-sized organization, you'll end up with lots of APIs. Each of those APIs will have their own team dynamics, microcultures, and product lifecycles. In previous chapters we've touched on the properties of the landscape of APIs and the things you'll need to think about as it grows.

Later in this chapter, we'll try to tie together the "macro" model of the landscape that we've built up with the "micro" model of the API product that we established earlier in the book. But before we get to the unification of our models, we want to explore three practices that can help you start managing your landscape.

In truth, managing a landscape of API products isn't easy. We've alluded to the complex nature of the landscape throughout this book. But, that complexity really hits home when you're the one who is responsible for making all the APIs in your organization safer, better, and cheaper.

With that in mind, we've outlined a few approaches that have helped us and the practitioners we've spoken to. Let's start with an important first step in any system design work: defining your boundaries by establishing your "red lines."

Socialize Your "Red Lines"

In the natural world, evolution happens because some things work while others don't. The things that work stick around in the long-term, while the things that don't work die away. Evolution is powerful. But, practically speaking, you probably can't afford to have your product, business, or organization "die off" for the sake of long-term evolutionary success.

That's why one of the first practical things you should do is define the "red lines" for your landscape context. What are the things that are nonnegotiable where you work? These are the things that you can't afford to experiment with. That could be because the risk associated with poor decisions in this area is too high, because it deters you from a known business goal, or simply because it goes against the company culture.

In our experience, these kinds of boundaries and constraints are often unspoken and ill-defined in large organizations. This can lead to problems when new people come in and waste time trying to drive innovation without understanding that a boundary has been set. It's useful to express these boundaries in a way that people can learn from quickly—as principles, policies, or even as "best practices."

For example, here are some of the "red lines" that we've run into at various organizations:

- Service outages are unacceptable, and we must achieve 100% uptime of client-facing applications at all costs.
- We can't use tools from company X due to a recent dispute.
- Team structures need to adhere to human resources' recently released mandates.
- Don't make technical decisions that contradict the founder's decisions.
- We can't store any data for users from Svenborgia.

Don't forget that "red lines" are not meant to be challenged. That means you're limiting your innovation potential whenever you introduce them. But, on the plus side, constraints can be a designer's best friend. They can help you channel the organization's energy into areas with massive improvement potential.

Platforms Over Projects (Eventually)

It's really difficult to get the most out of a landscape of APIs without continuous improvement. That's a central theme of this book, and it reflects our real-life experiences. But the problem is that a lot of organizations aren't built to work this way. Continuous improvement can also mean continuous cost, and that can be a big leap for an organization that hasn't yet bought into the value of API management.

Another way of saying this is that an organization should adopt a product (or platform) mindset for API management. That means that an enduring team designs, builds, and supports the landscape of APIs. They own the decisions and responsibility to improve the API products that live within it. This is different from a project mindset where an organization funds short-lived teams who fulfill landscape improvement projects.

Here are some examples of classic project approaches:

- A limited, six-month funding investment to improve API governance
- Engaging a consulting firm on a fixed-term basis to audit and improve a set of APIs
- Using a pool of centrally managed delivery teams for short-term technology improvement projects

From an organizational perspective, the project mindset is efficient, measurable, and manageable. But it also introduces barriers to change, execution, and holistic decision making. Without an enduring team, landscape features become disconnected and conflicting. Without enduring funding, fewer changes or improvements are introduced because of the overhead costs associated with gaining approvals.

If you're lucky, you'll be able to create an enduring team that has the trust of the organization to curate your landscape on day one. But, in many existing organizations, there is a need to earn that trust (and funding). To get there, you'll need to work harder and adapt a project perspective into a platform perspective by delivering value. Sometimes that will take a bit of negotiation. Taking the previous examples, you could try the following tactical approaches:

- Use part of the funding to build a business case for the next funding cycle. Repeat and build a case to establish an enduring team.

- Select a firm that will take a landscape perspective of your APIs so that they can advise on organizational and operational changes that you'll need for platform success.

- Define an API management specialization skill. Then find and use a consistent group of people who you can grow into an enduring team.

None of these approaches is perfect. But they highlight that you may need to take a practical approach to shift your organization to a platform mindset from the bottom up.

Design for Consumers, Producers, and Sponsors

Whether it's a product or a platform, success depends on meeting your user's needs. In an API landscape, you'll need to quickly figure out who the key consumers, producers, and sponsors for your system are.

Serving your consumers
>One of your early goals should be to improve the way that the landscape as we've defined it in Chapter 9 can serve the needs of API consumers. How will you shape the variety, volume, visibility, and other Vs of your landscape so that they meet the needs of consumers? A good starting point is to identify who your primary consumers are and the needs that they have. Then you can check the design and execution decisions you make against those needs. For example, if we were offering a meeting scheduling service, we'd prioritize the needs of developers using our scheduling API, but also the needs of teams who use internal APIs to fulfill those users' needs.

Serving your producers
>Being consumer-centric makes sense for a product. But, to embrace the platform perspective as we defined in "The Platform Principle" on page 228, we'll need to serve the needs of the teams that build and run APIs as well. How will you make it easier for API teams to produce APIs that meet the needs of consumers? Again, it's worthwhile identifying who your primary API producers will be. That could mean identifying a few key "archetypes," communities, or "tribes." For

example, you may identify that most of your teams use Java and the Spring Boot framework. Or you might establish that teams working on externally facing APIs have different needs than the ones working on internal APIs. However you define them, the goal is to serve the needs of these producers with the landscape decisions you make and shape the APIs they eventually output.

Serving your sponsors

Every platform has at least one owner or sponsor. These are the people who make the decisions about the goals of the system and provide the funding that is needed to operate, improve, and run it. When we talk about the theory of a platform, it's easy to forget about this group. But, anyone who has run an API management program in a large organization will be acutely aware of the importance of serving the needs of sponsors. If you don't think about your sponsors when you design your platform, it may not last for very long. In large organizations, it's a good idea to make your landscape of APIs easier for sponsors to understand and observe, especially if your platform funding comes from a nontechnical business team. How easy is it for the business to understand the API-enabled capabilities that they have? How easily can they map your landscape structure to their business strategies? Making it easier for your landscape to fit your sponsor's needs can help your long-term success.

Designing Platforms

The platform perspective isn't unique to APIs. In fact, there are already some great tools and methodologies you can use to help you design holistic solutions that help you take a needs-based perspective. We've had success adopting a service design approach (*https://oreil.ly/XvvdX*) in our bigger projects. There are also specific tools like the Platform Design Toolkit (*https://oreil.ly/rfJsA*) that can help guide you in the right direction.

Focusing on the participants in your landscape will help you keep your focus on the real needs and jobs of your people and your users. That will help you make better decisions about the landscape and your API products. But you'll still need to make bold, speculative decisions. That's why the spirit of testing, measuring, and learning is so important.

Test, Measure, and Learn

When it comes to dealing with big, "hairy," complex problem spaces, the most common advice you'll hear is to make small changes and learn from them. This "test and learn" approach lets you make a small investment in changing a system that rewards you with information about how to change it better. A landscape of API products certainly qualifies as a complex system that needs a test and learn approach.

We recommend that you develop a strategy for your API management program that is oriented around this idea.

The real challenge you'll have is in defining the right steps to take and the best way to measure your progress as you go. You organizational goals, your "red lines," and the technology and people you're working with will dictate the best way forward. For example, consider these two very different approaches to launching a landscape of APIs—one for a new, "greenfield," cloud-based platform and one for a complex, existing, "brownfield" platform of APIs:

Organic landscape evolution for a "greenfield"
1. Kick off the development of new API products. Start building before establishing any landscape-level features.

2. Create a cross-product team of API specialists.

3. Take the lessons learned and best features of individual APIs and make them landscape-level features.

4. Empower API specialists to bring landscape features back into their API products.

Structured landscape evolution for a "brownfield"
1. Identify candidate APIs that would benefit from improvement (and are safe to change).

2. Establish operational measures and "key performance indicators" to measure progress.

3. Implement landscape-level policies and test them with candidate APIs.

4. Observe measurements and make adjustments to the landscape.

5. Roll out landscape-level policies to more APIs.

We've talked a lot in this book about continuous improvement for APIs and API management. But to bring it to life, you'll need to get really good at taking small bites out of this complex problem. It's OK if you don't figure it out perfectly on your first go, but it's important to adopt a "test, measure, and learn" mentality so that you can get better as you grow. Defining the right measures and identifying the right steps isn't easy. But, the good news is that you can use the eight Vs of the landscape and the pillars of the API product as a frame to guide you.

Let's dive into those models and see how they work together.

API Products and Lifecycle Pillars

As we pointed out in Chapter 3, applying the appropriate level of "product think-ing" to your API efforts helps focus your teams on consumer-centric uses of your interfaces. This is your first-level opportunity to instill Clayton Christensen's Jobs-to-Be-Done approach (*https://oreil.ly/tuyRY*) to designing and implementing your APIs. And, at the business level, teaching your design and architecture teams to ask questions such as "How does this help us achieve our business goals?" and "What OKRs are we hoping to affect with this design?" can reduce the chances of your backend teams ending up simply releasing data-centric interfaces that don't have a clear user-driven workflow. With this JTBD and user-driven focus, it is easier for IT leadership to quiz teams on their contributions and help keep your API initiatives clearly tied to not just IT-centric KPIs but shared business-level OKRs as well.

Along with the AaaP strategy, we've also introduced what we call the API lifecycle pillars (see Chapter 4). While not true *cycles* (as in a fixed order that you repeat over and over again), the lifecycle pillars identify essential elements that support a healthy API program. You can use the pillars as a guide in creating your APIs. In this way, the AaaP model and the lifecycle pillars support one another at the single-API level.

However, as you've seen in the last couple of chapters that introduce the notion of the API landscape, companies rarely work in a world where there are just a few isolated APIs. Instead, most organizations are working to create an ecosystem of interdependent and interoperable APIs that help expose business value and reduce the cost and risk of using APIs and services to reach OKRs.

API Landscapes

So far this book has focused on how to continuously manage individual APIs and how these fit into the bigger picture of the API landscape. The eight Vs described in Chapters 9 and 10 were used to focus attention on individual aspects of this big picture, helping you to make sure that you consider everything that's important while you manage your growing and ever-evolving API landscape.

In this chapter, our goal is to bring together the perspective of individual API management and the context of the API landscape they are a part of. We will focus on our general theme that the interaction between individual APIs and API landscapes always should be a two-way street. *APIs contribute to the landscape* and should be as observable as possible so that the landscape can gain insights into how individual APIs are being designed and how they evolve. *The landscape guides and supports API product teams* by providing insights into the overall picture of principles, protocols, and practices in the landscape and by providing guidance and support.

The eight Vs (the landscape aspects) can be used to focus attention for the individual API lifecycle pillars. Our way to bring together the individual API and API landscape perspectives will be to discuss how the pillars are affected when an API is part of a landscape, and which landscape aspects are most important to consider when rethinking that particular pillar (and how to support API product teams relying on that pillar) in the context of the landscape.

Decision Points and Maturity

In "Decisions" on page 18, we made a point of saying that the code and interfaces we create today are "dumb"—that our releases just do exactly what they are told to do, and nothing more. Code can't *decide* or *explore* or *experiment*; it can only *do*. The decisions and creativity come from humans, and those decisions must be translated into code and APIs at some point in order to be realized.

A big part of decision making is knowing *when* to decide. It turns out that putting off a decision is often a smart option when it comes to helping to realize an API landscape. There are so many interdependent, interoperable elements in a growing ecosystem that deciding "too soon" can reduce the number of possibilities in the future and may even eliminate some of the best options for solving your architecture problems. Tom and Mary Poppendieck, authors of several books including *Lean Software Development: An Agile Toolkit* (Addison-Wesley), recommend that you "delay commitment until the last responsible moment, that is, the moment at which failing to make a decision eliminates an important alternative."

However, this practice of delaying commitment can be difficult for system-level IT managers and designers. The common question is *when* the "last responsible moment" is. Our goal with this chapter is to help you recognize common changes in the shape of your API landscape by walking through the pillars and calling out common challenges related to the different landscape aspects. This should help you compare the observable aspects within your company (variety, volume, etc.) with the examples we offer here. Hopefully our examples will give you enough of a guideline that you'll be able to identify pillars that need special attention due to your growing ecosystem.

Landscape Aspects and API Lifecycle Pillars

Just as the lifecycle pillars and the AaaP guidance work together to form a set of practices to apply to the work of designing, building, and releasing APIs in your organization, these same pillars can be helpful in managing a growing ecosystem or API landscape. In fact, we can create a simple matrix (see Table 11-1) that combines the previously mentioned landscape aspects and the API lifecycle pillars to give you a sense of the surface area you need to manage in an API ecosystem.

Table 11-1. API landscape lifecycle pillars and landscape aspects

	Variety	Volume	Vocabulary	Velocity	Vulnerability	Visibility	Versioning	Volatility
Strategy	✓	✓		✓				
Design	✓		✓				✓	
Documentation	✓		✓			✓	✓	
Development	✓			✓			✓	✓
Testing		✓		✓	✓			✓
Deployment	✓			✓			✓	✓
Security				✓	✓	✓		
Monitoring		✓				✓		✓
Discovery	✓	✓	✓			✓	✓	
Change management			✓	✓		✓	✓	

Every pillar mentioned in Chapter 4, along with every one of the eight Vs identified in Chapter 9, deserves attention. As your landscape grows, it does not just "get bigger." Instead, your ecosystem *changes shape*. In a small API landscape (e.g., a single team working on one related set of APIs), you don't need to spend much time creating guidance and standards on API styles or message formats. That is because everyone is working on the same team, using the same tools, and aiming for the same results.

However, as your API ecosystem grows, you'll be adding more teams, with varying goals. Some of these teams may be in remote locations, using different sets of tools, with a different history of API styles and guidance. A growing landscape can result in greater variety, a broader vocabulary, and varying levels of visibility, volume, velocity, and vulnerability. Growing landscapes change shape over time.

While it is important to review each of the landscape aspects as they apply to the lifecycle pillars, that would require a much larger book than we can offer you today. Instead, we've decided to focus on select aspects of each of the lifecycle pillars along with helpful examples and, in some cases, suggested guidance to consider when tackling the challenges along the way.

Ideally, you'll be able to use the following reviews as a guide while your landscape grows in scale and scope and you move through the maturity stages over time, as discussed in the previous chapter. Since each company's culture is different, you may find it useful to create your own blank matrix templates to use as a way to spur conversation among your teams and drive open discussion that allows everyone in your organization to contribute examples and guidance along the lines offered here.

With that in mind, let's take a tour through the API lifecycle pillars and highlight some of the more common landscape aspects that you will encounter as your ecosystem grows and changes over time.

Strategy

As a company's API landscape grows, the tactics and even short-term goals of its API strategy initiative may undergo changes. In "OKRs and KPIs" on page 162, we showed how questions about general digital strategy were informed by OKRs and KPIs, as well as the common uses and audiences for APIs (private, partner, public). While these continue to be critical as your landscape expands, the details for each of them will transform.

For example, the KPIs for your initial set of APIs might have focused on reliability, increased use within the company, and contribution to revenue or cost reduction. As your program expands to tens, hundreds, or even thousands of APIs, you may need to adjust your KPIs to focus on considerations unique to large API ecosystems. This is where you can apply the landscape aspects introduced in Chapter 9 to clarify your tactics and implementation directives to match your current ecosystem challenges.

Among the landscape aspects that should be considered when adjusting your strategy as your ecosystem grows, three of them stand out as needing special attention: variety, volume, and velocity. Let's review each briefly.

Variety

As you add more product groups, more teams, and more API consumers to your API landscape, your ability to control and constrain each element of API design and implementation will become less effective, meaning a natural tendency toward more variety. It is relatively easy to constrain a single team or small group of colocated teams to make sure they all follow the same design conventions and use the same formats, tools, and testing and release practices. However, as you add more locations (e.g., office halfway around the globe), begin to support APIs from other product groups (e.g., acquired companies), and work with products using vastly different technologies (STFP, mainframe systems, etc.), you'll find that you can no longer dictate just "how" things get done.

As your landscape grows, its variety naturally increases. Instead of trying to avoid this healthy diversity, it is important to change your API strategy to embrace differences and focus on overriding *principles* all teams share, instead of trying to get everyone to use the same *practices* across technology stacks and product groups (see "Principles, Protocols, and Patterns" on page 230).

Increasing variety is not a bad thing.

Volume

A large API landscape can also mean increases in varying types of volume—more APIs, more traffic, more teams, and so forth. However, you may still have limited resources available for managing this growth. This usually means you need to make choices about what new initiatives to support, what old ones to deprecate, and what APIs need to be kept as they are for the near future.

When it comes to making choices, focusing on APIs that are clearly bringing in more positive business, ones that are easier to update and maintain, and other business-centric goals can help you manage the increasing volume. You may need to start to invest in platforms that "scale better" at high traffic volumes. You may also need to move from on-premise releases to virtual machines in the cloud that are more easily scaled. You may have some APIs that will perform better in a Function-as-a-Service (FaaS) environment, and so on. And in some cases, it might make more sense to bring traffic back into your own local infrastructure to reduce distance and costs.

Volume is one of the most common aspects you'll need to deal with as your landscape grows, and there are many ways to address it.

Velocity

The last landscape aspect we'll call out here is velocity. Several customers tell us that "things are just getting faster and faster," and it's challenging to keep up. While sometimes this is true, other times it is not just the speed of change but the *number* of changes that becomes a problem. Velocity can be experienced in several forms.

As your ecosystem grows, more parts will need to change, and that means you notice change more often. Your API strategy will need to adjust to make sure changes are not disruptive (see "Change Management" on page 317) and that they are cheaper and less risky. Usually this means setting up barriers to large-scale changes (e.g., formal proposals, careful reviews, and sign-off) and *removing* barriers for minor changes (e.g., small changes in UI layout bug fixes, nonbreaking API changes, etc.).

Velocity can also be experienced as an increase in customer business. If you've implemented successful APIs that bring in more orders, but your back-office teams are still stuck doing things like credit reviews and customer approvals manually, you'll discover overwhelming backlogs and may lose critical revenue. Your API strategy reaches beyond just the technical details of designing and releasing code—it includes everyone in the organization.

Velocity is not just experienced as simple speed; it can also cause perceived slow-downs in some parts of the company.

Design

As discussed in "Design" on page 88, interface design is an important pillar of API product work. And new challenges are introduced when APIs are designed in the context of a landscape. As part of an API landscape, an API is not a standalone product anymore but instead can be seen as part of a "product family." How much that view should influence the design of individual APIs very much depends on the projected use of an API.

APIs that may see a lot of use, are projected to be highly visible, and will be used as "single-user touchpoints" still can be designed very much as individual products, with their design optimized primarily for the API consumers. However, in terms of implementation (which is not visible to the users of the API), it may still make sense to harmonize the API with the landscape, allowing developers to take advantage of support and tooling.

APIs that are more likely to be used as part of the API landscape, for example, in conjunction with other APIs of that "product family," should be designed with that usage pattern in mind. Design familiarity will play a larger role: developers using and combining various APIs from the same landscape can benefit when there is harmonization on the API design level.

Looking at these two scenarios, it becomes clear that API design plays an important role in both cases, but in strikingly different ways. For the former, harmonization is mostly an issue when it comes to implementation issues, while API design, of course, still can take design cues from the guidelines when it comes to identifying and solving API design issues. For the latter, harmonization becomes more important both at the API design and the implementation levels, meaning that guidelines play a bigger role in that scenario.

When it comes to considering how design should be approached in the API landscape, the considerations mentioned here can be complemented with the landscape aspects introduced in Chapter 9. Of these aspects, the design pillar is most impacted by considerations of variety, vocabulary, and versioning.

Variety

Variety happens as a natural result of an evolving API landscape. One reason for this is changing design patterns over time so that the same problem naturally gets solved in different ways, based on the context of established practices at design time. The second reason is that different products can fulfill different needs and target different consumers, and there may be no one design practice that is the perfect fit for all these different consumer groups.

For these reasons, variety should be allowed, instead of trying to constrain the solution space to one possible design. However, curating the design space through design guidance managed by a C4E (as discussed in "The Center for Enablement" on page 254) helps to constrain it in a way that helps designers, who have a set of design options in front of them and can make informed decisions based on which options are practiced in which way and supported by which tooling.

One of the antipatterns of variety shows up in design when the same problem is being solved in different ways in different APIs, without a good reason. This not only wastes team resources by inventing new solutions instead of using existing ones, but also negatively impacts consumer productivity because every API needs to be relearned. This is often referred to as individual APIs being treated like "precious snowflakes," each of them unique and different in their most intricate details, instead of promoting and supporting reuse where it makes sense.

In summary, design variety makes sense and should be embraced when there is a *product-driven reason* behind it. Otherwise, it is more economical and benefits the landscape when design uses established patterns.

Vocabulary

Aligning design vocabularies across an organization can help to create a more coherent design practice, and it can also help to avoid repeated (and in the worst case conflicting) attempts to create models for the same domain. On the other hand, defining and harmonizing vocabularies comes at a certain cost, so simply choosing the path of trying to harmonize everything across an organization may not be the most economical option.[1]

As a general rule, domain concepts that can be safely encapsulated in a service (i.e., that do not show up in the service's API) do not need to be harmonized at all. These are implementation details of the service, and making them visible outside the service would directly contradict the principle of encapsulation.

For concepts that are relevant for a service's API, we can distinguish two cases.

Domain-independent vocabularies should be easy to find in an organization. A simple example would be something like a list of countries or a list of languages. Any API using vocabularies should try to separate the API and the vocabulary and then list all vocabularies so that vocabulary use becomes observable.

Domain-specific vocabularies may need to be set up (instead of just being referenced) as part of the API design. Depending on the maturity of this aspect (as discussed

---

1 An example of this is the many attempts in larger organizations to create an enterprise information model (see "EIMs and APIs: Perfection Versus Pragmatism" on page 239). There are few cases where the enterprise is slow-changing enough to make this a feasible undertaking, and even in those cases, these EIM initiatives are rarely reported as successful undertakings.

in "Vocabulary" on page 261), the landscape may provide support for this so that defining and populating a new vocabulary can be done easily by API product teams.

Generally speaking, managing vocabularies for API design follows the idea that vocabulary harmonization is good and that observation and support can help with that. APIs listing their vocabulary use helps landscape managers to observe vocabulary usage and evolution, which in turn can lead to simplifying API design by reusing established vocabularies instead of reinventing them.

Versioning

One of the main goals of an advanced API strategy is to decouple the evolution of services so that they can individually evolve at the velocity that is best for them. This evolution means that the service implementation may change, and the API may change as well. From a design point of view, the former is still important as it may indicate that the product team has chosen to solve a problem in a new way.

To understand the rate of change in the API landscape, it is important to keep track of versions, as discussed in "Versioning" on page 273. Following the "API the APIs" principle (see "API the APIs" on page 233), this means that APIs should expose their versions so that changes in their implementation and design become visible.

Managing versions also becomes important from the client's perspective, as discussed in more detail in "Change Management" on page 317. An important part of API design, therefore, is to follow design principles that make it easy for consumers to handle new versions, ideally in a way that consumers can always learn about new versions being made available, but only have to do something about that when they decide that they want to take advantage of new features, for example.

In summary, design in API landscapes should always take into account that services will evolve continuously. *Designing for change* then means to make it easy both for landscape management and for service consumers to learn about new versions, while at the same time practicing design that requires as little effort as possible by consumers to adapt to new versions.

Documentation

As introduced in "Documentation" on page 91, documentation is heavily influenced by API maturity, even though some basic documentation is always a good idea—and, in the case of the AaaP approach (see Chapter 3), is even what API products get started with.

Documentation is a pillar that has a particularly wide range. For example, minimal reference documentation can be generated from technical artifacts such as OpenAPI descriptions. Documentation can be enriched with comments, examples, tutorials, and usage guides. It can even be integrated into the API itself so that the API is self-describing, optimizing the developer experience to the point where almost all friction of using the API is removed, and the API becomes a highly optimized self-serve product.

However, this final step of investing in documentation can be rather expensive and in all likelihood is a good investment only when the effort of creating highly refined documentation is offset by the number of developers benefitting from it.

The level of investment in documentation for individual APIs mostly will be a function of API maturity and the projected consumer community, as discussed in Chapter 7. However, the landscape should provide guidance and support once that investment decision has been made. Of the landscape aspects, the four that are most important in helping make the landscape support the documentation pillar of individual APIs are *variety*, *vocabulary*, *versions*, and *visibility*.

Variety

Allowing and managing a variety of documentation styles helps ensure that each team can pick the best style for the API they are developing and evolving. This choice will depend both on the *API style* and on the maturity and intended audience of the individual APIs.

Enabling teams to choose the documentation tooling and depth that fits their API design, its maturity stage, and its audience will help them to publish the documentation that fits their current needs.

If there are "clusters" of documentation requirements, then it's useful to have specific guidance and tooling as well as validation tooling that allows teams to integrate documentation checks into their delivery pipeline. In most cases, it will not be possible to check all aspects of documentation in an automated fashion, but often at least some sanity checks ("Are there sections about extensibility and about versioning, and are they called out and marked explicitly?") can be included so that teams know a bit better what the expectations are.

It is likely that documentation variety will evolve over time. Some styles of documentation may become historical, while new ones may get adopted. Ideally, variety in documentation styles should be decoupled from documentation content so that, for example, some important principles (such as the guidance about extensibility and versioning sections in the documentation) can be carried across specific documentation styles.

Vocabulary

As discussed in "Vocabulary" on page 261, one sign of maturity in API landscapes is to manage vocabularies across APIs so that it becomes easier for API producers to find and reuse existing vocabularies and for API consumers to use their understanding of vocabularies across APIs.

Managing vocabularies for better documentation means *managing documentation for these vocabularies* so that any API using a given vocabulary can reuse this existing documentation. Depending on how documentation is managed, this reuse can be "webby" and simply involve linking to existing documentation that is available elsewhere. Or, if the documentation style is a little less webby and more about creating self-contained documentation per API, then reusing documentation might mean including it in the API documentation.[2]

It is important to keep in mind that managing documentation vocabularies is also extremely valuable from the observation point of view: if APIs document the vocabularies they use in a way that is *supported* by the landscape, or at the very least *observable* for the landscape, then it becomes much easier to understand vocabulary use across APIs, suggest and focus on emerging vocabularies, and understand which ones are not used as widely anymore. Once again, observing APIs to better support the landscape and supporting APIs in a way that makes things observable are the two sides of the coin that provide the best way to combine benefits for individual APIs and for the API landscape.

Versioning

One of the main goals of APIs and API landscapes is to decouple implementations so that individual products can be evolved individually. This increase in product velocity naturally leads to an increase in product *versions*, as discussed in "Versioning" on page 273. While ideally the majority of versions should be nonbreaking from the API point of view, each version that results in changes of the minor version when using a semantic versioning scheme should still be documented. This helps consumers understand the changes that may have happened and allows producers to make their documentation useful across versions.

As discussed in "API the APIs" on page 233, documentation (like everything else *about* the API) should be part of the API. Following this principle, it also means that *documentation history* should be part of the API, allowing API consumers to understand the evolution of an API by traversing its documentation history.[3]

---

2 The webby way mentioned first is called *transclusion*, meaning that it is made accessible via the API documentation but retains its identity as the documentation of the vocabulary.

Guidance about versions can help make APIs easier to use and can help consumers stay updated about API versions and better decide when and how they want to adjust to API updates. Providing API product teams with guidance on how to produce and publish documentation across versions makes it easier for them to follow these practices. The landscape can provide support and tooling for testing so that API developers get more immediate feedback about how they document their APIs across versions.

For API landscapes using semantic versioning and following webby principles, one possible landscape guidance is to recommend that all API documentation should make all versions navigable using RFC 5829 links (*https://oreil.ly/byW2L*). This scheme includes a navigable version documentation history, as well as interlinked documentation of individual versions. Testing for the presence of these links could be done when APIs and their documentation get deployed, making it possible to validate at least the schematic part of the documentation practice.

In summary, documentation in API landscapes naturally will involve the versioning aspect, and by providing guidance and support for documenting versions in an observable way, landscape management can get some insight into API versions and their documentation.

Visibility

Documentation can potentially be a rather complex resource in itself, with quite a bit of content and structure to it. As discussed so far, it helps if there is existing tooling and support around documentation so that API teams may rely on certain production pipelines for their documentation instead of having to choose or build their own.

It is important to keep in mind, though, as discussed in "Variety" on page 293, that the main goal of guiding and supporting documentation should not be to tell teams "how" to produce it, but "what" they should be producing. There can be supported toolchains, allowing them to easily satisfy the "what" by following a supported "how," but separating the toolchain from what it is supposed to produce is important.

API documentation should always be visible, and with it, all the aspects that are important from the landscape point of view. This is important both for consumers of the documentation and for the landscape itself, which can then use this visibility as an important way to gain detailed insights into APIs and to provide deep links into documentation when required. This means that it is important for landscape

---

3 This is at least true for nonbreaking changes to the API. For breaking changes (major version changes in a semantic versioning scheme), a different scheme may work better, such as archiving the documentation of old versions (which in itself could be become a service provided by the API landscape).

guidance to address what needs to be observable from the landscape perspective and to add these aspects to guidance and tooling.

Development

On the surface (and what a nice pun that is!), *development* does not play such a big role for API landscapes. After all, the role of APIs is to *encapsulate* implementations, and thus how they are developed is out of scope from the pure API point of view. However, there clearly are no APIs without somebody developing an implementation, so the development pillar (as discussed in "Development" on page 94) is an essential part of API landscapes. Increasing the overall effectiveness of the API landscape is one of the main goals of managing API landscapes, so looking into how development fits into the landscape perspective is important.

Once again, looking at the web as the biggest known API landscape there is can be informative. It probably would have been the kiss of death for the web early on if somehow somebody had declared and enforced the constraint that all applications for the web must be programmed using the same language and development tools. After all, one of the main winning recipes of the web, in particular when compared to competing approaches in its early days, was that it gave development teams complete freedom in *how* to develop their solutions, as long as *what* they released worked as an application that could be used with a browser.

On the other hand, while it was essential for the web's success that development languages and tools were not mandated by web architecture, with web-based applications becoming mainstream, development support became a major factor of making web application development more effective. Web-oriented languages and frameworks such as PHP, ASP, JSP, JSF, Django, Flask, Ruby on Rails, Node.js, and many others have shaped the way web applications were and are developed. But they also go through a lifecycle themselves, and it is safe to say that the web not only has already outlived many of the languages and tools that have been used for web-based applications but will outlive the rest too, and any new ones that appear.

The lesson from this view of development practices and support on the web directly applies to API landscapes: it helps productivity and helps with certain protocols and patterns a lot when there are languages and tools for supporting the development of individual products. However, it is important to keep in mind that as protocols and patterns change, so will the languages and tools. And even without protocols and patterns changing, there still will be a steady stream of languages and tools claiming to be better solutions to existing problems.

Not looking at the development pillar from the landscape perspective, therefore, will cause you to miss important opportunities to leverage economies of scale, to establish and share development practices across teams, and to evaluate and adopt new languages and tools as they become available. For the landscape to support and realize these opportunities, the most important landscape aspects to keep in mind are variety, velocity, versioning, and volatility.

Variety

Looking from the API-as-a-Product standpoint (as discussed in Chapter 3), the initial stages of API conception are not concerned with implementation details or how to develop the API product. Everything is about the design and about discussing prototypes and seeing how early feedback might impact these early design stages.

After it is clear what the API product should look like, in this idealized picture the next task is to consider the best way to actually build the product. This decision should be based on the product design (making sure to pick the right tool for the job) and on the product team (making sure the team feels comfortable with the tool selection).

Since different APIs serve different purposes, target different consumer groups, and are developed by different API product teams, it is likely that there is no such thing as the single best development language and tool suite to use to develop every single API. Therefore, it is important to support variety in the landscape and to allow teams to experiment with new approaches when they feel the need to do so.

Balancing variety with the need to not create a landscape of implementations is not an easy task. One of the main considerations should be the goal to have some *continuity* regarding the variety aspect: it is acceptable to use a variety of languages and tooling, but it is advisable to limit these choices so that there is some continuity in the choices, so investments and education become worthwhile through economies of scale, and so there is always some "critical mass" around development choices. If there are more than a given number of API products using particular development languages or tools, then these might move from being "experimental" to being "implementation" choices.

Velocity

For individual APIs, velocity captures how quickly a first API product can be released and how quickly it can be changed and adapted to changing requirements. When it comes to development, velocity is impacted by the whole development and deployment pipeline, as discussed here and in "Deployment" on page 304. While it's important to use languages and tools that are good solutions for the implementation problem, the landscape can help by providing support and tools to make the development and deployment process smoother and faster.

Velocity is also impacted by the size of the developer community: the more teams are using languages and tools, the quicker they evolve, and the quicker issues with them are likely to be addressed and resolved. This means that velocity is not just a question of choosing languages and tools that are appropriate for solving a problem; it's also a question of how variety (discussed in the previous section) gets managed. If variety makes sure that there is always a critical mass to identify, address, and resolve issues, then managing velocity can be described as "picking the best solution for the given problem *where there is critical mass at the organization level.*"

Versioning

The practices around versioning have a clear impact on the development practices for APIs. As we discussed in "Versioning" on page 246, versioning is an important aspect of API landscapes, and responsible versioning becomes essential as the complexity of an API landscape grows in terms of landscape size, service dependencies, and the number of changes that are made throughout the landscape.

From the consumer point of view, versioning can be highly beneficial (when APIs are improved to provide services that consumers are interested in) or unnecessarily disruptive (when APIs change but the consumers are not interested in changing their consumption of the service). As discussed in "Velocity" on page 266, having a development process that allows the velocity required to quickly deploy changes, but also follows design practices that minimize the negative impact of new versions, will maximize the overall value that service agility can produce.

At the landscape level, it is important to make sure that development velocity is observable so that it is possible to observe the rate of change and to possibly provide ways to make information about various versions visible and accessible. Using standardized ways of meaningfully identifying (as discussed in "Semantic versioning" on page 247) and exposing version numbers is a good way to start and already can provide deep insights into the dynamics of the overall API landscape.

Volatility

The volatility of services in API landscapes, discussed in "Volatility" on page 247, introduces some challenges for existing development practices. The main issue is that by definition API landscapes are distributed systems, bringing with them all the fundamental challenges created by a decentralized model. Handling the volatility of API landscapes responsibly takes a different approach to programming in more tightly coupled settings, and when it's ignored, the overall stability of the landscape can suffer (for example, through cascading failures).

When it comes to handling volatility well, development languages and tools, as well as practices, make a big impact. As such, the role of the landscape is to specifically identify and nurture development that is well suited for the volatility inherent in API landscapes. This may not be necessary for all scenarios, but it's a good way to make sure that volatility is treated properly.

> ## GraphQL and API Availability
>
> Volatility may also be isolated in certain ways, meaning that some teams have to deal with it responsibly, and others not so much. For example, when following the Backend for Frontends (BFF) pattern (*https://oreil.ly/qoyqo*), there will be one backend application serving as the "aggregator" of various APIs, and this backend then exposes *one API* to frontend apps, possibly in a flexible query-based API model such as GraphQL. In this scenario, the frontend has a very simple API availability model: either GraphQL is available, or it is not. However, the backend might have a much more complex model to deal with. When translating a GraphQL query into various API requests, these APIs all should be considered volatile. A well-written GraphQL resolver would be able to deal with partial outages of the underlying APIs, responding with partial GraphQL responses. In this scenario, managing volatility *at the API level* has been delegated to the BFF backend, whereas the BFF frontend only has to deal with volatility *at the data level* (assuming the scenario of partial GraphQL responses), making handling it quite a bit easier for the development team.

Managing the inherent volatility of API landscapes as part of the API development process can have a significant impact on the quality of API products, and on the overall stability of the API landscape. Making sure that development languages and tools, as well as development practices, take this aspect into account will make a difference in how well products behave in the inherently volatile environment of the API landscape.

Testing

In "Testing" on page 98, we covered the importance of testing. We also set a rather high bar, saying, "No API should go into production without being tested." As your API landscape grows, this may become challenging. Since time and deadlines are always a factor in software, you may experience pressure to not just speed up the testing process, but also to *short-circuit* the process by skipping steps or reducing the depth or thoroughness of your testing. This is always a bad idea. However, as you'll see here, the way you test will need to evolve as your landscape grows.

Another challenge you're likely to encounter as you scale up your API landscape is that the cost of testing will go up—not only the actual cost of doing the tests (in time and effort) but also the cost of *not* doing the tests (e.g., the cost of failing to catch issues through tests). In other words, the cost of failure in general goes up. This can be particularly worrisome for system-level architects since system failures are usually very visible and can, if not handled well, be very costly for the business.

The good news is this problem has been faced many times before by experienced companies, and there are available solutions for meeting the API landscape testing challenge. We'll highlight some of the common ones here and, in the process, hope to give you some ideas on how you can start looking at your testing challenges and coming up with solutions that work for your company. With regard to testing, the four landscape aspects that are most important are volume, velocity, vulnerability, and volatility.

Volume

A common challenge as your API landscape grows is that the sheer number of tests needed for "coverage" starts to climb rapidly. And because most API ecosystems rely on calling other APIs, the number of tests grows *nonlinearly*. Adding one new API endpoint that is used by 12 other APIs doesn't just add one more set of tests—it requires a modification of 12 more sets of tests! If your testing practice relies primarily on human-driven test suites (e.g., people typing on screens and recording results), the demands of testing a growing API landscape can easily overrun your QA department's ability to respond.

The nonlinear growth of API testing is one of the big reasons to increase your company's reliance on automated testing. It is much easier to scale up automated tests (e.g., by adding more test instances to run in parallel) than it is to add more people to your QA team, train them, and supervise them as they run manual tests. Of course, introducing automated tests has its own up-front costs, but these can pay off quickly as your system grows.

Another volume-related challenge for testing is the amount of traffic your tests need in order to produce reliable results. In the early days of your API adventure, simulating 100 requests per second (RPS) may be reflective of your production traffic. However, as you add more teams authoring their own APIs and these APIs start calling each other more often, the sheer volume of traffic can balloon quickly. When production traffic runs at 1,000 RPS, passing tests at 100 RPS is no longer a good predictor of success once the component is released. It is important that you keep close track of production request levels and make sure your test environment continues to reflect production demands as your ecosystem expands.

Velocity

As we've mentioned, test velocity—the ability to complete tests in a reasonable amount of time—can become an issue as your ecosystem grows. A good rule of thumb is that unit or bench tests should complete in a few seconds, behavior or business tests should complete in less than 30 seconds, integration tests should complete in less than 5 minutes, and scale/capacity tests should complete in less than 30 minutes. If your testing platform can't keep up with this pace and your development teams are producing continuous-change-style updates, you'll run into a major backlog in the test/QA area again.

There are several ways to tackle this kind of volume challenge. We'll highlight three here:

- Parallel testing
- Virtualization
- Canary builds

One way to improve the velocity of your testing is to employ *parallels*. The most direct way to do this is to spread your automated tests across a set of machines and run them all at the same time. For example, if you have 35 tests to run after each build of a component, you could run all 35 tests in sequence on a single machine instance, or you could run all 35 tests in parallel on 35 machine instances. Assuming each test runs in 10 seconds or less, with the latter approach, you'll go from a test run that takes just over 5 minutes to one that takes less than 10 seconds. That's velocity. Of course, this assumes all tests *can* be run in parallel—that is, there are no dependencies on the order of tests (test 13 *must* be run before test 14, etc.)—which, by the way, is also a good practice. Parallel testing helps improve your testing velocity *before* you release into production.

While parallels can aid in dealing with velocity at the unit and behavior test levels, the challenge of increasing velocity for interop- and capacity-level testing can be handled with the introduction of virtualization elements. It can be both costly and risky to run interoperability testing of a new component against other services. What if the new component mishandles production data? What if the test target interacts with existing components in an unexpected and damaging way? In small ecosystems, the use of *mock* services as stand-ins for production components can scale well. However, as the landscape grows, mocks may have a difficult time keeping up with the velocity of change in the ecosystem.

A powerful solution to improving velocity in testing while maintaining safety is to use *virtualized* services, typically via a general virtualization platform that can consume production traffic and then replay it on demand in a protected test environment. This allows developers to reduce their efforts to keep mock services in sync with production features and functionality while they increase their delivery of the actual production components. As an added benefit, good virtualization platforms will allow developers to create *synthetic traffic* that does more than mimic well-behaving production services; it can also virtualize malformed or even malicious network interactions and allow developers to test their APIs and services in scenarios that are less than ideal. This helps deal with the vulnerability and volatility aspects covered next.

Another way you can improve your testing velocity is to run some of your tests *after* you release the service into production. This is sometimes called *canary testing* or *canary release (https://oreil.ly/DZKNC)*. In this case, after basic bench and behavior testing, you release the new service to a select set of accounts (which may have volunteered to be beta testers). After this partial release, you monitor the results (see "Monitoring" on page 311) and, if all goes well, roll the update out to a wider production audience over time.

The canary solution makes a handful of important assumptions:

- You still run basic tests to validate the component.
- You have the ability to perform a partial release of a subsection of your ecosystem.
- You have the proper monitoring in place to be able to assess the impact of the partial release.
- You have the ability to back out the change quickly (e.g., within a few seconds) and can revert to the previous production build without damaging functionality or data storage along the way.

Vulnerability

As the scope of your API landscape increases (e.g., more endpoints) and the scale goes up (e.g., more teams *using* those endpoints), your ecosystem becomes more vulnerable. We'll cover more of this in "Security" on page 308, but for now it is important to focus on how growing API landscapes mean increasing vulnerability, and ways to address that.

We've already mentioned that scaling up tests means making sure the traffic volume used in your tests matches that of production. This also holds true for cases where there is an increase in the number of teams or the number of other services that will be using a particular API. Your testing regime needs to account for many *different* API consumers making requests at the same time. For example, there might be cases where some type of consumer-driven state is passed between components. That means the cost of state handling can go up dramatically when you roll an API out to a wide consumer audience. It also means you may need more testing to validate that the state remains isolated between API consumers at the provider point, that large amounts of state don't overrun working memory as the number of API consumers increases, etc. Vulnerability can shoot up due to more use.

Vulnerability can also increase as the *type* of users of the API changes over time. The key here is that, at some point, your API users may not be just internal teams but key external partners or even third-party developers over whom you have very little control. Your tests need to reflect this possible change in the ecosystem and be designed to protect your system (and your data) from any mistaken or malicious activity by external users.

Much has been made in recent years of the "mandate" in which Jeff Bezos told his teams (among other things) that "all service interfaces, without exception, must be designed from the ground up to be externalizable."[4] While our experience with maturity models tells us you *may* not need to do this from day zero in your API plan, you *do* need to be prepared to deal with it as your landscape grows over time.

Finally, it is worth mentioning here that one of the most effective ways to improve your testing results is to write your code and your API contracts in ways that reduce the likelihood of test failures in the first place. For this reason, we find that many of the companies we work with that are able to properly respond to the increased scale and scope of testing are putting test experts on the development teams. In other words, they are "shifting left" when it comes to testing. By adding test skills to the teams writing the code and designing the APIs, it is possible to avoid mistakes that result in creating involved tests that take a lot of time to run and may not accurately reflect the conditions that exist in production. Consider reducing your system's vulnerability by improving the test expertise of your development teams.

Volatility

Lastly, as we've already mentioned, a growing API landscape means an increase in complexity—not just a larger ecosystem. What was a minor runtime bug when your company's API world contained just a handful of endpoints managed by a single team has the potential to render most of your system inoperative if it turns out *all* your API services depend on one single service running on a single machine at some faraway location.

A larger API landscape runs the risk of becoming a more volatile landscape. One way in which growing ecosystems become more volatile is that things like fatal dependencies creep into the system unseen. A simple example of this can be found in the 2016 "left-pad crisis" (*https://oreil.ly/5OnKJ*) in the Node.js community. Without getting into the messy details (see the linked article if you're curious), a small library was, over a small period of time, included in thousands of Node.js projects. A dispute with the author of this library led them to remove the library from circulation, and almost immediately thousands of builds crashed—including the build for Node.js itself! While it took less than an hour to find and fix the problem, it was a stark reminder of how large systems can become more volatile over time.[5]

And this kind of volatility isn't limited to cases where components "go missing" or are in some way unavailable. It is also possible that some API or component upon which

---

4 John Kim, "The API Manifesto Success Story," ProFocus (blog), updated September 26, 2019, *https://oreil.ly/AAmSO*.

5 Chris Williams, "How One Developer Just Broke Node, Babel and Thousands of Projects in 11 Lines of JavaScript," *The Register*, March 23, 2016, *https://oreil.ly/5OnKJ*.

your system depends will *change* in a way that breaks critical functionality in your ecosystem. You can train your own teams to reduce this likelihood when *they* update their code, but you will not have any control over third-party libraries or frameworks that make their way into your ecosystem. As your landscape grows, you're more likely to increase your use of external APIs, and they will increase the volatility of your landscape.

That means it is important to add tests that expose fatal dependencies and highlight the cost of critical failures of key components. The best place for this is in the interoperability or capacity test phase, where links to other APIs and services are exercised. As we mentioned in the previous section, a direct way to reduce vulnerability is to add testing expertise to your design and development teams so these kinds of problems can be addressed *before* a component or API workflow ends up in production.

In larger systems, even small bugs can have wide-ranging effects. Be sure to test for, and code around, cases where key components go missing or change in ways that make them unusable for others in the ecosystem.

Deployment

One of the major pillars of any API program is deployment. No matter what design or build process you use, it is not a "real thing" until the API or component has been published (see "Stage 2: Publish" on page 171), and deployment is how you get something published. At the start of your API program, you can focus on a clean, simple pipeline for releasing your APIs into production. Many organizations even use manual release processes (e.g., point-and-click in release tools, human-driven selection and execution of scripts, etc.) at the start of their API program. However, as your API landscape begins to grow, manual releases are difficult to scale and introduce a new level of needless volatility into your ecosystem.

The most common tactic for scaling deployment is to automate as much of it as possible. This is the one of the key lessons of the DevOps and continuous delivery movement. Jez Humble, coauthor of the book *Continuous Delivery* (Addison-Wesley), has been quoted as saying, "[The] goal is to make deployments—whether of a large-scale distributed system, a complex production environment, an embedded system, or an app—predictable, routine affairs that can be performed on demand."[6]

There are a number of advantages to automating deployment, especially when it comes to scaling deployment for your API landscape. We'll focus on four of the landscape aspects here: variety, velocity, versioning, and volatility.

---

6 Jez Humble, "What Is Continuous Delivery?" *https://oreil.ly/KVxP8*.

Variety

In most of this book, we've emphasized the value of supporting variety as your ecosystem grows. However, when it comes to the build and deployment process, variety can be a real threat to your landscape's health and stability. Running a process that results in a production deployment should be consistent, deterministic, and repeatable. If your team executes the `installOnboardingAPIs` process today, it should produce the *exact same results* if that process is run several days later. Deployments should be nonvariant.

That means driving variability out of the system. The build and deployment processes are a great place to implement approaches like Six Sigma, Kaizen, Lean production, etc. That means focusing on eliminating minor variations in the release and making sure to build up deployment technology that collects *all* the release artifacts (code, configuration, etc.) in one place for easy publishing. It also means tracking the operating system and other supporting dependencies carefully and making sure these are the same for each repetition of that same deployment. Good CI/CD platforms will give you the opportunity to design and implement a reliable and repeatable deployment process.

Six Sigma, Lean, Kaizen

There are a number of models aimed at continuous improvement and driving out variability while increasing quality. Six Sigma, Lean, and Kaizen are probably the best-known of these models, but there are others. And even each of these three has several variations (e.g., Lean Six Sigma, etc.). If your company doesn't already have a program along these lines, we recommend you look into it. There is a decent article on Formaspace (*https://oreil.ly/DAmop*) comparing the top three that might be a good place to start.

While driving out variability in your deployments is critical, you may still need to support a variety of CI/CD toolchains. It is not a requirement that all parts of your organization (from mainframe to handheld) across the globe use the *exact same platform* for deployment. However, we advise constraining your platform variants as much as possible, since most of these deployment platforms represent a large investment of time and money.

Velocity

Speeding up the deployment process is often mentioned as a prime goal when companies work to transform their IT processes. There are two aspects of deployment velocity to consider as your landscape expands. The first we call *type 1*: shortening the time between releases for a single API/component. The second we call *type 2*: increasing the overall speed of all release cycles in your IT group.

The first case (type 1) is the one most people think of when they think about deployment velocity. And it is an important one. We often talk to our customers about reducing the "feedback-to-feature" loop or, for new projects, getting from "idea to install" faster. Speedier deployment can reduce the risk and cost of experimenting with a new product or service, and that can improve your company's ability to learn and to innovate over time. Again, automated, deterministic deployments can help you increase your release speed.

The second case (type 2) is something quite different. In this instance, you need to release *more* things into production over the same time period. That means more teams doing releases, more releases landing in production, and more changes to your landscape. If you are relying on a single central release team for all your production deployments, it will be difficult to gain this type 2 deployment velocity. There are limits to scaling a single release team.

A better approach is to start distributing the responsibility for releases to a wider community. This is another reason that automating as much of the release process as possible is valuable. The more automation you have in place, the more humans can focus on edge cases and expectations in order to get things working properly and consistently. Just as in other pillars that we've covered here in this chapter, you can more safely speed up the process by distributing it and/or running parallel processes. This results in *more* releases overall without necessarily speeding up individual release cycles for everyone.

 Distributed Release Management at Etsy

Mike Brittain, engineering director at Etsy, has created a very nice set of slides and video presentation on Etsy's version of distributed releases called "Distributed Release Management" (*https://oreil.ly/ ixT3G*). If you're interested in pursuing this idea, Brittain's presentation is a good place to start.

When speeding up deployments, be sure to take into account the value of velocity type 1 and velocity type 2.

Versioning

We spent some time discussing versioning in general in Chapter 9 (see "Versioning" on page 246). While we made the case that design and implementations should avoid versioning the API's *public interface*, the story is different when it comes to the *internal interface*. API consumers should not be bothered with bug fixes or minor (nonbreaking) changes; they should be alerted only when the interface breaks and/or when new features are available. But internal users (the developers, designers, architects, etc.) should be able to see every minor tweak and change of the release package—even small things such as changes to supporting assets like logos, etc.

One way to make sure you expose small changes in the deployment packages is to *version the release* using the semantic versioning pattern (see "Semantic versioning" on page 247) of *MAJOR* (breaking change), *MINOR* (backward-compatible new feature), and *PATCH* (no interface change, bug fix). We've also seen customers include an additional level: *RELEASE* (i.e., *MAJOR.MINOR.PATCH.RELEASE*). With this added value, it is easier to track every build and/or release cycle down to the smallest change. And that can be important when a production release acts in some unexpected way. The ability to trace the package using the *RELEASE* number can be helpful in determining what is different in the package.

Most release tools will also allow you to assign an independent build number to each release. That way, you don't need to amend the semantic versioning pattern and you still get detailed tracking on every build and production package. Whatever you decide to do, remember that *internal* releases get detailed identifiers and *external* interface identifiers need to change only when there is a breaking change.

Volatility

As you might expect, increasing the velocity of deployment—both type 1 and type 2 (see "Velocity" on page 305)—runs the risk of increasing the overall volatility of your system. For this reason, many organizations attempt to slow the pace of release. However, this is usually not a good idea. Instead, there are three things you can do to make sure your deployment pillar doesn't introduce unexpected volatility into your ecosystem:

- Ensure nonbreaking changes in releases
- Maintain deterministic, nonvariant deployment packages
- Support instant reversibility of installs

As mentioned in "Versioning" on page 246, deployments should—whenever possible—*avoid versioning* in the sense that most of us think about it. Our experience is that you can make meaningful changes to a running system without having to "break it" each time. Jason Randolph of GitHub calls this *evolutionary design* and explains the value of this kind of design work this way:[7]

> When people are building on top of our API, we're really asking them to trust us with the time they're investing in building their applications. And to earn that trust, we can't make changes [to the API] that would cause their code to break.

Rudolph goes on to explain that you can leverage *design* elements to make it easier to introduce nonbreaking changes. You can also create tests (see "Testing" on page 98) that check for breaking changes and include them in your build pipeline to reduce

---

7 Randolph's talk is sadly no longer available on the web.

the chances of disrupting production. Taking the "no breaking changes pledge" can limit the possibility of added volatility as you scale up your deployments.

Another key to reducing volatility for deployments is ensuring each release package is fully self-contained and, as we mentioned earlier in this chapter, deterministic (see "Variety" on page 305). When you can safely predict the results of a deployment (e.g., when you are confident which elements in production will be affected by the release), you can reduce the likelihood of surprises in the production update. Also, anyone responsible for placing a package into production should be able to execute the release in production, or some other environment (on a dev machine, on a test server, etc.), and get the same results. This is critical for testing the release and for uncovering interoperability bugs and other extra-package errors that might occur in production.

Finally, an important aspect of deployment volatility has to do with *reversibility*. As we mentioned when discussing velocity (see "Velocity" on page 305), type 2 velocity (*more* overall releases) can threaten stability by increasing volatility. Ensuring non-breaking changes and nonvariant deployment can certainly help reduce disruption in production, but it cannot prevent it 100%. In cases where unexpected bugs creep into releases, it is essential to be able to *instantly reverse* a change; to back it out *within seconds*. This is a kind of worst-case-scenario solution. Furthermore, backing out the change means doing it without damaging any collected/stored data. In other words, all your deployments need to account for reversibility of any data schema/ model changes. This will mean changes to the way your teams design and implement production updates.

Security

In "Security" on page 104 we talked about the importance of basic security elements (identification, authentication, and authorization). We also discussed ways to reduce the overall attack surface and add resilience and isolation to each component and/or API released into production (see "Vulnerability" on page 244). As you might imagine, each of these elements becomes more important as your landscape grows. And, true to form, they become more challenging, too. Security is a wide-ranging and complex subject—one that we won't be able to get into in depth here. However, we'll highlight three of the most relevant landscape aspects here and discuss how they affect overall system security.

Velocity

A big challenge to maintaining proper security in an expanding API ecosystem is the velocity of change to the landscape itself. More components are added, usually at a faster pace, and more interconnections are added for more users. Many of our customers operate security infrastructure that requires explicit access control definitions before a component or interface can be released into production. This works when the pace of change and breadth of the ecosystem are relatively limited. However, as the landscape increases in scale and scope, up-front access control definitions can become a bottleneck. They can hold up production releases and slow feature and bug fix rollouts.

A common way to deal with the velocity problem for the security pillar is to make sure components are designed and built to operate in a secure manner even when access control profiles are not yet in place.

Another way to maintain security while speeding up the release process is to introduce automated security testing. Scripting security tests is not a perfect solution (it is hard to test for malicious attempts in scripts), but it can help; running security tests during the build cycle can help you catch problems early, reduce the cost of fixing them, and decrease the likelihood of experiencing runtime damage.

Vulnerability

A growing API landscape means an increased surface area and a resulting increase in vulnerability. Having lots of teams releasing lots of components and doing it all quickly makes it tough to keep up with the possible vulnerabilities introduced into your system. As we just mentioned, adding security tests during the build phase can help, but it is not the only thing you can do to tackle a growing vulnerability aspect in your API landscape.

When each component release is treated as a "one-off" security event, it can be incredibly difficult to monitor, validate, and track your vulnerability space. An important way to deal with this increase in both scope and scale is to 1) rely on blanket policies as a starter for component-level security profiles and 2) push responsibility for the work of tracking and reporting security-related activity as close to the team level as possible.

Relying on policy-driven security implementations (rather than code-specific implementations) has several benefits. First, declarative policies are easier to read and debug than imperative code. Second, most security proxies allow you to treat each policy as a reusable unit (a kind of micro-policy) and then combine these policies into a strong profile package that you can more easily monitor and track. Finally, many security platforms allow you to manage policies via scripting and/or command-line tools that are compatible with CI/CD systems so that you can make your security policy a release package element that all teams must learn to deal with.

And that leads to the second part of the approach: pushing tracking and reporting responsibility toward the developer teams. It is not likely that a single security team (especially one hosted at the corporate level for a global enterprise) can sufficiently closely monitor and respond to component-level security events. Instead, it is much more reasonable to expect the team that developed and released that component or

API to keep an eye on things. However, they can do that well only with adequate tooling and support. As your ecosystem grows, it is important to convert central expertise into distributed tools and practice. You can do this by moving some of your company's security expertise into developer teams (as we recommended for testing). Another way to scale your security skills is to create tools such as design-level practices, build-level testing, and production-level dashboarding. By investing in tools to help scale out your existing security knowledge, you can successfully broaden the scope of your reach and improve the overall safety of your API landscape.

Visibility

And that leads to the last aspect to highlight here: visibility. In the world of security, it is the things you *don't* know that can hurt you. And you can't anticipate all possibilities. Instead, along with adopting practices like "zero trust," policy-driven security rules, and build-time security tests, you can also add increased visibility through the use of logging and dashboarding.

Dashboards are important because they offer a real-time view of network activity. This gives teams from all areas of the company a chance to watch their interfaces and components in action. And that includes the security teams. The initial value of dashboards is to simply "make visible" the common traffic on your network. As time goes on, teams can fashion filters to focus on traffic that they have learned is an important indicator of system health (or lack thereof).

Often the data points that appear on dashboards are the kinds of KPIs and OKRs (see "OKRs and KPIs" on page 162) we've discussed earlier in this book. It is up to security teams to identify key values worth monitoring and make it easy for all developer teams to supply this real-time information. Most often this information can be pulled from gateways and proxies used throughout the ecosystem, but sometimes individual components will need to be coded to collect and emit important metrics on requests for authentication, validation, access grants/denials, and more. By providing development teams with the data points and patterns security experts expect to see and ensuring component-level compliance during prerelease testing, you ensure that your security operations can properly respond to the added scale and scope of your company's growing API landscape.

Typically, logs can be used as part of an "after-action" exercise that helps you and your security team understand what happened and (ideally) gives clues on how to prevent a repeat of the same problems in the future. Instituting a robust and reliable logging practice for all your development teams is key to making sure this information is captured for possible use in a security postmortem discussion. But just *collecting* the information in the form of logs is not enough. You also need to make sure to store the information in a form that enables easy data access, filtering, and correlating so you can find and inspect just the records you need. A good way to do this is to adopt a practice of *distributed collection* (e.g., each team is responsible for collecting tracking information) and *centralized storage* (e.g., a single platform where all logs get sent for later filtering and review). Central security guidance can also provide recommended and required tracking data points and actions, and you can write build-level tests to ensure all teams comply with the guidance before their work gets released into production.

Monitoring

Monitoring has several useful purposes, including identifying bottlenecks, tracking internal KPIs and external OKRs, and alerting teams to performance anomalies such as unusual traffic spikes, unexpected access grants, and more. In the early days of your API program, monitoring can be handled with relatively small, focused tools and a few simple dashboards and log inspection practices. However, as with many of the other API pillars, as your API landscape grows, the challenges of volume, visibility, and volatility can overrun your existing tooling. We'll call out some common challenges and possible solutions here.

Volume

A common challenge to the monitoring pillar as your API landscape expands is that the sheer volume of monitoring information starts to overwhelm your ability to deal with it. This usually happens when the organization has a centralized monitoring management model, where a small group of people with monitoring skills are tasked with collecting, managing, and interpreting the incoming real-time and historical log data. At some point the volume gets beyond what a single team can handle—and expanding the central team does not make this better. Instead, as we suggested in "Vulnerability" on page 309, a better strategy is to push the monitoring expertise closer to the teams developing the APIs and components. Distributing the work of collecting and managing the tracking data is the first step. Once teams *own* their tracking data, they can start developing filters and correlations that result in meaningful insights about that data.

However, single-component or single-API monitoring is only part of the challenge. As your landscape grows, the interplay between these components needs to be monitored, too. A good tactic to meet this new challenge is to create a central repository of tracking data that can be focused on correlations across the various APIs in your organization. In this case, the central data store is often a filtered, correlated subset (often time-compressed) of the *actual* tracking data owned by the component/API teams. This centralized data is a selective, abbreviated view of the entire operation— one that can be used to spot patterns and anomalies. When they are identified, the teams can then find pointers into the tracking details to help root out problems and confirm insights.

Note that the practice here is:

- Get teams to collect and manage their tracking details.
- Stand up a central repository that pulls selective, filtered data from team tracking stores.
- As trends/problems emerge at the central level, rely on the details at the team level to confirm/resolve any issues.

Visibility

The practice of creating a central repository for filtered/correlated data is a key element in maintaining and even improving monitoring visibility. As a corollary to the point we made in "Security" on page 308 about how you can't anticipate all possible problems, for the monitoring pillar it is important to remember that you can't anticipate all possible data points to track. For that reason, early efforts at logging and monitoring often include lots of values that have no known relation to the current state of your network. They do have a relation, just not one that humans might *know* at any point in time. This can lead to teams truncating data collection by dropping "unrelated" values from the logging streams. This is not usually a good idea.

Instead, it is smart to log everything and *monitor* only a selective set of data points. This follows our earlier guidance encouraging teams to own their own data collection and storage while allowing central monitoring entities to pull filtered, correlated versions of that data into a shared set of dashboards for everyone to see. While teams keep an eye on a more detailed (but limited) view of the system, central monitoring operations can keep a wider (but less detailed) view of the same system. This is a down-to-earth instance of Heisenberg's Uncertainty Principle.

Heisenberg's Uncertainty Principle

In 1927, Werner Heisenberg published a physics paper that contained the observation that the more precisely the position of some particle is determined, the less precisely its momentum can be known, and vice versa. In the IT world, this usually is commonly experienced as the trade-off between detailed understanding of a small part of the system and knowing how that small part of the system affects the whole system. Attempts to gain both a detailed understanding of each part and a full understanding of how the parts interact—at the same time—are less and less reliable as ecosystems grow. That is why we share the guidance that *teams* maintain a detailed view and the *central monitoring operation* maintains a broader, less detailed view.

Another important aspect of visibility for monitoring systems is the related quality of *observability*. As landscapes grow, it becomes harder to observe their behavior. You can use monitoring, or more specifically the publishing of monitoring data, as a way to improve overall observability. Unexpected results, bugs, and other confusing phenomena often occur because humans can't see how a system works and/or how components of the system are related to each other. Our experience is that, upon uncovering an odd ("edge case") bug in a complex system, people are apt to say something like, "Huh, I didn't know that was possible" or "I didn't think it worked like that." Improved monitoring and dashboarding may not *prevent* something from going wrong, but it can help reduce the likelihood of a surprise when something doesn't go as planned.

Volatility

Finally, again to echo what was stated in "Security" on page 308, it is our experience that larger systems are more likely to experience a higher degree of volatility than smaller systems. This observation was expressed by computer scientist Mel Conway in his 1967 paper: "The structures of large systems tend to disintegrate...qualitatively more so than with small systems."[8]

While his observation dealt primarily with the development phase of large projects, we see the same kind of behavior at runtime in large systems. One small bug has the potential to crash the entire system, and as the system grows, that crash becomes more and more costly. This can lead companies to assume the quality of their ecosystem is degrading over time, but the truth is these kinds of bugs were most likely always there. It's just that now that the overall system is larger, their reach—their risk—is higher than before. You can reduce the risk of a single bug disrupting your entire landscape and gain a better perspective on the overall system quality by maintaining a solid monitoring program.

Discovery

As discussed in "Discovery" on page 110, the *discovery and promotion* pillar of the API lifecycle consists of all activities that help to make an API findable and usable. For individual APIs, this often means understanding the context in which it should be discoverable and potentially helping make it easier to find and use.

In complex and constantly growing API landscapes, discovery follows the same general trajectory witnessed over time for websites and pages on the web. Initially, it was sufficient to have a curated list of sites and pages that were compiled into categories in an attempt to make them findable. This approach was practiced by Yahoo! as the initial primary discovery mechanism on the web and worked well as long as the number of sites and pages was relatively small, the rate of change was small, and it was appropriate to have one categorization scheme for all content on the web.

---

8 Melvin E. Conway, "How Do Committees Invent?" *Datamation*, April 1968, *https://oreil.ly/PXGIt*.

This approach clearly did not scale well, though, and was rapidly outgrown by the enormous growth, change frequency, and diversity of content on the web. Starting in 1996, Google (which was initially called *BackRub* and a Stanford-only campus-provided service) radically altered discovery by introducing two major changes:

- *Search by content* replaced search by category, meaning that instead of relying on a categorization scheme created by a third party, search was now directly driven by full-text search of the actual content.
- *Ranking by popularity* replaced manual ranking, replacing third-party decisions of how to sort content by computing content relevance as a function of popularity on the web (as given by inbound links).

There is, of course, a lot more to the story of how discovery evolved on the web, but it is important to have the general trajectory in mind. While this approach does have some side effects (making popular sites even more popular and making it harder to find less popular sites), it generally worked well enough for users to find it useful, and therefore most discovery tasks on the web today are driven by this general model.

In the world of APIs, *content* has a different meaning, as APIs are not so much content by themselves but instead are *service descriptions*. *Popularity*, however, is a concept that can translate relatively easily into the world of APIs, where it is not too far-fetched to conceive of an API dependency graph as the equivalent of the web's link structure.

So far, there is no clear sign of who will become the "Google of the APIs." And since many API landscapes contain mostly APIs that are in the private/partner space, rather than being public, it is not quite clear whether the same trajectory of discovery will be seen for APIs as was seen on the web. However, for discovery and promotion to be scalable, it is important for relevant information to be made available in a way that it can be used for automation and tooling. The major landscape aspects playing into this are variety, volume, vocabulary, visibility, and versioning.

Variety

API documentation can be produced in many forms, and the form it is produced in is dictated by the investment decisions in this lifecycle pillar. Investment is driven by API maturity, as well as by the intended audience for an API. Investment is also driven by the support and tooling that may be made available at the landscape level.

With the increasing popularity and importance of APIs, sophisticated solutions for API documentation and discovery are available. Often these are integrated suites, combining aspects of documentation, discovery, code generation, and other DX factors. While these suites are definitely valuable, it should be kept in mind that they necessarily have built-in bias (such as preferred API styles) and like all tooling should be used in such a way that they can be augmented or replaced when necessary.

The ideal solution for making sure that discovery can be assisted by tooling, while remaining open and declarative at its core, is to expose all information necessary for discovery *in the API itself* (see "API the APIs" on page 233 for the principle) and then let support and tooling pick up this information and use it for landscape-assisted discovery. This follows the general principle of exposing everything relevant in the API itself and is discussed in greater detail in "Vocabulary" on page 315.

Volume

As the API landscape grows in volume, it is important to build up discoverability as an aspect that can not only help *find* APIs, but also *rank* them. Finding is necessary but not sufficient, as everybody who has ever used a web search engine that reports millions of hits for a given search term knows.

Discovery thus requires more than just ways to find APIs; it also requires ways to better understand and thus rank them. It is likely that the understanding of "useful ranking" will evolve over time in any given API landscape. Initially, ranking might not even be necessary since there aren't that many APIs. Then it might become a necessity because of the increasing volume of APIs. Useful ways to perform ranking might change over time too, as volume grows and as the definition of "best matches for a given search" evolves over time.

To be able to grow along this axis of continuously changing and improving discovery, it is important to keep in mind that APIs should make as much information available about themselves as seems useful at any given point in time and that this set of information can continually evolve as the landscape and the discovery needs for APIs change over time.

From the landscape point of view, it is important to provide support and tooling that makes it easy to become easily discoverable in the API landscape. Depending on the discovery model, this set of tasks might look surprisingly similar to SEO on the web, where there is a balance between the information that can be harvested and used by discovery services and the level of cooperation that individual providers are willing to invest.

Vocabulary

Discovery means making APIs easier to find, and while the general principle discussed here follows the pattern of how large-scale discovery on the web moved from Yahoo!'s categorization model to Google's full-text search and popularity-based ranking model, it is helpful to consider some other developments on the web.

In 2011, Schema.org was started (*https://oreil.ly/NIcHO*) as a collaboration between the major search engines Bing, Google, and Yahoo! in an effort to create a single schema across a wide range of topics that included people, places, events, products, offers, and so on. The main goal of the project is to allow web publishers to mark up their content as they see fit and to allow search engines to use this markup as another input to their search and ranking algorithms.

It is worth noting that this specifically applies to web content, and not to APIs. But the *principle* is what matters most: Schema.org keeps evolving as a vocabulary of terms on the web that publishers can use to mark up their content. This is possible because the vocabulary itself and its use by vocabulary users and consumers are decoupled. As the vocabulary evolves, content can be marked in more sophisticated ways, and the production and consumption of vocabulary terms are loosely coupled.

For API landscapes, similar principles can be established. The landscape can support and promote the usage of terms to increase discoverability, and it can provide support for producing marked-up content (e.g., in documentation and/or API home documents) as well as for validating it. Deployment pipelines can even automate tests for the presence of some terms: for example, testing for "API style" and, if no such term is found, raising a warning and asking the API team to include this information and make it discoverable.

Visibility

As discussed in "Volume" on page 315, one of the primary aspects to keep in mind when thinking about discovery in API landscapes is volume. And as we saw in that section, the main way to manage volume is to make as much information about the API visible in the API as is necessary. The set of "necessary" information will evolve over time, of course, so the main thing to keep in mind for visibility is to be able to start small and to have a plan for how that can be continuously evolved into a bigger set of information exposed in individual APIs.

By keeping the aspect of visibility in mind and keeping in mind that the set of visible information is likely to evolve over time, discovery can be continuously evolved in the API landscape in the same way as it continuously evolves on the web. Discoverability is never "finished," and the way it is approached is to evolve the information that is available to discoverability tooling and to observe the landscape's evolution and consider what changes would best help improve discovery.

Versioning

APIs in an API landscape tend to change, and making that easy is one of the goals of having an API landscape in the first place. Enabling change without breaking all consumers with every new release is also a goal that is inherent in many APIs and API landscapes. With good change management practices, it is possible to better decouple API producers and consumers and to allow them to evolve independently.

Ideally, API teams can evolve their products and release new versions at their own speed. However, while this makes it easy for the API teams, it makes it harder for

API consumers to keep track of versions and to be able to find older versions and explanations of changes between versions.

One possible way for landscapes to make it easier to see and understand APIs and their versions is to require APIs to document *all* versions. By making the version history available through the API, it can be more easily made discoverable, allowing consumers to discover information about an API's version and possibly to understand its evolution throughout the history of the product.

This aspect can become trickier for breaking changes of the API, where the API implementation may have changed completely and it is harder to keep documentation and versions discoverable at all times. In these cases, it may be helpful to provide support so that API teams do not have to spend additional effort keeping legacy versions around and instead can rely on the landscape either still making some information available or informing consumers that an old version is still known, but that detailed information is not available anymore.

Change Management

One important pillar of the API lifecycle is *change management*, as discussed in "Change Management" on page 112. Part of the general API journey should be to minimize disruptions of the API ecosystem as an API evolves. Often, one way to help with that is to follow change management principles that may revolve around extensibility models and only make safe changes according to these models; another approach may be to never change released APIs and instead have an operational model that makes it feasible to run many different versions in parallel.

Planning for change is one of the central issues of API landscapes and their ongoing evolution, and thus change management is a pillar that is very much dependent on how the API landscape supports API changes with guidance and tooling. To help individual APIs with their change management, the aspects of vocabulary, velocity, visibility, and versioning are the most relevant ones and are discussed in the following sections.

Vocabulary

One important aspect to keep in mind when considering change management for APIs is the impact of *vocabulary evolution* on *API evolution*. Vocabularies are a common and well-known aspect of API design, and designing a vocabulary into an API always means that vocabulary updates result in API updates. While with the right extension model these updates can be nonbreaking, they still trigger the whole chain of updating the API and its associated resources, and possibly similar activities for API consumers.

Vocabulary management also can be decoupled from an API, turning the vocabulary itself into a resource that can evolve and thus allowing the API to remain stable even when the vocabulary changes. As discussed in "Vocabulary" on page 261, one popular way of doing this is by referring to a *registry*, either managed by some external authority or possibly managed and hosted as part of the landscape. In this model, vocabulary changes do not necessarily trigger API changes, and there is the added benefit of better *vocabulary sharing* across APIs.

For these reasons, thinking about vocabularies at the landscape level makes a lot of sense and can support and simplify the design and evolution work of individual API product teams. At some level, the idea of vocabulary support at the landscape level is related to the concept of a *data dictionary*, but that term most often is related to specific aspects of database schemas, whereas the idea of vocabularies is to be independent of implementation and essentially just be data types that are managed by themselves and can be reused across various APIs.

Velocity

Making changes should primarily be driven by product planning and iteration, based on feedback and feature rollout. Change management is necessary to make this easy, and first and foremost should not get in the way of making changes. Velocity (as discussed in "Velocity" on page 266) is one of the main goals of moving to APIs and API landscapes, and understanding how velocity is assisted or hampered by the landscape is an important ongoing activity.

API product teams should be encouraged to provide feedback about how they feel their velocity has been helped or hindered, and this feedback is important to keep in mind when creating guidance about how to improve change management and when building up support and tooling at the landscape level. Change management is one of the pillars that should always be taken seriously, and one reason for that is its direct link with velocity.

However, once again it is important for API products to consider the context of their change management efforts, possibly delaying more sophisticated ways of managing change in later API maturity stages. The answer to the question "If an API changes in the landscape, does anybody care?" varies based on who is depending on this API.

If nobody uses the API (so far), it could be argued that *any* change management is wasted effort and therefore impacting velocity. On the other hand, if usage picks up, there is the conundrum that with broader usage, better change management helps with keeping up velocity, but now that there are users, changing the API to support better change management itself has become more complicated. This means that to maintain velocity, in particular through advanced stages of the maturity journey, considering change management from the beginning is a good investment, and one that should be supported well at the landscape level early on.

Versioning

Generally speaking, APIs should follow the model of semantic versioning (as described in "Semantic versioning" on page 247). They don't have to use the exact same scheme, but the distinction of change "levels" is useful:

- For *patch* versions, there is no observable change at the API level, so this kind of change is only interesting for consumers to possibly check whether an implementation has been changed to address a bug.

- For *minor* versions, which are by definition backward-compatible, consumers might be interested to learn about the changes, but they might also choose to ignore them if the service is sufficient for them.

- For *major* versions, consumers must take action, as these introduce breaking changes. Consumers must be notified when major versions are rolled out, and should also be notified about how much time remains before the version they currently depend on is removed from use.

There are many different ways in which these mechanisms can be managed by individual APIs. Since change management and dependency management are central to the robustness of an API landscape, a good guidance is to have some coherence about these issues so that it becomes easier for API consumers to deal with the velocity of changes in the API landscape.

After all, having the ability to change and update APIs at high velocity is a good thing, as long as the negative side effects are kept in check.

Visibility

Managing visibility is a tricky balance when it comes to change management in API landscapes. Generally speaking, API consumers would like to use an API as undisturbed as possible, unless they learn of new features that they want to use, in which case they are willing to invest in adapting their API consumption to the changed API. Making change management visible and therefore allowing consumers to write code that can react to this information helps to improve the resilience of an API landscape.

As mentioned in the previous section, it is important to build change management into the API landscape so that the velocity of changes does not disrupt services more than necessary. One of the main considerations just discussed is *what* to make visible. It is recommended to use a model that reflects the semantic versioning scheme of *patch*, *minor*, and *major* versions.

From a security point of view, it may be advisable to not expose patch versions to the public, or even to partners. After all, these changes are not supposed to change the API or its behavior, other than potentially resolving implementation problems.

Minor versions should be made visible, as this helps consumers to understand their availability. Consumers should *always* have a way to inspect the version history, and ideally what has changed between minor versions should always be documented. Major versions, of course, must always be visible because they introduce breaking changes.

Making versions visible in a unified way helps API consumers adapt to that model of change management in the API landscape and can even allow them to use and reuse tooling to react to it. For this reason, treating versioning in a way that is consistent across APIs adds considerable value (in the form of better stability) to an API landscape. Providing guidance about what to do, providing support for how to do it, and having tools to verify that APIs actually follow the guidance will help to make change management less challenging for API producers, while allowing API consumers to benefit from robust change management practices throughout the landscape.

Summary

In this chapter, we set out to combine the lifecycle pillars introduced in Chapter 4 with the landscape aspects (the eight Vs) introduced in Chapter 9. The most important goal of this exercise was to highlight the move from focusing on *one* API to focusing on *many* APIs so that on the one hand individual APIs can flourish in the API landscape, and on the other hand the API landscape as the constraining and supporting fabric around APIs can continuously evolve. The main factors in this evolution are *feedback by observation*, allowing the landscape to understand the evolution of API practices, and *support through guidance and tooling*, allowing the landscape to turn the observations into actionable ways to facilitate change over time.

The landscape/lifecycle matrix (see "Landscape Aspects and API Lifecycle Pillars" on page 286) is a way to show the relationship between landscape aspects and lifecycle pillars. The way we addressed the complexity of the resulting grid was by focusing on those combinations of landscape aspects and lifecycle pillars that deserve special attention.

Our general model of relating landscape aspects and lifecycle pillars is to look at *observability* in individual APIs so that from the landscape perspective, it becomes possible to observe how individual APIs behave. This follows the general "API the APIs" principle. The second step, then, is to use these observations to identify areas in which API development could be best guided and supported by investing in pillars. We always apply the "why/what/how" model (see "The Center for Enablement" on page 254) to make sure that *API guidance* and *implementation guidance* are cleanly separated. This allows API and implementation practices to evolve independently, meaning more continuity in the API landscape because implementations can change without changing API-level practices.

Finally, this chapter was an opportunity to bring together several elements discussed elsewhere in the book. We touched on the notion of maturity as an indicator of when the shape of your landscape is changing, and we mentioned the process of distributed decision making as a tool for sharing responsibility and guiding actions throughout a growing organization. Each company has its own culture, common practice, and levels of expectation. Ideally, the material here will give you some ideas on how to develop your own unique landscape/lifecycle matrix and learn to use your company's internal decision-making process to continuously improve your ecosystem as it matures over time.

CHAPTER 12

Continuing the Journey

We demand rigidly defined areas of doubt and uncertainty!
  —Douglas Adams

API management is a complex subject, and we've had to cover a lot of ground in this book to explore it. After a brief discussion of the challenge and promise of API programs (Chapter 1), we examined the foundational concept of API *governance* (Chapter 2) and what it means to do decision-based work. Focusing on decisions led us to a model of decision making with elements we could distribute or map. Mapping decisions gave us a powerful, nuanced way of managing API work.

With this focus on decision-making as a foundation, we started our API journey in earnest by introducing the first important API management factor: *a product perspective* (Chapter 3). Treating the API as a product that solves a problem for a target audience gives you a guiding light for deciding which decisions matter the most. We started with this product approach by focusing on the work of creating a *single* API product. Our experience tells us that the context of *local optimization* for an identified use case (such as Clayton Christensen's "Jobs to Be Done") is important. Starting from a single use case is also easier to grasp than starting by tackling the complex landscape that inevitably comes as you add more and more APIs to your system.

In this first set of chapters, we also explored the local context of an API by taking a tour of the API pillars (Chapter 4), learned about API styles (Chapter 6), and worked through the stages of your API product lifecycle (Chapter 7). With these tools, you can establish a solid foundation of API practice that can result in consistent, coherent APIs built in a way that supports tracking and managing the flow of work from the create step through to the retirement phase of your APIs.

The next important API management factor we covered was that of your company's overall organization and culture. This topic is much too broad (and important) to be left to just a couple of chapters here, but we want to be sure to highlight two fundamental organizational elements we all deal with when it comes to introducing and maintaining a healthy API program. The first of these is nurturing a company-wide ethos of continuous improvement (Chapter 5). Creating an organization-wide environment that has the right levels of psychological safety and a relentless striving to experiment to make things better is a tough job. And it is an essential element for a successful API program over the long term. But company-level efforts are only the start. You also need to create similar levels of trust and experimentation at the team level. For that reason we also devoted a chapter to the concept of API teams (Chapter 8). Here we discussed roles within a team and the larger task of designing and maintaining the teams themselves. By leading with an overall dedication to continuous improvement backed up by a concentrated effort to support effective teams, you can—over time—grow a strong, healthy culture in your company that leads to high-quality APIs.

Finally, we added the third factor of API management: scale. We introduced you to the API landscape and the 10,000-foot view of the complex system. The last section of the book focused on the concept of *system optimization* and the decisions that go along with it. We introduced the notion of API landscapes (Chapter 9) and how your API landscape affects the API lifecycle (Chapter 11). Working at this landscape level can be quite challenging. Here, all the elements we covered earlier—governance, products, culture, and scale—come together in a complex mix of interactions. Our hope in these last couple of chapters was to give you some guidelines and share some advice on what kinds of challenges to expect as you create your company's unique blend of APIs that make up your organization's singular system-level landscape.

That's a lot of information, frameworks, and models—but at the heart of API management are those four fundamental parts: governance, products, culture, and scale. No matter what kind of APIs you have, what industry you are operating in, or the size of your company, you'll need to manage APIs from all of those perspectives. Ideally, we've given you a set of tools in this book to help you start doing that today.

Continuing to Prepare for the Future

It's hard to say what the future will look like, but we're certain that the connectedness of software isn't a passing trend. As architectures become more reliant on components being interoperable or integrated, the demand for API management will grow, even as the protocols, formats, styles, and languages that underpin it change and evolve. Indeed, since we released the first edition of this book just a few short years ago, there has been a surge of interest in managing multiple APIs (what we call *landscapes*). There has also been a growing attention paid to lowering the barriers to use, reuse, and integration—all things we discussed in 2019.

We've tried to write this book in a way that will be useful for you regardless of the specific technology choices you face. The core concepts of governance, product, culture, and scale are essential and timeless for API management. So, even as everything changes around you, you'll have a set of concepts and frameworks that will help you make sense of it.

You can use the API-as-a-Product approach to help drive your design and implementation choices. This will give you the freedom to create APIs that fit your users' long-term needs instead of finding yourself at the mercy of short-term industry trends and hype cycles. You can also distribute API decision-making based on the goals, talent, and context of your organization instead of trying to clone the working culture of the latest successful startup.

Above all, we encourage you to embrace the complexity of the system you are managing rather than fight it. Get an understanding of how time and scale change the work that needs to happen. Use the API product lifecycle and the landscape journey to frame your working context. Play the "what if?" game with the landscape variables to assess your system: What if the variety increases? What if velocity stops being important? Your answers to these questions might not be prescient, but they'll definitely be enlightening. And they most assuredly will lead you to opportunities to continually improve your system.

Continue Managing Every Day

When you're faced with a big problem in a complex, complicated domain, it's easy to feel overwhelmed. At the beginning of this book, we talked about decision quality. One of the most important elements of making a good decision is the information you have available to you. That includes learning how other people have solved similar problems, understanding your current context, and gaining more certainty about the future impact of any decision you make.

It is important to spend time gathering that kind of information about API management in order to make better decisions. At the same time, if you spend too much time gathering information, you'll never get a chance to learn by doing. When you're dealing with the uncertainty of a complex adaptive system, the reasonable way to move forward is to take small bites out of your problem. Tackle one small thing, learn from it, and move on to the next thing.

In our experience, the best way to do that is to apply techniques like Deming's PDSA cycle, introduced in "Incremental Improvement" on page 127. Use the data you have today and come up with a theory. Take that theory and plan an experiment. Find a safe place in your organization to try the experiment. Measure the results, and start again. You don't need Agile processes, Lean methods, Kanban boards, DevOps tooling, or a microservice architecture to start managing your APIs. All those things are useful and have their place, but you don't need them to get started. All you need is a theory, a good measurement, and a willingness to execute and experiment safely and consistently.

When it comes to a complex domain like API management, this is the best way to move forward—and the good news is you can start doing that *right now*. Find something in your API system that you think can be improved, and use what you've learned in this book to perform an experiment. Learn as you go, and grow as you learn. Before you know it, you'll have an API management system that works for you as much as you've worked to build it.

Even better news is that you can continue this cycle of tackling small problems for as long as you want. This is the *continuous* part of *Continuous API Management*. The challenges will always be different, and the solutions will evolve over time along with technology and experience. But the general approach will stay that same.

It's a long journey. But our experience, and that of most of the companies we've talked to, tells us that it doesn't have to be a difficult one. If you're armed with the API management knowledge that we've gathered in this book and have a willingness to search for a solution that fits your company's unique needs, you'll have a big advantage. Your path will be clearer, and you'll have a much better chance of making progress.

The more progress we make, the closer we can get to reaching our goals. And continuing that is a good thing for everyone.

Index

W

Z

About the Authors

Mehdi Medjaoui is an entrepreneur in the API industry, cofounder of OAuth.io, and creator of APIDays conferences, the main worldwide series of API conferences held every year in seven countries. As a lead API economist, Mehdi advises API decision makers about the impact of API adoption in their digital transformation strategies at the micro and macro levels. He designed the API Industry Landscape, has been a coauthor of the *Banking APIs: State of the Market* industry report since 2015, and serves as a European Commission expert on the APIs for Digital Government (APIs4DGov) project. He also lectures on entrepreneurship in the digital age at HEC Paris MBA and is a board advisor at several API tooling startups.

An expert in protocol design and structured data, **Erik Wilde** helps organizations to get the most out of APIs by helping them with their API strategy and program. Erik has been involved in the development of innovative technologies since the advent of the web and is active in the IETF and W3C communities. He obtained his PhD from ETH Zurich and taught at ETH Zurich and UC Berkeley before working at EMC, Siemens, CA Technologies, and, most recently, Axway.

Ronnie Mitra works as a consultant helping technology and business leaders with large-scale digital transformation. He's also a coauthor of the books *Microservices: Up & Running* and *Microservice Architecture*.

An internationally known author and speaker, **Mike Amundsen** consults with organizations around the world on network architecture, web development, and the intersection of technology and society. He works with companies large and small to help them capitalize on the opportunities in APIs, microservices, and digital transformation present for both consumers and the enterprise.

Colophon

The animal on the cover of *Continuous API Management* is the Welsh shepherd (Welsh: *Ci Defaid Cymreig*), a collie-type breed of domestic herding dog native to Wales. Appearing in black-and-white, red-and-white, and tricolor varieties, with a high incidence of merle markings, Welsh shepherds have longer limbs and a broader chest and muzzle than the border collie.

Welsh shepherds are extremely strong-willed and energetic dogs, and they function mostly independently of human direction once trained in herding duties. However, they lack the low posture and strong eye contact of the border collie (lupine predation traits that allow a dog to manage a herd with less effort), making them less popular candidates for modern livestock supervision.

Due to a combination of breeding for behavioral characteristics rather than features, and dilution due to cross-breeding with the border collie, the Welsh shepherd is not recognized as a standardized breed by any major kennel organization. In recent years, efforts have been made to preserve the breed, mostly for domestic purposes.

Many of the animals on O'Reilly covers are endangered; all of them are important to the world.

The cover image is from J. G. Wood's *Animate Creation*. The cover fonts are Gilroy Semibold and Guardian Sans. The text font is Adobe Minion Pro; the heading font is Adobe Myriad Condensed; and the code font is Dalton Maag's Ubuntu Mono.

Lightning Source UK Ltd.
Milton Keynes UK
UKHW031902171121
394142UK00004B/4